Easter Island
Earth Island

PAUL BAHN AND JOHN FLENLEY

Easter Island
Earth Island

With 200 illustrations, 15 in color

THAMES AND HUDSON

For Jos and Peter; and Eleanor, Frances and Yvonne

Frontispiece: Sunset at Ahu Ko Te Riku, Tahai, Easter Island

Designed by Pat Mueller

© 1992 Thames and Hudson Ltd, London
Text © 1992 Paul Bahn and John Flenley

First published in the United States in 1992 by
Thames and Hudson Inc., 500 Fifth Avenue,
New York, New York 10110

Library of Congress Catalog Card Number 91-67308

Printed and bound in Yugoslavia

CONTENTS

PART III THE AFTERMATH

PREFACE

*This tiny mote of land lost in the endless empty seas
of the southeast Pacific.*

William Mulloy

The sheer remoteness of Easter Island is overpowering – it is five or six hours by jet from the nearest land; to reach it by boat takes days. The small island is pounded so hard by the ocean on all sides that, now that it has an airstrip, very few boats go there any more. Since the 19th century, the island has been known to its inhabitants as Rapa Nui (Big Rapa), a name owed to Tahitian sailors who thought it resembled the Polynesian island of Rapa, 3850 km (2400 miles) to the west. The early islanders themselves may never have had a real name for their island, which constituted their whole world. Yet somehow this remote, battered speck produced one of the world's most fascinating and least understood prehistoric cultures, a culture which has long gripped the public's imagination because of its unique, huge, stone statues or *moai*. These have become one of our 'icons' of the ancient world, instantly recognizable in their frequent appearances in cartoons or advertisements, where they are usually – and erroneously – depicted simply as blind, brooding heads gazing gloomily out to sea.

In view of the worldwide public fascination with the island, it is odd that no serious general account of its history and archaeology has appeared in English for over thirty years. Yet we now know far more about the development and downfall of its unique culture, and it is a story with an urgent and sobering message for our own times. There have been many popular books, but if one leaves aside those filled with fantasies about lost continents and visiting astronauts, they are dominated by the works of Thor Heyerdahl, which set out to buttress a single and now largely discredited theory. A more balanced and up-to-date account is badly needed, and it is hoped that the present volume will fill this gap.

Today, Easter Island is generally considered a strange, fantastic, mysterious place, and this is reflected in the titles of popular books and television programmes; indeed, one recent book about the island is even subtitled *The Mystery Solved*, though which particular mystery this referred to is not explained. For the archaeologists who have devoted their lives to the study of this fascinating place, there are no mysteries exactly, but there are plenty of intriguing questions to be answered. No one could fail to feel awe and wonder on contemplating the bare landscape of rolling hills; the huge craters with their reedy lakes; the hundreds of enormous stone statues toppled and scattered about the place; the abandoned quarries; the ruins of platforms, houses and other structures; and the rich rock art. Easter Island has been called the world's greatest open-air museum, and indeed the entire island can be seen as one huge archaeological site.

At a conservative estimate, there are between 800 and 1000 giant statues or *moai* on Easter Island; the total is uncertain because survey work is still incomplete, and there are probably many lying hidden by rubble and soil at the island's quarry. More than 230 of the statues were erected on *ahu* (platforms), each of which might carry from one to fifteen statues in a row. Contrary to popular belief, the figures are not absolutely identical: in fact, no two are exactly alike in height, width or weight.

Despite variations in form and size, however, the classic *moai* consists of a human head, gracefully stylized into an elongated rectangle, together with its torso down to the abdomen. Beneath the overhanging brow, the nose is long and straight or concave, the chin prominent and pointed, and the ear-lobes often greatly distended and carved to appear perforated, with discs inserted. The arms are held tightly at the sides, and the hands, their long tapering fingers (which have no nails) almost touching, rest on the protruding abdomen.

What motivated the islanders to create these extraordinary towering figures? Perhaps, as we shall see, on their platforms around the coast they served as a sacred border between two worlds, between 'home' and 'out there'. On a tiny island such as Rapa Nui the feeling of being alone and cut off from the outside world must have been overpowering.

How did the islanders transport the statues over long distances and erect them on the platforms? Were they *really* devoid of timber and rope, as the first European visitors thought? The answers are almost as diverse and contradictory as the variety of scholars working on the problem.

Further clues to the island's rich cultural development are provided by its cult of the 'birdman', which survived until the end of the 19th century. The birdman was seen as the representative on earth of the creator god Makemake and was of enormous symbolic significance to these isolated people who could not come and go as the birds did. Indeed, the striking motif of the birdman appears repeatedly in Easter Island's abundant rock art, especially near the village of Orongo, which was the centre of the cult. One can even see birdlike features in some of the giant statues. But what prompted the rise of this enigmatic cult?

Scholars have searched for answers to this series of riddles in the Rongorongo phenomenon, the islanders' 'script' comprising parallel lines of engraved characters preserved on a series of wooden boards. According to legend, Hotu Matua, the first settler, brought sixty-seven inscribed tablets to the island with him. We shall explore just how much progress has been made in interpreting the twenty-nine surviving tablets now scattered around the world's museums.

In this book, we take a look at these different topics, particularly in the light of the intense archaeological activity of the past four decades. We also address the issue of the islanders' origins. Where did they come from, and when? How many of them were there? How and why did they travel to the island in the first place? What did they bring with them, and how did they survive? More puzzling still is the question of why, not long after the first European visits to the island, the statues were toppled over and left in disarray, often deliberately beheaded. All the evidence points to a dramatic change in the islanders' way of life, which included the onset of violence and warfare. What cataclysm could have had such a devastating impact on the island's culture?

As we shall see, the answer to this last question carries a message that is of fundamental importance to every person alive today and even more so to our descendants. Given the decline of the island's culture, we should consider the parallels between the behaviour of the Easter Islanders in relation to their limited resources and our cavalier disregard for our own fragile natural environment: the earth itself.

This is more, therefore, than an account of the rise and fall of an extraordinary prehistoric culture; if Easter Island is seen as a microcosm of our own world, then this is, indeed, a cautionary tale relevant for the future of all humankind.

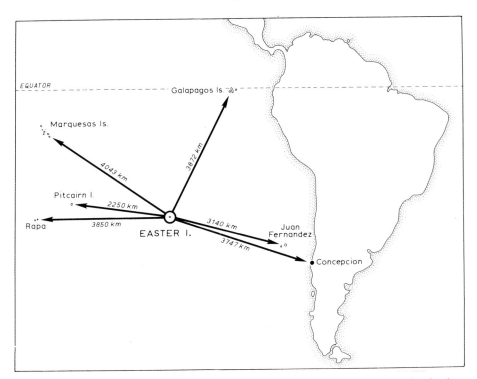

1 ABOVE *Easter Island lies isolated in the vastness of the Pacific Ocean, thousands of miles from its nearest inhabited neighbours.*

2 OVERLEAF *A four-masted schooner lies at anchor off the coast beyond a giant stone statue, or moai, on the ceremonial platform Ahu Ko Te Riku.*

INTRODUCTION

EUROPEAN DISCOVERY

Easter Island has been a source of both bafflement and fascination to the outside world ever since the first recorded visits by Europeans. Equally, nothing was ever quite the same after this European contact, and certainly not after the arrival of missionaries, the first Europeans to take up residence, in 1864.

There are some Spanish claims of a visit to the island by Alvaro de Mendaña in his voyages to the South Pacific during the late 16th century; he certainly discovered some islands, including the southern Marquesas group, but there is no proof of a visit to Easter Island, and surviving records are not sufficiently precise to follow his route. Others think this was the island reported in latitude 27°S by the English buccaneer John Davis in 1687, though it scarcely matches his description of a low and sandy island only 500 miles from Chile, and with 'a long tract of pretty high land' some 12 leagues to the west. It is likely that he was wrong about the latitude; besides, none of his crew went ashore, and his account makes no mention of the numerous great monoliths which would certainly have been strikingly visible at this time.

We may never know for sure which, if any, vessels called at the island in the 17th century or earlier, but one scholar, Robert Langdon, believes that a lost Spanish caravel, the *San Lesmes*, was shipwrecked on a reef east of Tahiti around 1536, some of its crew intermarrying with Polynesian women; their descendants eventually reached Easter Island and donated Basque genes, which are still found there. There is some genetic support for Langdon's theory: recent analyses of HLA (Human Leucocyte Antigen) groups, a tissue-typing system useful in the preparation of medical transplants, have revealed that eighteen people of 'pure' Easter Island stock possess a combination of genes that is frequent among Basques (the 'Basque haplotype'). They can be traced back to one islander of the late 19th century, and prove that at least one Basque passed through. However, there is no chronological dimension to these analyses: that is, one cannot assume that the Basque genes arrived via the *San Lesmes* or any other early ship. There were hundreds of whalers in this part of the Pacific during the 19th century, and Basques were usually pre-eminent in this industry. We know virtually nothing about the routes or landfalls of all these doubtless lusty crews.

Thus the officially accepted discovery by the outside world was made by the Dutch commander Jacob Roggeveen on 5 April 1722; towards 5 p.m., the island was spotted by the *Afrikaansche Galei*, one of a company of three ships under Roggeveen's command. The first sighting was noted in the ship's log:

> About the 10th glass in the afternoon watch, *De Afrikaansche Galei*, which was sailing ahead, headed into the wind ... giving signal of seeing land ... a low flat island ... we gave ... to the land the name of the Paasch Eyland [Easter Island], because it was discovered and found by us on Easter Day.

The next day columns of smoke were seen rising from various places, 'from which it may with reason be concluded that the island, although it appears sandy and barren, nevertheless is inhabited by people'. (The Dutchmen later found that what looked like sand from a distance was, in fact, 'withered grass, hay or other scorched and burnt vegetation'.)

Owing to 'very unstable weather, with thunder, lightning, heavy rain and variable winds from the northwest', a landing was not possible that day. Next morning, a canoe travelled the distance of nearly 5 km (3 miles) out to the ships, bearing a 'Paaschlander', a well-built man in his fifties, with a goatee beard. He was 'quite naked, without having the least covering in front of what modesty forbids being named more clearly. This poor person appeared to be very glad to see us, and marvelled greatly at the construction of our ship.'

On the following day, the Europeans did make a brief visit to the island itself, and provided the first recorded comments on its material culture:

> Concerning the religion of these people, of this we could get no full knowledge because of the shortness of our stay; we merely observed that they set fires before some particularly high erected stone images ... these stone images at first caused us to be struck with astonishment, because we could not comprehend how it was possible that these people, who are devoid of heavy thick timber for making any machines, as well as strong ropes, nevertheless had been able to erect such images, which were fully 30 feet high and thick in proportion.

It is ironic that Roggeveen had been searching for the island recorded by Davis thirty-five years before; Roggeveen's journal did not appear until 1838, but his officer Carl Behrens did publish a romanticized, unreliable account in 1739.

One clue that the Dutch may not have been the first European visitors is the sheer lack of surprise shown by the islander who visited the ship. If the islanders had, indeed, had no contact with the outside world, and believed Rapa Nui to be the whole world, one would imagine that the arrival of three sailing ships full of white-skinned people would be akin to UFOs landing today and would arouse panic and terror; but Roggeveen's visitor displayed merely a friendly nonchalance and curiosity.

The early European explorers from Roggeveen onward made useful observations about the island's ethnography and antiquities, but their reports were prone to exaggeration (especially of the statues' dimensions) and contained

3 Duché de Vancy, the artist on the French expedition to Easter Island in 1786, portrayed the islanders as having strangely European physiognomy and as being quick to steal any of the visitors' possessions that took their fancy. The expedition's leader, Comte de La Pérouse, is shown measuring a giant statue with its pukao, or stone head-dress, still in place.

frequent inaccuracies: the Dutch, for example, thought the statues were made of clay, and represented figures 'hung round with a long garment from the neck to the soles of the feet', and the Spaniards said the statues had lips stretching from ear to ear, and no hands, while the famous drawing produced during French explorer Comte de La Pérouse's visit in 1786 (ill. 3) gives both the people and the statues a somewhat European appearance. Some made extremely brief visits (the Dutch only came ashore on one day, while the French, under La Pérouse, spent only ten hours on the island), or wrote down their recollections long afterwards. Others said little: the Spanish expedition from Peru in 1770 did not publish a word, leaving us with only the ship's log.

Scientific study really began with Captain James Cook's visit of 1774. Cook had left Plymouth on 13 June 1772 with two ships, the *Resolution* and the *Adventure*, with the intention of sailing round the world along the most southerly latitude possible in the hope of finding the fabled southern continent. This expedition was the first in history to cross the Antarctic Circle, and sailed closer to the South Pole than anyone had before.

However, the weeks sailing in those icy waters weakened the crew, and scurvy developed. Cook suffered a severe gall-bladder infection, and was saved by a broth of fresh meat made of the beloved dog of his naturalist Forster.

It was under these conditions that Cook ordered the expedition to sail north, hoping to reach some Polynesian island where the crew might recuperate. On 1 March 1774 they sighted Easter Island, and searched its rocky coast for a suitable landing place. The next day, two islanders in a small boat gave them bananas, while another came aboard and measured the ship's length. Cook and some men then went ashore to buy supplies, trading tinsel, nails, glass and clothing for sweet potatoes, bananas, sugar cane and chickens. Being still weak, Cook himself stayed on the beach, but a small detachment was sent inland to reconnoitre. Mahine, a Tahitian accompanying Cook's expedition, could converse with the natives to some degree.

Cook had been informed of the 1770 Spanish visit to the island just before he left England, but clearly his landfall here was not planned. The British rested at the island for four days, and then sailed on. As Cook himself recorded, 'We could hardly conceive how these islanders, wholly unacquainted with any mechanical power, could raise such stupendous figures, and afterwards place the large cylindric stones upon their heads.' Four years earlier, the Spanish captain Felipe González y Haedo – whose visit was the first since Roggeveen's – had written something similar in his own log, adding, 'Much remains to be worked out on this subject.'

The earliest known archaeological probings were carried out by men from the German gunboat *Hyäne*, commanded by Captain Geiseler, which visited the island for a week in 1882. Although their main aim was to collect ethnographic material for Berlin's Kaiserliches Museum, they also excavated the floor of a house at Orongo, and some *hare moa* (stone 'chicken houses').

The first true archaeological work was done by an American team from the

4 OPPOSITE *The unmistakable profile of a thin-faced Easter Island moai, or giant statue, on the slopes of the Rano Raraku quarry.*

USS *Mohican* in 1886, and from then until recent decades concentration focused, inevitably, on the conspicuous and impressive remains: the statues, quarries, platforms and stone houses. The Americans (primarily paymaster William Thomson and ship's surgeon G.H. Cooke) accomplished an extraordinary amount of work in only eleven days, including a reconnaissance survey that noted 555 statues; detailed recording of 113 platforms and of the ceremonial village of Orongo, as well as descriptions of many villages, caves, tombs, petroglyphs and paintings; brief excavations in the crater of Rano Raraku; the gathering of much information on legends and language; and the collection of many objects including two Rongorongo tablets.

A pioneering and courageous Englishwoman, Mrs Katherine Scoresby Routledge, spent an eventful seventeen months on the island during the First World War, a stay which led to an excellent book; she also conducted extensive surveys and many excavations, as well as taking a series of superb photographs which form an invaluable archive of the island and its monuments at that time. She was so bent on retrieving as much information as possible before it was too late that she even ventured into the island's leper settlement to interview elderly Easter Islanders about their memories and customs.

In 1934/5 a Franco-Belgian expedition brought the archaeologist Henri Lavachery and the ethnographer Alfred Métraux to Easter Island for five months. The former concentrated his attention on the rock art, while the latter produced a monumental study of the island's technology and customs. Rapa Nui's pastor, Sebastian Englert (1888–1969), made the first complete survey of the *ahu* and carried out invaluable work on language and traditions.

Then, in 1955, came a milestone in Easter Island studies, when Thor Heyerdahl's first expedition brought in a team of archaeologists, including William Mulloy (1917–78) who was to become the foremost expert on the island's archaeology. This expedition carried out excavations in a variety of sites, developed a provisional three-period sequence, and obtained the first radiocarbon and obsidian dates. It also took pollen samples, and carried out interesting experiments in the carving, transportation and erection of statues. Two large monographs were rapidly published, as well as more popular works. Until his death in 1978 Mulloy continued his work on the island, involving not only excavation and survey but also (and most spectacularly) the restoration of several monuments and of part of Orongo. His ashes are buried on Rapa Nui.

During the last few decades, a good deal of new research has been done on the island, often by people who studied under, or were otherwise inspired by, Mulloy; indeed, their work forms the nucleus of this book. By developing the work of their predecessors and investigating aspects of Easter Island history that had been neglected, they have made great progress in filling some of the gaps in our knowledge of the rise and decline of this unique culture.

5 OPPOSITE *The monumental platform or ahu known as Vai Uri at Tahai, the statues silhouetted against the dramatic evening sky.*

Discoverers and Explorers

6,7 LEFT *Captain Cook nearly lost his life during his search for the fabled southern continent, but in March 1774 he found his way to Easter Island.* BELOW *The expedition's artist, William Hodges, produced this painting of rows of coastal statues; the skeletal remains in the foreground suggest that the violent breakdown of the island's culture had already begun.*

8–10 ABOVE *William Mulloy, who was part of Thor Heyerdahl's 1955 expedition team, became the leading expert on the archaeology of Easter Island until his death in 1978.* RIGHT *Mulloy's forerunners included the intrepid Katherine Scoresby Routledge (top), who spent seventeen months on the island during the First World War, and Father Sebastian Englert (bottom), who made the first complete survey of the island's statue platforms.*

CHAPTER 1

THE ISLAND AND ITS GEOGRAPHY

Easter Island, a tiny speck in the South Pacific, is the most isolated piece of inhabited land on the globe and the easternmost inhabited island of Polynesia. It is located at latitude 27°S, longitude 109°W, some 2250 km (1400 miles) southeast of Pitcairn, its nearest inhabited neighbour and home to the descendants of the Bounty mutineers. The nearest point in South America is Concepción in Chile, 3747 km (2340 miles) to the southeast. The Galápagos Islands, which played a key role in Charles Darwin's development of the theory of evolution by natural selection, are 3872 km (2420 miles) to the northeast.

To the south lies only the vast emptiness of the Southern Ocean, where countless mariners including Captain Cook once searched in vain for the supposed great southern continent. Eventually they found Antarctica, but much further south than predicted, and covered in the world's greatest ice sheet. Today, perhaps those scientists who live at the South Polar Station could claim greater isolation than the Easter Islanders. But the polar researchers have a transitory existence, and depend on a constant supply of resources from the outside world. By contrast, Easter Island has been permanently inhabited for many centuries, for most of which time it was self-sufficient and probably in complete isolation.

Nowadays you approach the island at the end of a five-hour flight in a large jet belonging to Lan Chile, the Chilean airline. Leaving Santiago in the morning, you travel westwards only slightly more slowly than the sun, and thus arrive not much later than you set off. Alternatively, you start from Tahiti at the other end of the run, and face a similar length of flight. In this direction, however, the time change works against you, so that the six-hour flight takes more like ten hours on the clock. But be thankful for small mercies – at least you do not have to face the complication of crossing the international date line and thus arriving, like the lady in the limerick, before you set off. The date line is in the Pacific, but far to the west, between Tahiti and Fiji.

The first sight of the island is a relief. Although you know the plane is guided by a radio beacon, there is always that slight tension in the guts. What if the plane overshot? Would it have enough fuel to go anywhere else? Suppose there was a storm or fog and the airport was closed?

The Landscape

When first seen from a plane window, the island gives little hint of the amazing sights in store. In general shape it is like a delta-winged bomber, that is, triangular and roughly symmetrical, with sides of 22, 18 and 16 km (13, 11 and 10 miles): it therefore covers only 16,623 ha (166 sq. km or 64 sq. miles). Its three main peaks – one near each corner of the triangle – are not like the craggy pinnacles of Hawai'i or Tahiti. Rather, they are firm and rounded, like the aptly named Paps of Jura in the Scottish Hebrides. The highest breast, Terevaka in the north, rises to 510 m (1674 ft) above sea level. The lesser pap of Poike in the east reaches only 460 m (1510 ft) and Rano Kau in the southwest only 300 m (985 ft).

As the plane draws closer, however, the strange details of the landscape appear. Cliffs along many parts of the coastline have been formed by the constant crashing of the waves, revealing black rocky columns reminiscent of Fingal's Cave on Staffa, another of the Scottish Hebridean islands. Caves are present here too, but mostly high up in the cliffs. Rano Kau is a pap with a serious problem, for in its centre is a monstrous circular crater, 1.5 km (c. 1 mile) across.

Other smaller craters are now seen to be dotted about, which would give a slightly lunar appearance were it not for the obvious grassy vegetation. On Poike, as well as a small central crater, there are three strange rounded knolls in a line running to the coast. A few offshore stacks are pounded by the sea, especially the two at the southwestern tip of the island, Motu Nui and Motu Iti.

All too soon, the plane lands on the airstrip which crosses the island from north to south, and which has now been extended in case it should be needed to receive the NASA space shuttle on an emergency landing. Any visiting geologist will soon be able to confirm the first impressions gained from the craters and columns seen from the air. The island is, indeed, volcanic in origin. Despite desperate searches for granite or for sedimentary rocks such as limestone or sandstone, no trace of minerals derived from a continental formation has ever been found on the island, apart from a bit of sand at Anakena beach. This is a blow to those searching for a 'lost continent', for granite and sedimentary rock are characteristic continental rocks. Volcanoes, however, may occur in continents or oceans, and most oceanic islands are considered by geologists to be volcanoes which have grown from the bed of the ocean until finally they have poked their noses above the water.

Modern geological theory accounts for such features rather well. All the major oceans have mid-ocean rifts at which liquid rock is constantly emerging from beneath the crust and solidifying. These rifts mark the boundaries between plates in the Earth's crust, beneath which upwelling convection currents bring the molten rock to the surface. A corresponding amount of rock is taken away from the crust at the edge of the oceans by a process of

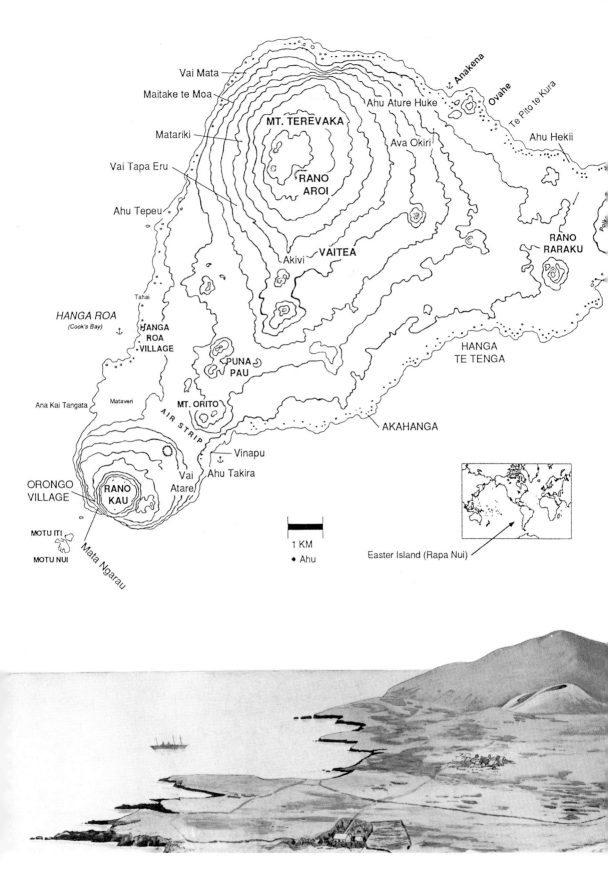

Vai Mata
Maitake te Moa
Matariki
Vai Tapa Eru
Ahu Tepeu
Tahai

HANGA ROA
(Cook's Bay)

Ana Kai Tangata
Mataveri

ORONGO
VILLAGE

MOTU ITI
MOTU NUI
Mata Ngarau

MT. TEREVAKA

RANO
AROI

Akivi

HANGA
ROA
VILLAGE

PUNA
PAU

MT. ORITO

AIR STRIP

Vinapu
Vai
Atare
Ahu Takira

RANO
KAU

VAITEA

Ahu Ature Huke

Ava Okiri

Anakena

Ovahe

Te Pito te Kura

Ahu Hekii

RANO
RARAKU

Poik

HANGA
TE TENGA

AKAHANGA

1 KM
● Ahu

Easter Island (Rapa Nui)

La Pérouse Bay

Ana o Keke

OIKE

TONGARIKI

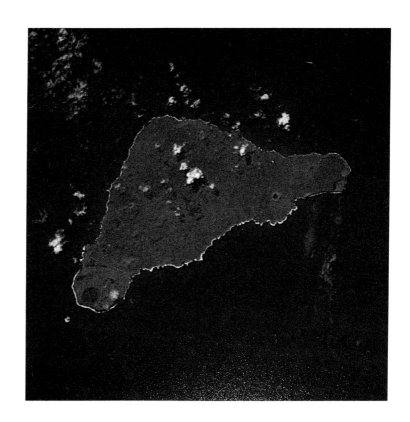

Easter Island – An Overview

11–13 LEFT *General map of the island: note the ahu or platforms ranged along north, west and south coasts.* BELOW *The island's volcanic origins are clearly revealed in this watercolour sketch made by Katherine Routledge in 1914, looking north and east from Rano Kau.* ABOVE *The monstrous crater of Rano Kau, at the most southerly tip of the triangle of land that emerges from the South Pacific, is visible even from space.*

subduction, in which one tectonic plate slides under another. This leads to mountain building – in this case the Andes at the eastern edge and the Southern Alps of New Zealand at the western edge of the Pacific. Sometimes the ocean rifts branch, and at these points, known as 'hot spots', the upwelling is particularly active. Easter Island is over a 'hot spot', so it is not surprising that enough outpouring of molten volcanic rock has occurred to build a mountain nearly 3000 m (nearly 10,000 ft) high – for that is the true height of the Easter Island volcano, as measured from the ocean bed. Were it not for the fact that over 2000 m (6500 ft) are covered by the sea, we should recognize Easter for the majestic mountain it really is.

Does this mean that Easter Island is still an active volcano which might burst into violent eruption at any time? Probably. The whole volcano – at least the part we can get at above the sea – is not very old by geologists' standards. By the potassium-argon dating method, it has been shown that even the oldest part (Poike) is only about 2.5 million years old. Next youngest is Rano Kau, whose many outpourings of lava can be clearly seen as layers in the cliffs: the lowest – and therefore oldest – layers date to perhaps only 1 million years. Youngest of all three peaks is Terevaka, the main eminence on the island, which is perhaps 240,000 years old. It released a large lava flow on the southeast side very recently – only 2000 or 3000 years ago according to one estimate. But the last major activity for which we have a date is *c.* 12,000 years ago, which geologically speaking is merely yesterday. This could have come from one of the numerous subsidiary cinder cones which dot the slopes of Terevaka; there are about seventy ancient eruptive centres on the island, each with its cone of ash. However, there has been absolutely no volcanic activity during the centuries of human occupation, and this is confirmed by the total absence of the phenomenon in the island's folklore.

Volcanoes produce a great variety of rock types, and a surprising range of these is present on Easter Island. All three peaks are constructed mainly of basalt, which is simply solidified lava. Typically, it is a hard, almost black rock which might be mistaken for coal at a distance. It often occurs in layers representing distinct lava flows, a feature that is especially clear in the cliffs of Rano Kau. Vertical joints, producing the columnar appearance, are formed by the shrinkage of the lava as it cools and solidifies. The numerous caves, made famous in Thor Heyerdahl's book *Aku-Aku*, are mostly lava tubes. They are formed when an outpouring of lava solidifies on the outside, but the inside continues to flow downhill, leaving a tubular cavity. On Terevaka, some of the roofs of these caves have collapsed, revealing in each case a long cavern 10 m (33 ft) or more in height, with remaining areas of roof sometimes as thin as 30 cm (1 ft) (ill. 72). It is the abundance of these caves that causes most of the rainfall to drain away underground, contributing to the rather arid nature of large parts of the island. In fact, there are no permanent surface streams anywhere on the island; one stream does flow intermittently from Terevaka to the sea during heavy rainfall, but overall the absence of a high central plateau prevents gully erosion and the development of either streams or valleys.

Much of the superficial basalt on Terevaka has a very rough surface, giving it an appearance very like a fresh lava flow. It may be this that has led one geologist, P.E. Baker, to propose that it is a mere 2000 years old, and it remains to be established whether this estimate is correct.

Some of the basalt is extremely hard, and a deposit of it at Aroi on Terevaka was exploited to make some of the hard tools used to carve the giant statues, as well as to make house-foundation slabs (ills 113 and 69). Most of the tools that required a sharp edge, such as spearheads and woodworking implements, were made from obsidian, a black volcanic glass formed when lava cools so rapidly that it has no time to crystallize into basalt. There are numerous obsidian outcrops on the island; the most important are around Rano Kau and on Motu Iti. The mineralogical characteristics of each source are distinctive, so we can tell that people thought the Motu Iti obsidian of sufficiently high value for them to make the risky boat trip out to the islet for the express purpose of obtaining this material.

The giant statues are, with some exceptions, made of porous volcanic tuff from Rano Raraku, a subsidiary cone on the side of Terevaka. Tuff is a rock formed from volcanic ash thrown out during an eruption, and subsequently compacted and hardened. It remains, however, much softer than basalt, which is doubtless why it was used for carving.

Most of the satellite cones of Terevaka are located on lines of weakness radiating from the peaks. They are mostly made of volcanic cinders or 'lapilli'. Sometimes these too have become compacted and hardened. It is one of these deposits of 'scoria' at Puna Pau, coloured red with oxidized iron as volcanic rocks often are, which provided the *pukao* or 'top-knots' which surmounted many of the statues (see pp. 157–62).

The coastline of Easter Island is unusual in a Polynesian island in that it lacks a coral reef. A little coral does grow, but the ocean temperature, falling to 21°C (70°F) in winter, is too low for corals of the reef-forming types. There is nothing surprising in this, considering the latitude, which is outside the southern limit of the tropics. It does mean, however, that the coast is unprotected in storms. The result of the waves' ferocity has been erosion, leading to steep cliffs up to 300 m (985 ft) high around Poike, Rano Kau and the north side of Terevaka. Only the south coast seems to have escaped erosion on this scale, and has a gently shelving shoreline in many areas. Even this, however, cannot avoid the effect of exceptional wave action. Such an event occurred in 1960, following a powerful earthquake in Chile. This triggered a *tsunami* (tidal wave), which carried fifteen statues weighing up to 30 tons each about 90 m (300 ft) inland from the platform of Tongariki.

The coastline has remarkably few sandy beaches. Only at Anakena on the north coast, and less notably at La Pérouse Bay nearby, are these features found. This makes it difficult to land anything larger than a canoe in most areas, and tradition has it that Hotu Matua, the first discoverer of the island, circumnavigated it in his two canoes before landing at Anakena.

Under the influence of the subtropical temperatures and the moderate rainfall, Easter Island rocks have slowly weathered to give a variety of reddish or brownish clay soils that are potentially quite fertile, although at first sight the island must have appeared ill suited to cultivation: in places, 80 to 95 per cent of the surface is covered in loose rocks, though elsewhere (for example, on Poike) they cover only about 10 per cent and there are loams and clay soils. Not surprisingly, the soils are best developed on the oldest rocks (Poike) and least so on the youngest (Terevaka). The variation in erosion of basalt means that soil is sparse in some areas but abundant and fertile in others (there is, for example, deep soil cover on the older, flatter south coastal area). But almost everywhere on the island, apart from the steepest parts of the cliffs and the youngest lava surfaces, there is soil sufficient in quantity and quality to support the growth of trees. This puts paid immediately to any suggestion that the present almost treeless nature of the island is the result of inadequacy in the soil.

The Climate

Similarly, the lack of trees cannot be blamed on inadequacy of climate. In terms of temperature, conditions are almost idyllic for the growth of many species of tree. The mean annual temperature is 20.5°C (69°F), with only slight variation between seasons. The warmest months are January and February with 23.4°C (74°F), and the coolest are July and August with 17.8°C (64°F). Variation between day and night is only moderate, and frost is unknown. Rainfall is rather irregularly distributed throughout the year, with a mean of 1198 mm (c. 47 in). The wettest months tend to be March to June, and droughts may occur in several months, but especially in September which is commonly a very dry month. Rainfall also varies greatly from year to year (from 1550 mm [61 in] in 1948 to 766 mm [30 in] in 1953) as well as monthly. There are also marked differences over the island despite its small size, with the centre receiving far more rain than the north coast, as a result of the interplay of temperatures, topography, and the direction and intensity of winds.

The rainfall records are not very complete, but it is clear that severe droughts sometimes happen. Could these have prevented trees from surviving? Certainly this is not so in the 20th century, for there are introduced trees of considerable age, and of several species, round the main village of Hanga Roa and at other spots on the island. Whether the droughts might have been more severe in the past, as some scholars such as Australian ethnographer Grant McCall have suggested, is an open question at this stage, but one to which we shall return later.

The island is certainly a very windy place. Winds are a major climatic factor here, and few days are free of them. They blow mainly from the east and

14,15 OPPOSITE *Seen from the air, the island's most southerly point, Rano Kau; (below) a close-up view of the crater.*

southeast between September and May, and from the north and northwest for the rest of the year. Severe storms are known, and the lack of a good harbour has caused real problems for shipping. Although these storms could have created difficulties for vegetation, there is nowhere in the world where wind *alone* can prevent the growth of woody vegetation. It may be limited to a wind-pruned shrub (as on many coastal cliffs in Britain, for instance), but it is not eliminated, even when the wind bears a damaging salt spray from the sea. In any case, there are locations on Easter Island, notably inside the crater of Rano Kau, which are totally protected from the wind. In fact, Rano Kau is a sort of natural hothouse, and its interior slopes support vines, figs and Bougainvillea which have flourished unrestrainedly since their introduction by Father Sebastian Englert. In general, then, Easter Island is potentially quite a fertile place. Large parts of it would be capable of supporting permanent agriculture or forest.

One drawback, however, is the lack of surface water. The high temperature and humidity cause rapid chemical weathering of the soil which, in turn, frequently leads to leaching; the high soil temperatures mean the evaporation rate is also high. The inevitable result of excessive evaporation and porous soils is poor drainage and weak moisture retention. The only reliable sources of freshwater naturally available to the first settlers were the three crater lakes (Rano Aroi, Rano Kau, Rano Raraku), apart from a few springs on the north coast, and pools formed in lava tubes. Not surprisingly, the settlers eventually pecked out some stone basins to catch and retain rainwater.

A description of Easter Island would be incomplete without mention of Sala-y-Gómez. This is a small reef, 415 km (260 miles) away to the northeast. It is only 300 m (985 ft) long at low tide, and shrinks to a mere 70 m (230 ft) at high tide. It is constantly swept by salt spray, and only four species of land plants grow there. There is a small depression which sometimes contains fresh water. Sea birds abound in the breeding season. Although it is possible to land only at times of exceptional calm, the Easter Islanders insist that they used to visit Sala-y-Gómez on a regular basis, to collect sea-bird eggs and young as a food supply. To achieve the return journey by canoe must have been a hazardous and exhausting affair.

Fauna and Flora

Islands are important natural laboratories, where evolution has carried out its work on a scale much easier to understand than on a large continent. Easter Island, thanks to its extreme isolation, has always been naturally poor in both fauna and flora. It has no indigenous land vertebrates, and only two small lizard species which are thought to have arrived as stowaways with the human settlers, who also almost certainly brought, deliberately, the edible Polynesian rat, later to be ousted by the European rat. On present evidence the settlers did not introduce the pig, which is surprising if they came from Polynesia where this animal was commonly domesticated (Chapter 3). But they seem to have had the dog for a while (see p. 91) and, later, after this animal's disappearance, retained a memory of it, because when the cat was introduced they gave it the name *kuri* which applies elsewhere in Polynesia to dogs. Rabbits enjoyed a brief abundance after their introduction in 1866, but later became extinct, wiped out by the islanders. Sheep, pigs, horses and cattle were introduced in 1866 and survive to this day, in fluctuating numbers.

The only conspicuous land bird is a small hawk, which apparently survives mainly by eating insects. It too is introduced, as are the Chilean partridge and a species of quail. The human immigrants did bring with them the fowl *Gallus domesticus*, which was a major item of diet and was known by its Polynesian name *moa*. At times chickens have become feral in large numbers. Some Easter Island chickens still lay pale blue eggs, and it has been claimed that this is an original character. Similar eggs are laid by fowls in South America, which perhaps argues for a contact between the two places in the past; but whether it implies an immigration of people, and if so in which direction, is not so clear (Chapter 2).

Migratory sea birds used to come by, but their numbers and variety have now dwindled. Before human occupation, sea birds must have nested not just on offshore islets, as they do today, but also on the main island and probably in vast numbers, like those on the uninhabited Henderson Island far to the northwest. On the islet of Motu Nui, in the 1930s, Alfred Métraux collected not just the sooty tern for which the island is famous, but also petrels, grey terns, noddy terns, boobies, tropicbirds and frigate birds.

Sea mammals and turtles do not seem to have been abundant after the arrival of human settlers, judging from the scarcity of their bones in archaeological sites, though turtle shells were sometimes used to make decorative objects; fish were clearly less limited, since 126 species have been recorded, but compare this figure with the 450 species available in Hawai'i or the more than 1000 in Fiji! The lack of a coral reef also meant that shellfish were highly restricted in their numbers and variety, though they were heavily exploited.

The island's invertebrate fauna is also small and has some introduced forms. There are a few species of isopods, spiders, insects, worms, a snail; a cricket and scorpion are said to be introduced, like an irritatingly ubiquitous large type of cockroach.

Although the present-day visitor to Easter Island might, with a little searching, find well over a hundred species of flowering plants and ferns growing, there is no doubt at all that the majority of these are recent introductions to the island. Many are ornamental plants, like the nasturtium and lavender; others are clearly crop plants, such as the avocado and the french bean. There are some large timber trees, including the blue gum and the Monterey cypress. Many are simply widespread weeds, like the fleabane and the dandelion. Sometimes the introduction is a matter of history, but more often it is unrecorded and – especially in the case of weeds – accidental. A few species are mentioned in the island's legends as having been introduced by the first settlers.

In 1956 the Swedish botanist Carl Skottsberg found only forty-six indigenous plant species, and knew of no other oceanic island of comparable dimensions, geology and climate with such a poor native flora. Even allowing for some important species that are now extinct (Chapter 4), it is clear that Easter Island's environment was somewhat special. The study of the native flora rests on its taxonomy, means of dispersal and known distribution outside the island. Certain species, for example, are endemic and, since they have no extra-island distribution, they must presumably be native. Others are known to occur on most tropical and subtropical coastlines. Their seeds float on sea water and remain viable in it, so there is no difficulty in believing them to be native too. In other cases, the likely means of arrival is by wind – this almost certainly applies to the ferns, whose spores are very light. A third possible method of arrival is by bird transport. This could include adherence to the feathers, feet or beak of a bird, or transport in its gut. A number of Easter Island grasses and sedges might well have been transported in the plumage of birds.

It is worth remembering that long-distance transport to Easter Island may have been less of an obstacle in the past than it is now. We know that a number of species (the endemic ones) have been there long enough to diverge by evolution from their relatives elsewhere. We also know that the island is at least three million years old, and for most of that period the Earth has been in the grip of successive ice ages. By removing water from the ocean to form massive polar ice caps, these ice ages lowered sea level by at least 100 m (328 ft), and possibly twice that much at times. Submerged islands (seamounts or guyots) abound in the Pacific (ill. 17). Although many of these are now too deep to have been exposed by the ice age lowering of sea level, the general history of Pacific islands is one of progressive lowering by a combination of marine and subaerial erosion and tectonic sinking (ill. 16), so that seamounts may have been higher in the past. All these factors combine to suggest that during much of Easter Island's existence, the possibility of 'stepping stone' dispersal would have been much greater than now.

It is also true that some of the mechanisms of dispersal may have been more powerful in the past. During the ice ages, the polar regions were subject to greater reductions in temperature than tropical regions. The difference in temperature between the tropics and the poles would therefore have been greater, and since this difference is what drives the 'Hadley circulation' (the basis of the trade winds), it is often argued that trade winds may have been more powerful in glacial times, although more latitudinally restricted. The westerly winds now prevalent in the forties latitudes may also have been stronger and there is evidence that this wind-belt moved towards the equator. Conversely, at times of higher temperature than now, such as the early to middle post-glacial (*c.* 9000 to 5000 years ago) and last interglacial (*c.* 120,000

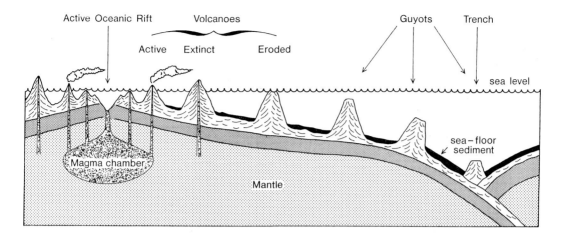

16,17 ABOVE *Volcanic islands such as Easter Island are formed by outpourings of molten rock from beneath the Earth's crust. Many of these islands, however, subsequently become submerged as the tectonic plate on which they rest is carried beneath an adjoining plate by the geological process of subduction.* BELOW *An apparently isolated island may be surrounded by numerous submerged peaks; the Pacific is known to contain hundreds of such 'hidden islands'.*

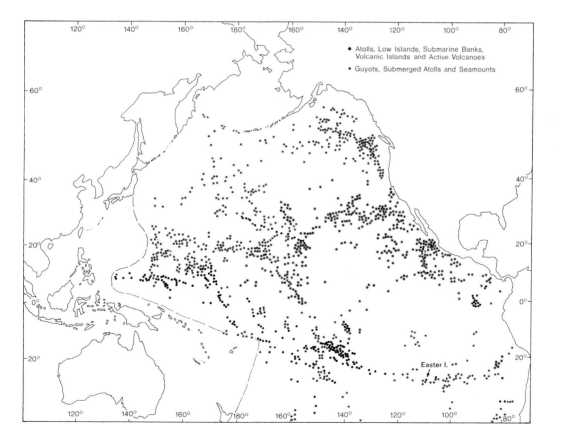

years ago), cyclones extended to higher latitudes and may have been more frequent than now; we may be seeing the start of a similar phase, caused by the Greenhouse Effect. There is thus a strong possibility that the wind speeds available to carry plant matter to Easter Island were greater in the past.

Another, perhaps more important reason why dispersal could have been more effective in earlier times is that, on many islands, not only were bird populations greater in the past, but also the number of species was much higher. We shall see in Chapter 4 that recent discoveries of fossil bones on several Pacific island groups such as Galápagos and Hawai'i have demonstrated the former existence of species that no longer occur there. Many of these were endemic species, now extinct. On Hawai'i, about twenty-five species are known to have been eliminated since human immigration. Some of these were apparently flightless, but others were perfectly capable of the long-distance migration that is common in birds. A number were ducks, a group for which the crater lakes of Easter could have been a suitable habitat.

It has been reckoned, therefore, that about half of Easter Island's native plant species could have arrived by bird, a third (all ferns) by wind and a sixth by water. The question of *where* they came from will be considered more fully in the next chapter. It will suffice here to state that, according to Skottsberg, most of the island's flora came from southeast Asia via western Polynesia, and only to a small extent from South America.

We have already mentioned that Easter Island's environment is somewhat special. The remarkable fact is that Skottsberg found only one species of indigenous tree (2 per cent) and two of shrubs (4 per cent). This is quite out of line with other 'high' islands of the Pacific, which have a large woody flora (70 per cent), and has led to its flora being described as 'disharmonic'.

The indigenous tree that Skottsberg identified, *Sophora toromiro*, is itself scarcely more than a shrub. It is endemic to Easter, although Skottsberg regards it as close to the species from the Juan Fernández Islands. The genus is common on islands of the southern oceans. The seeds of some sophoras can float in sea water for at least three years, and retain their viability for up to eight years. Thanks to the depredations of the inhabitants, and the introduction of browsing and grazing animals by Europeans, the toromiro declined, so that by the time Thor Heyerdahl visited the island in the 1950s he could find only a single, almost dead specimen in the crater of Rano Kau. Since then, no botanist has recorded it, and the species appeared to be extinct.

Miraculously, phoenix-like, it rose from the grave in Sweden. Seeds collected by Heyerdahl from the last surviving specimen on the island germinated in the botanic gardens at Göteborg. The species is now flourishing there, as well as in the botanic gardens at the University of Bonn. Attempts have been made to reintroduce it to the island; the first attempt was unsuccesful, and there was concern that perhaps some vital ingredient was no longer present in the island soil. The outcome of the latest attempt is awaited with great interest.

18 OPPOSITE *A moai on the coast at Tongariki. Its base was later damaged in an experiment intended to establish whether the statues could have been swivelled in an upright position to their final resting place. The foundations of a boat-shaped dwelling lie in the foreground.*

PART I

THE ORIGINAL 'BOAT PEOPLE'

When the subject is enigmatic Easter Island no man's knowledge is either complete or secure.

Father Sebastian Englert

20 *A present-day Easter Islander, descendant of the original 'boat people'.*

19 OPPOSITE *The beach at Anakena, with Ahu Nau Nau and its row of statues visible against a group of palms planted in an attempt to reintroduce them to the island. The moai in the left of the picture was restored to its platform by Thor Heyerdahl's 1955 expedition.*

CHAPTER 2

WHERE DID THEY COME FROM?

East or West?

The most fundamental question concerning the Easter Islanders, the one on which many other issues depend, is where did they come from? Deeps surround this volcanic island for a radius of 15 km (*c.* 9 miles), and it is definitely not the remnant of a lost continent, so its inhabitants – like those of all other Pacific islands – must have arrived from elsewhere and colonized it. But where was this elsewhere? In view of the island's geographical position, there are two basic choices: east (South America) or west (Polynesia).

The idea that the Pacific islands were settled from the New World was initially put forward in 1803 by Father Joacquin de Zuñiga, a Spanish missionary in the Philippines; he based his view on the prevailing winds and currents. A specific link between Easter Island and the mainland was first suggested in 1870 when, at a lecture given by J.L. Palmer at London's Royal Geographic Society, Sir Clements Markham mentioned apparent analogies between the island's platforms and statues and those at Tiahuanaco, Bolivia. A number of German scholars in the 1930s also published papers seeing the origin of Easter Island culture in prehistoric Peru.

In the second half of this century, the question of where the Easter Islanders came from has been dominated by the much publicized claims of the Norwegian explorer and adventurer Thor Heyerdahl. He accepts that Polynesians eventually reached the island from the west, and that it is their traits which dominated its anthropology and culture in recent periods; but he firmly believes that they were preceded by settlers from South America, to the east.

Since the question of where the islanders came from clearly has important consequences for the assessment of their cultural origins and development, we must begin by taking a look at the evidence for the two possible sources.

The relevant evidence is varied, and little of it taken alone could be seen as decisive; as we shall see, however, the cumulative effect does point in one direction rather than the other.

Thor Heyerdahl and the Kon-Tiki Expedition

The prevailing winds and currents in this part of the Pacific are of crucial importance, for they are used by Thor Heyerdahl to support his claim that

Polynesia could only have been settled from the New World. Indeed, the fact that southeast trade winds blow for most of the year encouraged Heyerdahl to attempt to prove his theory with the famous Kon-Tiki expedition of 1947.

In a trip of great daring and imagination, Heyerdahl and his crew of five set out from Peru on a raft made of balsa wood, in order to demonstrate that a simple vessel could drift to eastern Polynesia on this 'one-way marine escalator'. Their supplies included canned foods and a solar still for making drinking water from the sea – essential equipment for a journey that was certain to last a number of months. On encountering powerful whirls at the eastern end of the South Equatorial Current, they were forced to west as much as possible to avoid being swept back.

The six men – and a parrot – were crowded into a tiny bamboo cabin, sleeping on straw mattresses on reed matting. From a distance the vessel looked like 'an old Norwegian hay loft...full of bearded ruffians'. Initial anxieties about the logs becoming sodden or the ropes suffering from friction proved ill-founded, but the long heavy steering-oar often had to be wrestled with. There were dangers, such as a huge whale shark which had to be fought off with a harpoon, and occasional storms during one of which a man fell overboard, but was eventually rescued; the parrot, however, was washed overboard and never seen again.

The freshwater supplies became brackish after two months, but heavy showers replenished them. The ocean also provided food, since bonitos and flying fish would land on the deck, and once literally in the frying pan. Dolphins and pilot fish were constantly around the raft, and the crew amused themselves with the sport of luring sharks with tit bits and then hoisting them on board by the tail.

Finally, having become one with the elements, and after months of perfect solitude, the crew knew that they were approaching land when they saw hundreds of sea birds. After 101 days at sea, the Kon-Tiki crashed on to a reef in the Tuamotus, east of Tahiti.

Following the apparent success of the Kon-Tiki voyage, Heyerdahl went on to expand and refine his theory. He had first seen Polynesia as having been colonized from the coasts of both South and Northwest America, but after Kon-Tiki he limited his theory to South America alone. Furthermore – and somewhat paradoxically – he decided that the Polynesians had indeed managed to arrive in canoes from the west, but quite late in Easter Island's prehistory, eventually massacring most of the Amerindian settlers. He has taken his view still further, suggesting in his most recent book that Polynesians were, as he puts it:

brought to Easter Island, either with their consent or against their will, by navigators from a more culturally developed area of ancient Peru, using either force or cunning. Maybe the 19th-century Europeans were not the first to sail from Peru into the Pacific as slave raiders.

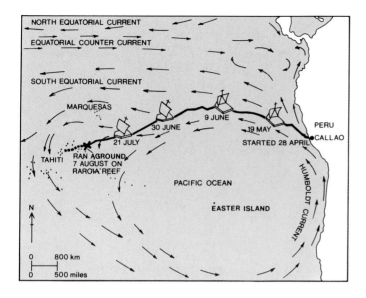

21–23 *In 1947, Thor Heyerdahl set out to prove that Polynesia was first settled from South America.* OPPOSITE *and* LEFT *Carrying a six-man crew, the Kon-Tiki, a raft made of balsa wood, survived the onslaught of occasional storms and powerful currents to drift westwards for 101 days before being wrecked east of Tahiti.* BELOW *Heyerdahl wrestling with the heavy steering oar. Despite the heroism of his expedition, it demonstrated no more than that a westward drift voyage was possible – and then only after a craft had been towed far out to sea to avoid the inshore Peruvian currents.*

Voyagers from the New World?

The Kon-Tiki voyage, therefore, was of decisive importance in the archaeological study of Easter Island, for it led to what many consider to be Heyerdahl's obsession with his theory of colonization from the east. Clearly believing that the Kon-Tiki proved his theory concerning the 'permanent tradewinds and forceful companion currents', he has bolstered his claim with selective evidence of the folk memory, botany, material culture, linguistics and physical anthropology of the island, building up a complex picture of the island's history – a picture that we must now examine more closely.

Heyerdahl presents, for example, the striking folk memory of an individual islander: Alexander Salmon, a half-Tahitian who lived on the island in the late 19th century, claimed that Hotu Matua came from a land in the direction of the rising sun in two big double-canoes with three hundred followers; they came from a group of islands to the east called Marae-toe-hau (Place of Burial), a very hot country.

These first South American settlers, as Heyerdahl sees it, introduced a series of plants to the island, including the sweet potato, toromiro, totora reed, chili pepper, cotton, and bottle gourd. He has always believed that the totora bullrush (*Scirpus riparius*) – the dominant plant of all three crater swamps of Easter Island – is identical to that of Peru; he claims that Olof Selling's (still unpublished) analysis found that its pollen suddenly began to deposit during the earliest human settlement period and was associated with soot particles. He also claims that pollen from freshwater plants was absent before humans arrived, and that totora and tavai (*Polygonum*, another aquatic plant) must have been brought in by humans because they generate only by new shoots from suckers, and not by seeds.

Over the years, Heyerdahl has put forward a whole list of tool-types and features found on Easter Island which he believes to be characteristic of the New World (though not necessarily of any single archaeological complex), but rare or absent in Polynesia – for example, stone pillows, shallow grinding-stones, basalt bowls, stone picks, stone fish-hooks, and bone needles – and he places equal stress on South American civilizations as sources of Easter Island's stonework and statues. In particular, it has often been suggested that the superb façade of closely fitted blocks at Ahu Vinapu I (ill. 31) is similar to Inca walls at Cuzco, Peru; and the kneeling statue 'Tukuturi' (ill. 24), discovered on the flank of Rano Raraku by Heyerdahl's 1955 expedition, has repeatedly been compared to kneeling statues from Tiahuanaco, and thus has been assumed to be an early prototype from which arose the more classic island statues, themselves compared somewhat paradoxically to standing statues from Tiahuanaco. Ironically, Heyerdahl himself once wrote that the classic *moai* have 'no similarity whatsoever to statues ... on the continent to the east'! He sees the fitted stone blocks of Easter Island as Early Period structures different from any known Polynesian pattern of architecture ('no Polynesian fisherman would have been capable of conceiving, much less building such a wall'); and he considers three aberrant statue types on the island (boulder heads, rectangular pillars with human traits, and kneeling figures) to be characteristic of pre-Classic Tiahuanaco. Heyerdahl has repeatedly pointed to superficial resemblances between the 16th-century Marquesas statues (see p. 108) and those of San Agustín in Colombia (of uncertain date, probably the early centuries AD), regardless of distance and chronology, although neither group has any specific resemblances with material from coastal Ecuador, which lies between them, together with 6400 km (4000 miles) of open sea! Furthermore, where domestic architecture is concerned, he sees two house-building traditions on Easter Island, with the Polynesians producing the boat-shaped pole-and-thatch dwellings (ills 68–70) and the Amerindians being responsible for the 'earlier' sophisticated corbelled structures.

In a somewhat tortuous argument, Heyerdahl also regards Rapa Nui's wooden carvings as non-Polynesian in inspiration and motif, especially the 'emaciated hooknosed long-eared goateed male figure' (ill. 154). Although he admits that these carvings must be from the Late Period (by which time he accepts the Polynesians had arrived), he insists that the objects display 'aberrant elements surviving from the Middle and even Early Periods'. Strangely enough, he sees the obsidian *mataa* (spearpoints), which did not occur before the Late Period, as bearing a strong resemblance to tools in Peru and the Andes. He has also made much of Edwin Ferdon's claim that four cupmarks on a rock at Rano Kau were a solar observatory, citing this as evidence of a heliolatry foreign to the rest of Polynesia and thus imported from sun-worshipping New World cultures.

The Easter Islanders' language has provided Heyerdahl with further evidence; the islanders' term for the sweet potato, for example (*kumara*), is similar to the pan-Polynesian term *kuumala*, which has often been derived from the Quechua (South American) word *cumar*. He notes that both Routledge and Englert had heard fragments of an incomprehensible ancient language, but that even the islanders could not understand these words by the time missionaries settled there, so they were not recorded. Heyerdahl chooses to assume that this ancient tongue came from South America; he believes that the original languages of Tiahuanaco and southern Peru were suppressed by the Inca long before they could be recorded, and hence it is impossible to find linguistic evidence for pre-Inca migrations from the mainland into Polynesia.

As for the Rongorongo 'script' preserved on a series of wooden boards, Heyerdahl has, in the past, tried to show some relationship with several South American scripts: for instance, he has mentioned a picture writing of the Cuna Indians of Panama and northwest Colombia, who painted on wooden tablets used for recording songs. He has also pointed to primitive writing systems found among the early historic (post-Columbian) Aymara and Quechua tribes of the Titicaca area who, like Rongorongo, use a 'boustrophedon' system, where the direction of lines is alternately reversed, so that one has to turn the tablet upside down at the end of each line. Similarly, he compares only selected

The Stonecarvers: from East or West?

24–26 LEFT *The famous kneeling statue 'Tukuturi' was discovered on Easter Island in 1955 on the flank of the Rano Raraku quarry by Thor Heyerdahl's team.*
ABOVE *Heyerdahl has repeatedly compared 'Tukuturi' to a kneeling stone figure from Tiahuanaco, the pre-Inca sun-worshipping centre in the Andes, but the similarities are not proof of Amerindian influence on Easter Island.* RIGHT *A squatting stone statue from Ra'ivavae, an island in the Cook-Austral chain near Tahiti, has much in common with the Easter Island example, demonstrating that a tradition of monumental stonecarving existed just as much in Polynesia as in South America.*

motifs and signs from Easter Island's abundant rock art and script with the total array of alleged ideograms on the monolithic gateway at Tiahuanaco in Bolivia.

In his study of physical anthropology, Heyerdahl points out that the skeletal material we have is primarily or exclusively from the later periods, by which time Polynesians were well established on the island. So the race of the earlier populations is still, for him, an open question. Nevertheless, he has recently claimed that new analyses of Easter Island skeletal material by American anthropologist George Gill have revealed 'traits that deviated from the Polynesian norm: many of the crania, for example, had curved "rocking-chair" jawbones, an un-Polynesian feature known from the aboriginal population of America'.

Heyerdahl has clearly spent decades assembling evidence to support his theory of Amerindian cultural superiority – yet does it hold up under close examination? Careful scrutiny reveals the flaws in his apparently convincing argument; as we shall see, he relies on the selective use of evidence, which results in a misleading conclusion.

Kon-Tiki – The Hidden Evidence

The Kon-Tiki voyage, while in many ways spectacular, is in fact far from conclusive proof that Polynesia was first settled from South America. The Kon-Tiki herself was modelled on a type of craft developed by the Peruvians only after the Spanish introduced the use of the sail. Prehistoric Peruvians did voyage with small three-log rafts off their coast, but propelled them with paddles; they also used one- and two-man reed-bundle floats, and inflated sealskin floats, depicted in thousands of prehistoric representations. Moreover, the desert coast of Peru lacked both the light woods needed for rafts and the large trees required for canoes. In southern Chile, sewn three-plank canoes existed, but here too the sail was unknown, and propulsion was by paddle and drifting with currents.

Furthermore, the Kon-Tiki's encounter with the South Equatorial Current – and the fact that she was towed out fifty nautical miles from the Peruvian coast – means that her journey cannot truly be termed a drift voyage; Eugene Savoy's 1969 attempt to repeat the trip without being towed away from the coast led to his raft being caught in the 250-mile wide Peru current and carried to Panama. Subsequent experiments have confirmed that, at best, the South Equatorial Current and the southeast trade winds would carry a vessel from Peru to the Marquesas or the Tuamotus, not to Easter Island. In any event, the comparison of Kon-Tiki with the drift voyage of a prehistoric vessel is hardly fair; Kon-Tiki was an intentional navigated voyage with a known, if general, destination, and the crew had the benefit of radios, maps and sophisticated navigation instruments. We must conclude that Kon-Tiki showed nothing more than that, by using a post-European-contact kind of sail-raft and modern survival equipment, it is possible to survive a 101-day voyage between Peru and Polynesia.

Winds, Currents and Navigation

Heyerdahl's argument relies on the prevailing easterly direction of the winds and currents in the region, yet this is by no means a constant: Heyerdahl, like de Zuñiga before him, overlooks the fact that the easterlies are subject to seasonal and annual variation, when the direction of winds and currents is from west to east. For example, Roggeveen, as we have seen, was prevented from landing on the island on 6 April 1722 by stormy winds from the northwest, and William Thomson noted that while in summer the wind blew from the southeast, in winter it blew from the southwest or west. There are also the 'El Nino' events to be considered – cyclical changes in the circulation of the ocean and atmosphere over a large part of the South Pacific, so named ('The Child') because they commonly occur around Christmas – westerly wind reversals that can become the prevailing wind over much of the region for a considerable period. During these episodes, the South Equatorial Current slackens or even reverses.

If the winds and currents can tell us little in themselves, we must turn to the navigational skills of the ancient Polynesians and South Americans, to see which group was best qualified to make the long and hazardous journey to Easter Island.

We have abundant, excellent, documented evidence of the amazing navigational skills of the ancient Polynesians who travelled across vast stretches of the Pacific carrying people and resources, colonizing such far-flung islands as Hawai'i and New Zealand, and usually progressing in a generally easterly direction, albeit with some counter movements. In fact, we know from the journals of explorers and missionaries that Polynesian mariners of the 18th and 19th centuries knew how to sail against the wind – prevailing southeasters posed no obstacle to sailing canoes or other sailed vessels, which simply tacked or lay close to the wind, and were helped by their long steering-oar or by paddles; and the Polynesians were well acquainted with the westerlies and frequently used them to sail eastward. Indeed, the exploits of the Polynesians throughout their history in colonizing every habitable island over 30 million sq. km (c. 11½ million sq. miles) of Pacific Ocean have been described as 'the great seafaring saga of all time', one that we shall examine more closely in Chapter 3.

On the other hand, we have no solid evidence for any ancient South American ocean voyaging of this type; there is no indication that in the early centuries AD (or indeed later) South American Indians had the capacity to move themselves and their domesticates over such great distances. Instead, their vessels seem to have hugged the shore, although finds of pottery indicate that some South Americans did reach the Galápagos Islands, 960 km (600 miles) west of Ecuador. It is known that this part of northwest South America, unlike Peru, did have prehistoric sailing rafts, with sails, that were capable of long voyages. However, there are few islands near the American coast that might encourage the development of off-shore voyaging of this type. Most South American sailing took place in the zone of very settled weather – the winds and currents only become strong well out to sea. After the Kon-Tiki expedition, Heyerdahl learned from South Americans how to steer a raft by manipulating the centre-boards and sail, so that the vessel could be handled as easily as any boat and could sail in any direction. But if the South Americans could do this, why not also the Polynesians? In addition, it is worth remembering that sailing off this continental coast is very different from voyaging between islands, in that you always know where you are, and you merely have to sail east to reach some point of the shore.

There is also the extreme isolation of Easter Island, so remote that it is pretty unlikely that it could be found more than once with any degree of reliability. And even if a very occasional stray vessel did reach that tiny speck from east or west, there is little chance that it could have gone to its homeland and back, let alone directed other vessels to the island. Most specialists consider two-way voyaging from the island to have been impossible during its prehistory, and many believe that it was settled only once.

Yet despite these facts, Heyerdahl is asking us to believe that not only did some enterprising voyagers from ancient Peru make it to Easter Island, but that they also went further west, kidnapped some Polynesians and brought them back. Assuming that the Peruvians maintained contact with their mother country, this all implies that the South Americans were fully capable of sailing eastward despite the prevailing currents and winds!

It is, clearly, far more sensible to base oneself on the proven skills and long-distance voyages of the ancient Polynesians, and to assume not only that they were fully capable of reaching Rapa Nui, but perhaps also of sailing further eastward to South America and possibly even returning safely to Polynesia (there are some prehistoric finds in Chile, for example, which could well be of Polynesian origin, though finds of Easter Island spearheads there may simply reflect the export of the island's artifacts since the 19th century). Any possible New World influences in Polynesia may not necessarily have had anything to do with Amerindian voyaging. . . .

The navigational skills of the ancient Polynesians are clear, therefore, and feature in a number of the Easter Islanders' compelling traditions and legends; indeed, virtually all the islanders' rich folk memories and legends support the case for colonization from the west.

Oral Traditions

One of the best-known legends of Easter Island is that Hotu Matua, the island's first king, came from the west, heading for the sunrise, and that his

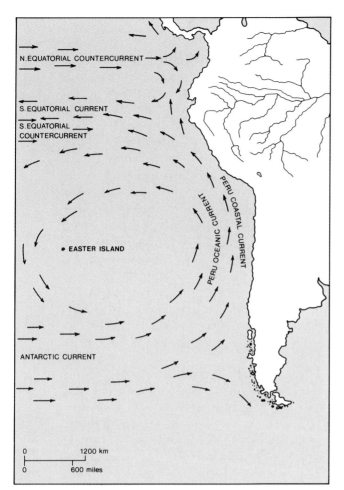

The Seafarers: Peruvians or Polynesians?

27–29 TOP LEFT *The map of prevailing ocean currents appears to support Heyerdahl's belief in the colonization of Easter Island from Peru – but the Peru coastal current tends to carry vessels north to Panama, while the ocean currents and winds often change direction.* TOP RIGHT *A Peruvian fisherboy on a reed float.* ABOVE *Polynesian mariners used canoes like this New Zealand type and vessels with sails to cross vast stretches of the Pacific.*

home was an island called Hiva. It is noteworthy that this name occurs several times (Nuku Hiva, Fatu Hiva, Hiva Oa) in the Marquesas Islands, 3360 km (2100 miles) northwest of Easter Island, because Father Sebastian Englert, one of this century's foremost experts on the island's culture, believed that this is where Hotu Matua came from. It would be ironic if Easter Island had been colonized from Fatu Hiva, the very place where Heyerdahl first began his quest to prove the opposite.

Furthermore, it is said that when Hotu Matua felt death approaching, he went to the sacred site of Orongo (the island's westernmost point) and called out to his homeland. In fact, Polynesian tradition sees the westernmost part of a land as the departure point of souls. Routledge heard that tale, and specifically noted that Hotu Matua 'looked over the islet of Motu Nui towards Marae Renga...his old home'. Similarly, according to Alfred Métraux, the islanders only knew the name of the land of their first ancestor, 'a big island located to the west called Marae-Renga. It was warm there and had lots of trees' – this was certainly a Polynesian island. Surgeon Palmer of H.M.S. *Topaze*, which called at Rapa Nui in 1868, said that the islanders of his day believed that the island of Rapa, 3850 km (2400 miles) to the west, was their original home.

A leading specialist in Polynesian archaeology, Yosihiko Sinoto, having worked in the Marquesas for many years, remarked that 'when I first visited Easter Island it was like going home.' The two places have so many similarities in their material culture and language, as will be seen below, that Kenneth Emory, the eminent specialist in Polynesian archaeology, became convinced that the prehistoric culture of Easter Island could have evolved from a single landing of Polynesians from a Marquesan island, fully equipped to colonize an uninhabited volcanic island.

Heyerdahl's approach to oral traditions is extremely selective, therefore: his model starts from a myth, and then he tries to support this picture with concrete evidence. He thus chooses to dismiss legends that the islanders came from the west (i.e. East Polynesia). The fact that all the island's folk-tales only began to be collected in the late 19th century, by which time the population had come very close to extinction, and that the few survivors may have had a less than perfect knowledge of the old traditions and legends, and besides had acquired terrible knowledge of Peru's existence through slave raids, should encourage the greatest caution, but Heyerdahl firmly believes his chosen scenario.

However, 'memory material' in modern anthropology is interpreted mainly as a clue to contemporary social relations, and its value as a historical record is very limited. Many scholars are reluctant to use this material to cover deficiencies in archaeology; but while scientists prefer to work from the archaeological and ethnographic evidence, using oral traditions only to provide confirmation or colour here and there, Heyerdahl does the precise opposite. Even within the selected story that Heyerdahl chooses to believe, he regards some parts as reliable (the direction from which the colonists came, the description of their land), but rejects others as allegorical (for example, that the first two separate arrivals were brothers, and the fact that even the legend pointing to an eastern origin says the homeland was a group of islands).

In fact, there is very little reason to pay the slightest attention to Heyerdahl's tale; for a start, it claims that Hotu Matua found the island empty, but also contradicts this by saying that his brother Machaa was already there, having set out two months previously. The chances of two such voyages managing to reach the same isolated speck just by heading west beggars belief. We shall see below that botanical evidence also destroys some aspects of these tales. But even more crucially, Thomson recorded the story in 1886 after a mere eleven days on the island; yet only twenty-eight years later Mrs Routledge, who spent sixteen months there intensively gathering information, *never encountered that story*. Instead, her informants either did not know (like most of Thomson's) or claimed that their ancestors came from two neighbouring islands known as Marae Renga and Marae Tohio.

In short, it is extremely dangerous to rely on oral traditions: as Mrs Routledge wisely pointed out,

> It was even more difficult to collect facts from brains than out of stones...it is particularly difficult to arrive at the truth from the untutored mind...when memory was vague, there was a constant tendency to glide from what was remembered to what was imagined.... The information given in reply to questions is generally wildly mythical.

Elsewhere she added that 'the Polynesians are notoriously inexact in their statements. They frequently do not themselves know when they are speaking the truth and when they are relying on imagination.'

So all the recorded folk tales from the island need to be taken with a large pinch of marine salt. But if oral tradition is to be included, as Heyerdahl insists it must, then his preferred version of the islanders' origins seems to be wildly inaccurate, inconsistent and aberrant; all the other versions gathered both before and after point to the west.

Folk memories can be equally misleading in the study of the island's plants: pollen analysis has shown, for example, that toromiro (*Sophora toromiro*) and hauhau (*Triumfetta semitriloba*) trees were on the island thousands of years before humans arrived, yet oral tradition says that these species, along with all other useful plants, were introduced by Hotu Matua, the first king: so much for the reliability of oral traditions!

Since the island's legends frequently contradict each other and cannot be seen as decisive evidence, perhaps we can make some progress by taking a look at the more tangible botanical information that is available.

Botanical Evidence

Taxonomy provides a clear challenge to Heyerdahl's theory of colonizers from the New World, in that the island had no maize, beans or squash – staple resources in South America – at the time of the European arrival or even in the first pollen analysis done for Heyerdahl's own investigation. It also disputes Heyerdahl's claim for the Peruvian origin of the totora, for the island's variety of totora is distinct from Peruvian ones (though similar to a Chilean kind), and it can reproduce by seeds, which could therefore have been transported to the island by the wind, the ocean or on birds' feet. There is nothing bizarre in such a method of transport. Charles Darwin washed the seeds of fifty-two species of plants from the feet of water birds. The tavai also probably reproduced by seed, and could have been introduced by birds from any number of places. Indeed, the fact that it occurs in South America does not prove Heyerdahl's case, for it could have been transported on birds' feet from South America to, say, the Marquesas in some distant time period, only to be taken by people from there to Easter Island. This would not be surprising, for the plant is credited with medicinal value. Pollen evidence is unclear about this plant's antiquity on the island.

The name for totora is the same in Hawai'i as on Easter Island, revealing that the word must have been carried from a common homeland where a similar reed was present before these islands were settled. In any case, all this argument has become academic recently, since pollen analysis by John Flenley shows the reed has been present on Easter Island for at least 30,000 years! It provides no evidence whatsoever for a link with the New World. Besides, we know that during Roggeveen's visit in 1722 natives 'came swimming on bundles of tied reeds' – they had no reed boats of the type associated with this plant in South America.

Heyerdahl's theory of the South American origin of the chili pepper is equally dubious. According to the Spanish account of 1770, chilis were brought out by the islanders together with sweet potatoes and bananas; Heyerdahl asserted that no other plant on the island could possibly be confused with chili peppers, while others suggested that it was probably confused with the indigenous plant *Solanum* whose native name of *poporo* or *poroporo* is also applied to the chili peppers now growing on the island. It is especially noteworthy that Captain Cook's botanist, George Forster, who devoted rather more time to such observations only four years later, never reported chili peppers.

In fact, the Australian researcher Robert Langdon believes that the whole chili pepper story rests on a mistranslation of the word *guineos* as a noun, rather than as an adjective describing the bananas ('guinea plantains'). However, he also believes that a different mistake has masked the presence of the American plant manioc (tapioca/cassava) on Easter Island: in the original Spanish account of 1770 the word *yuca* was used, which was translated as taro or left untranslated. It remains to be seen what credence can be placed in Langdon's theory: for a start, it relies on the testimony of a couple of 18th-century Spanish pilots, neither of whom presumably was very skilled at botanical identification. Secondly, Forster, the first botanist to visit the island, clearly recorded taro rather than cassava only four years later; and Langdon himself points out that Thomson made no mention of the plant in his careful list. It is hardly a crop that can be missed, for it is not seasonal, and has a large and distinctive top growth; yet it does not appear in any account until the thorough botanical survey of 1911! Langdon is driven to imagine a scenario whereby the final Polynesian settlers who came to the island neglected the plant, which was unfamiliar to them; so the manioc supposedly reported in 1770 became extinct, but the plant was reintroduced before 1911. . . . Clearly, an awful lot of assumptions are being made here.

As for cotton, none of the first three European expeditions (Roggeveen, González, Cook) reported seeing any, and we know that La Pérouse, the next European visitor in 1786, sowed some cotton seeds. The first botanical survey of the island, in 1911, found a few isolated semi-wild specimens of cotton, and claimed these had been introduced in the 1860s. Moreover, no word for the plant was recorded in the early dictionaries or vocabularies of the island. The only textiles seen by the first European visitors in 1722 were made of *tapa*, the beaten bark of the paper mulberry: at that time, even Polynesians who knew the cotton plant (such as Tahitians) did not know that it could be spun and woven, whereas the prehistoric Peruvians were the greatest experts the world has ever seen in spinning and weaving cotton. The total absence and ignorance of woven textiles on Easter Island is damning evidence against any link with Peru.

The one remaining possible botanical link between island and South American mainland is the sweet potato (*Ipomoea batatas*), which was certainly present on the island by 1722; Heyerdahl implies that it came direct from South America, though he has also admitted it might have come from the Marquesas. Even if it reached there from the New World, this would in no way imply any direct contact between Easter Island and the mainland. As yet we simply do not know how and where the plant was introduced to Oceania from South America, if that is indeed what happened (there are wild species in Southeast Asia). Many scholars believe it could have been distributed by birds or other natural means. On linguistic evidence, according to specialist Douglas Yen, it is probable that it was carried to central East Polynesia somewhere between the 3rd and 8th centuries AD, and was widely dispersed from there. Unfortunately, although its pollen grains are large and distinctive, they do not seem to preserve in sediments, and none has been recovered from Easter Island's crater-cores that could shed light on its history in Rapa Nui.

The latest thinking, therefore, is that no solid evidence exists for the transfer of any known plant between the New World and Polynesia. And even if the sweet potato was somehow obtained from the New World, this is very different from the transfer of a whole range of Amerindian material culture and religion, as well as of adequate numbers of Amerindians themselves. These are the areas to which we must now turn our attention.

Art and Artifacts

What can archaeology itself, in the form of artifacts, art and structures, tell us about the origin of the Easter Islanders? The studies and excavations of this century, and especially of the past few decades, have led almost all specialists in the archaeology of the South Pacific to see Rapa Nui's artifacts as clearly of Polynesian origin, and thoroughly familiar within the context of east Polynesian material culture.

Rapa Nui's fish-hooks, for example – despite Heyerdahl's claims – are typically and distinctively Polynesian, displaying continuity at least back to a group dated at Ahu Vinapu to AD 1220, and therefore on balance argue against any significant non-Polynesian element in Easter Island culture; for example, the use of sharply incurved points, in contrast to the barbed forms of Hawai'i and New Zealand, is also characteristic of early periods in the Marquesas. The two-piece hook, on the other hand, was a local development, comparable to innovations in Hawai'i and New Zealand.

The island's stone adzes correspond to the simple forms of a very early stage in east Polynesian adze development (as found especially in the Marquesas, as well as the Society Islands, Samoa and Tonga). Rapa Nui seems to have been isolated before the development of fully tanged forms in the rest of east Polynesia, but had some later innovations of its own, such as a quadrangular pecked adze with a deeply grooved butt. Much of the island's other material culture likewise reflects affinities with east Polynesia (particularly the Marquesas), innovations due to long isolation, and adaptation to local conditions (such as a comparative scarcity of large shells for tools, and an abundance of obsidian). The absence of Polynesia's typical food-pounders on Easter Island, like that of certain adze types which developed by AD 1000 in central Polynesia, points to a colonization in the first centuries AD.

Heyerdahl did find evidence of repeated South American visits to the (far closer) Galápagos Islands in the form of over 2000 fragments from at least 131 pots, 44 of them clearly pre-Inca types from South America. But, just as there is no trace of textiles, not a single prehistoric potsherd has ever been found on Easter Island – yet these are the two most characteristic and abundant products of Peruvian culture. Even if South Americans had brought no pottery with them, they could still have manufactured some on the island: Carlyle Smith, one of the archaeologists taken to Rapa Nui by Heyerdahl in 1955, found a source of excellent potter's clay on the island, in a damp area on the west slope of Rano Raraku. He made a small pottery vessel with it, and fired it successfully. Clearly any Amerindian potter could have done so too.

The same argument does not apply to Polynesians, however; although the

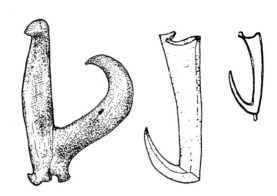

30 *A simple bone fish hook from Easter Island (right) – almost certainly made from the thigh bone of a deceased fisherman – can be compared with pearl-shell hooks from the Marquesas Islands (centre and far right), which suggests that the Easter Island fishermen who made such hooks were of Polynesian descent.*

early prehistory of western Polynesia is characterized by decorated *Lapita* pottery, which developed into a plain ware by the first millennium BC, pottery seems to have disappeared entirely by AD 200 in Samoa and Tonga, and by AD 300 everywhere else. In fact, after that date, it is probable that no society anywhere in Polynesia made pottery at all, perhaps because of the comparative poverty of clay resources on these basalt and coral islands. In other words, any Polynesian colonizers of Easter Island would be unfamiliar with pottery-making, unlike the Amerindians.

Ironically, at one point it appeared that pottery had been found: Heyerdahl showed the islanders potsherds from Peru, hoping that similar material might turn up on Rapa Nui. Sure enough, before long, a man produced some polished red sherds from a single vessel, which he claimed to be from a looted grave at Ahu Tepeu. The archaeologists found no pottery there, and indeed the episode turned out to be a hoax, the sherds being from an old pot from Chile. The islanders had been anxious to find what 'el señor Kon-Tiki' needed, and an excited Heyerdahl understandably could not believe his ears when he learned the truth, so badly did he want pottery to be found.

It is worth noting that some prehistoric pottery has been found in the Marquesas Islands, which were settled by the 1st century BC, but it was all imported from the west. Some stone bowls on Easter Island are identical in rim-shape to coarse-ware pottery bowls from Samoa; it has been suggested that such stone bowls, which appear to be replicas of late Polynesian Plain Ware ceramics, may be a tantalizing clue to early settlement of Rapa Nui.

A further argument against strong South American influence is the complete absence of the pressure-flaking technique on stone tools throughout Polynesia. This technique, involving 'pushing' flakes off a core, as opposed to striking them, was widespread in the New World; it appeared early and lasted a very long time, so any Amerindians reaching Easter Island would undoubtedly have used it, especially as the island's obsidian is eminently suited to the method. This was one piece of negative evidence which left William Mulloy – previously known for his work on Amerindian culture – 'unconvinced an American Indian had ever set foot on the island'.

So much for artifacts. But what of the monumental platforms and carvings? There are indeed some superficial similarities visible here and there between Easter Island and South American forms – after all, there are only so many shapes which simple monolithic human statues can take – but there is also much contradiction, wishful thinking and subjectivity underlying Heyerdahl's assertions. Even the few American anthropologists who strongly believed in contact between the New World and other parts of the Pacific found it very peculiar that Heyerdahl should be pointing to resemblances between Rapa Nui and the Tiahuanaco culture centred on Lake Titicaca in the highlands of Peru and Bolivia, rather than with a coastal complex. Moreover, the Classic Tiahuanaco phase begins around AD 800, and its influence on the coast starts 200 years later, so if the first settlers reached Easter Island before AD 400, as Heyerdahl believes, how could they bring Tiahuanaco culture across with them? This was the period of Mochica culture on the Peruvian coast. To overcome the contradictions, he would have to dismiss two early Rapa Nui radiocarbon dates (AD 318 from reeds in a grave at Ahu Tepeu I, and AD 380 from charcoal in the Poike ditch) as being invalid (e.g. the charcoal could be natural), and place the first settlement at the next earliest date of AD 690 (from Tahai).

Secondly, the accurate mortarless fitting of large polygonal blocks began in Peru after AD 1440, but Easter Island has similar dressed stonework before AD 1200 (at Tahai). Heyerdahl assigned Vinapu I (with fitted blocks) to the Early Period, but it has been shown that it probably dates to AD 1516, whereas Vinapu II is actually earlier (AD 857) and displays a rougher, typically east Polynesian facing of vertical slabs – in fact a block from Vinapu II is actually incorporated in the foundation of Vinapu I! So while a later date for Vinapu I corresponds better to the age of fitted blocks in the Andes, it postdates a clearly Polynesian structure on the same site.

In any case, Easter Island's platforms conform to the tradition and plan of the *marae* (shrines to ancestral gods, and socio-religious centres) of east Polynesia, not to those of Andean temples: in fact, Ahu Tepeu I (which produced the 4th-century date) bears a very marked resemblance to a *marae* on Timoe Island, near Mangareva – indeed, Mangarevan *marae* are more similar to Easter Island's platforms than to any other stone structures in Polynesia, suggesting a connection or, more likely, a common origin in the Marquesas. As for the stone walls, Andean specialists have pointed out that they cannot match the type exactly among classic Inca masonry. Moreover, unlike the solid blocks used in Peru, the Easter Island 'walls' are actually a facing of slabs that masks a rubble core, so any resemblance with Cyclopean blocks is equally superficial.

It has been suggested that the islanders' skill with stone was derived from their expertise in carpentry and woodworking, such as in producing the planks needed for canoes. But it was not a skill unique to Rapa Nui, since house platforms in the Marquesas, described as the finest in Polynesia, were built with beautifully fitted but unshaped Cyclopean basalt blocks: the dance-platform of Uahake-kua was built of stones weighing 3 to 5 tons each. One can also mention the immensely tall – 5 m or 16 ft – stone trilithon 'Haamonga a Maui' of about AD 1200 on the island of Tonga (ill. 33), reminiscent of the Stonehenge trilithons, and made of quarried coral blocks weighing 30 or 40 tons. Polynesians were no strangers to stoneworking or Cyclopean blocks. They were also quite capable of producing sophisticated corbelled structures, whatever Heyerdahl claims; there is no strong evidence that these were earlier than the boat-shaped dwellings (indeed, some of those at Orongo incorporate kerbstones from the boat-shaped houses in their stonework!) and, in fact, it is far more likely that the stone houses with corbelled roofs are a local invention stimulated by the availability of abundant flat, thin basalt slabs and, perhaps, a growing scarcity of materials for pole-and-thatch dwellings – perhaps even by the necessity of producing structures which could better withstand the elements. In any case, corbelling also exists in Hawai'i, and was clearly within the repertoire of 'Polynesian fishermen'. The boat-shaped houses certainly resemble elliptical structures of Mangareva, Rapa and the Tuamotus; the stone kerbs that outline some on Easter Island also occur in Mangareva and the Society Islands.

Furthermore, Heyerdahl's 'boulder-heads' are, in fact, recarved fragments of Rano Raraku tuff that used to be intact statues of classic type. The rectangular humanoid pillars appear to have been in use in the 19th century at Vinapu, and are thus more likely to be a very late form than very early.

Where the kneeling statue 'Tukuturi' is concerned, it has often been pointed out that there is no evidence for its early date – we have no idea about its original position – and several scholars, including Sebastian Englert, have seen it as stylistically a very late sculpture that resembles a Polynesian *tiki* (its posture is well known on Easter Island, and is used by singers in festivals). A recent attempt to pinpoint it led to four radiocarbon dates, two recent, one early, and one in-between, so the question remains unresolved. The kneeling statue of Tiahuanaco cannot be said to share more than its posture with the Easter Island example, and the latter's face is in any case too weathered for sound comparisons to be made. The treatment of Tukuturi's body is far less angular and more naturalistic, and its face is at quite a different angle: the more one looks at the two, the less alike they seem.

Very few specialists in either Polynesian or South American sculpture have been even remotely convinced by Heyerdahl's analogies. Heyerdahl has also compared much of Easter Island's other art with that of South America, and here, some of his examples are more plausible than others. Unfortunately, a few features such as supposed 'felines' and a 'turkey' seem to be figments of the imagination: William Thomson found that a single petroglyph of a birdman at Orongo with the face of Makemake, the main deity, was similar to a decorated stone he knew from Peru (though he stressed that he knew of no other similarity between the island's relics and those of Peru). However, his

Monuments and Masons

31–33 *Certain resemblances between Inca and Easter Island stonework helped convince Heyerdahl that there had been Peruvian contacts.* TOP *The well-fitted façade of the ahu, or statue platform, Vinapu I, on the coast of Easter Island.* ABOVE *An Inca wall of closely fitted blocks at Cuzco, Peru, showing the famous twelve-angled stone.* RIGHT *The Polynesians were, in fact, equally capable of shaping great blocks of stone to produce impressive monuments such as this trilithon of cut and fitted coral on the island of Tonga.*

 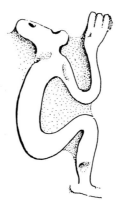 

34–36 LEFT *An Easter Island rock carving portraying the 'birdman'.* CENTRE *A Hawaiian rock art figure which, although lacking a beak, is astonishingly similar to its counterpart on Easter Island.* RIGHT *A net float from the Solomon Islands likewise portrays a seated human with a bird's head.*

cursory sketch of that figure lacks its bird-beak (in fact, he failed to mention birdman figures at all), while his unfortunate and inaccurate description of claw-like hands and feet was seized on by Heyerdahl as indicating 'feline' features and hence a link with the New World (although it has been argued that even if feline images were found on the island, they could easily postdate European contact, and in any case prove nothing about cats in Polynesia, let alone an American origin).

A further error of this type was Lavachery's illustration of a painted face in a cave on Motu Nui with 'tear-streaks' – another South American trait for Heyerdahl although, in fact, the lines on the face simply seem to define the shape of the nose.

As for Heyerdahl's attempt to link Easter Island's famous 'birdman' motif (ill. 34) with the New World, there are equally good if not better analogies in other directions, such as some remarkable resemblances between the Easter Island motifs and others in the Solomon Islands, where seated humans with frigate-bird heads are carved as net floats and canoe prows; while American rock-art specialist Georgia Lee has recently studied petroglyphs in the Hawaiian Islands, depicting squatting anthropomorphs in profile, some almost in basrelief, which 'bear an uncanny resemblance' to the birdmen of Easter Island. Rather than jump to simplistic conclusions about direct contact between the two places, however, she sensibly prefers to see the similarity as reflecting a shared Polynesian heritage.

Another factor which has recently come to light is that Hawaiian rock art includes an 'eye-mask' motif, which bears a remarkable resemblance to those of Easter Island as well as to some big-eyed faces in the art of the Marquesas.

The wooden statuettes of male figures on Rapa Nui recall certain wooden

37–39 LEFT *A typical Easter Island 'eye-mask' motif.* CENTRE *A rock carving of a face from Hawai'i.* RIGHT *The recurring 'eye-mask' face also appears in the Marquesas Islands.*

images of Hawai'i with similarly emphasized ribs and backbones, while elongated earlobes with earplugs are also prominent in the Marquesas – two factors that render Heyerdahl's ascription of American origins highly questionable. Furthermore, closer examination of the cupmarks at Rano Kau, cited by Edwin Ferdon as evidence of heliolatry on the island – a claim seized upon by Heyerdahl – reveals that they would be a hopelessly inaccurate solsticial observatory, especially since the horizon is obscured at this location. Hence, another New World trait proves to be a mirage.

All in all, the available archaeological evidence shows strong continuities leading up to the recent, better-known and undoubtedly Polynesian materials: these continuities, in artifacts and in the siting, planning, building and use of typically Polynesian ceremonial platforms, are in sharp contrast to the 'clear break' necessary to Heyerdahl's theory of the arrival of two totally different populations. Even if one were to allow some of Heyerdahl's resemblances to South American specimens, it is clear that the vast majority of Easter Island's material culture points to an origin in the west. Can the fields of language and physical anthropology cast further light on this matter?

Linguistics

Almost all recent work on this topic derives the language of Easter Island entirely from Polynesia: some of the words, such as *poki* for child, are unique to the island, and are symptomatic of the islanders' long isolation from their roots (it is generally reckoned that Easter Island became isolated from the rest of eastern Polynesia before the colonization of Hawai'i and New Zealand); however, Thor Heyerdahl inevitably regards these local words as being non-

Polynesian, from an alien (i.e. New World) substratum. For example, he points to the words for 'one' to 'ten' recorded by the Spanish visitors in 1770; yet, as Métraux showed, the Spaniards were on the island for only six days and were totally unfamiliar with Polynesian languages, so any information obtained by them is almost certainly garbled. Only four years later, Cook – who had a Tahitian with him, who could converse with the islanders – recorded correct proto-Polynesian words for one to ten on Rapa Nui. Similarly, Heyerdahl's attempt to trace the word *kumara* to a South American origin – specifically the Quechua (South American) word *cumar* – is far-fetched: in fact, nowhere on the South American coast was there a people cultivating any kind of sweet potato under a name even remotely resembling *cumar* or *cumara*. The Quechua word for sweet potato is *apichu*.

A few other researchers, notably Robert Langdon and Darrell Tryon, are also trying to turn the old Rapa Nui tongue into a link between Polynesia and South America: they claim that, at the time of contact, Rapa Nui's language was made up of three elements, one of west Polynesian origin, one from east Polynesia, and the third of unidentified origin. The first two elements were allegedly fused on the island of Ra'ivavae, 500 km (311 miles) south of Tahiti, and this language was then carried to Easter Island no earlier than the 16th century. The third element, comprising words unknown in other Polynesian languages, was the remnant of a non-Polynesian tongue which could only have come from the east in ancient times.

However, other specialists such as Roger Green have shown that there is only weak and selective evidence for this view, and, in fact, no satisfying evidence at all for the existence of a pre-Polynesian language on Easter Island. Langdon and Tryon conjure up a very complex picture, with influences going back and forth across the ocean, and with repeated borrowings which are unmarked and undetected in Easter Island linguistics. The standard, orthodox view is far more straightforward and accounts for the evidence more economically and quite satisfactorily: this is, therefore, a case for applying Occam's razor and choosing the simpler, common-sense explanation: i.e. the language of Easter Island is a member of an eastern Polynesian subgroup.

Certain words in the island's language show clear links with the 'Central Eastern' group of Polynesian languages, while others seem linked to western Polynesia, and not the central eastern area. All place-names are Polynesian. Attempts at glottochronology, using changes in language to estimate the length of time since the islanders became cut off from their homeland, point to their having parted company with eastern Polynesia between AD 300 and 530, probably around AD 400.

The language does stand apart from the others of the region in a number of ways, because it retains many features that have been lost or replaced on other islands. It seems to have a transitional or 'developmental' position between the tongues of western and eastern Polynesia. This suggests strongly that it was the first language to split off from eastern Polynesia; in the course

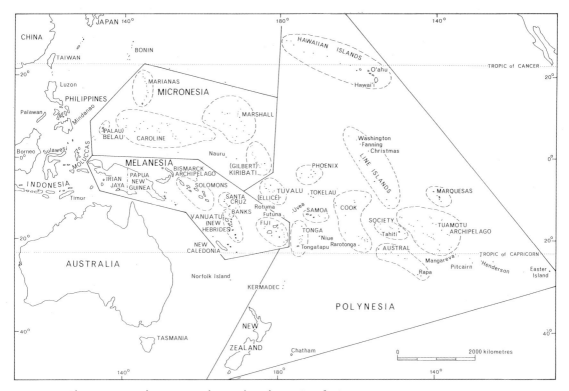

40 *Place-names and regions in the south and west Pacific Ocean.*

of its long isolation it lost some features and adopted others, while the other islands innovated a shared set of new features or lost inherited ones.

Heyerdahl's comparison of Easter Island's rock art and script with those of Bolivia is as dubious as his theory concerning the island's language: in fact, there are far more remarkable similarities between some Rongorongo motifs and designs employed in the Solomon Islands, which have led some scholars to believe that the Easter Island 'script' originated in Melanesia. Although the implied theory of a direct migration from there to Easter Island is no longer tenable (the Marquesas Islands are now seen as the obvious source), it is still clear that there were related influences at work here.

All current specialists, such as the Russians Butinov and Knorozov, say that the island's 'script' is clearly Polynesian, with its signs reflecting local environment and culture; they noted the use of boustrophedon (named after the way an ox ploughs a field) in Peru, but saw no affinity between signs in the two places, concluding that Easter Island did not borrow its 'script' from Peru, although there remained the possibility of some influence in either direction.

The foremost Rongorongo scholar, Thomas Barthel of Germany, says that the names, phrases and allusions so far deciphered on the Easter Island boards are unequivocally of Polynesian origin: he has found references to Tahiti, Bora Bora, Pitcairn, and to common Polynesian plants that have never grown on Easter Island. Consequently, he believes that the 'script' originated elsewhere in eastern Polynesia – perhaps on Huahine or Raiatea – and came to Rapa Nui with Hotu Matua.

But is there any evidence of the arrival of two different peoples on the island? Or should one assume, as has been argued, that arriving voyagers or castaways would probably have been killed or enslaved rather than allowed an opportunity to introduce new behaviour patterns?

Physical Anthropology

From the very start of anthropological analysis of the island's human remains, the results have always pointed west: measurements of skulls led a number of scholars, including leading British anatomist Sir Arthur Keith, independently to indicate a Melanesian origin rather than a Polynesian, though Polynesian types were present; while the 19th-century French scholar Hamy found affinities between the island's skulls and those of Papua New Guinea. More recent analyses have shown that Easter Island head shape and dentition have close affinities with those of Hawaiians. Current thinking is that the Easter Islanders are undoubtedly Polynesians, with no admixture with other groups; any morphological extremes found can be attributed – like those in language or material culture – to long development in isolation.

Analysis by Rupert Murrill of the bones collected by Heyerdahl's Norwegian expedition concluded that the islanders are and were Polynesian. Studies of blood groups led some scholars to suggest, with reservations, that South American Indians could have been a source of the island's population, but Murrill deduced from the same data that both the islanders and the Amerindians came from the same gene pool in east Asia: so much for blood groups! Roy Simmons studied the blood-group genetics of living islanders and other Polynesians, and suggested that they were the products of drift voyages from every direction, including South America, but stressed that such conclusions cannot really be deduced from blood-group, gene-frequency comparisons. In short, blood typing alone is meaningless for a comparison of two groups of people whose other physical features are as dissimilar as the 'short, coppery, barrel-chested Peruvian with round head, straight hair and slightly hooked nose' is from the 'tall, brown, stocky Polynesian with a wide range of head shape, wavy black hair, and a rather flat, wide nose'.

Heyerdahl's attempt to link the islanders' crania with those of the American continent using George Gill's analyses is a complete misrepresentation of Gill's results: Amerindian skulls display a flat jaw-base, a broad flat nasal root and a straight suture of the palate and it is Polynesian skulls that have the 'rocker jaw', a deeply depressed nasal root, and a jagged, arched suture of the palate. Indeed, the rocker jaw is the most characteristically Polynesian skeletal trait

The Polynesian Face

41–44 TOP *Captain Cook's artist William Hodges portrayed two Easter Island inhabitants on the expedition's visit to the island in 1774. The practice of artificially elongating the ears, perhaps to carry disc ornaments, is known to have existed in Polynesia at that time.* ABOVE *The profile of this native of Easter Island (left) was recorded in Tahiti in 1824; such heavy facial tattooing was also common elsewhere in Polynesia, as in the case of Fangui, a Maori chief (right) from New Zealand.*

known to physical anthropology, one that is considered virtually diagnostic of Polynesian ancestry. Its frequency of occurrence on almost all islands from New Zealand to Hawai'i ranges from 72 to 90 per cent, but it is extremely rare among Amerindians.

The Easter Island skeletal material Gill has examined so far is of Polynesian type in all these and other features, though its percentage of rocker jaws is comparatively low (48.5 per cent). So far, no South American Indian trait has been found in skeletons from the island.

Gill's preliminary analysis of fifty skulls, together with his reinterpretation of Murrill's data, suggests close ties between Easter Island and the Marquesas. The skeletons are clearly those of Polynesians, and although he has scarcely begun evaluation of possible Amerindian traits, he feels that 'any Amerindian genetic contribution detected is going to be a small one'.

Heyerdahl has also made much of selected early descriptions of the islanders' physical appearance, in particular their fair skin. Although the earliest voyagers give conflicting accounts of the islanders' racial characteristics, as on so many other points, the perceptive Captain Cook wrote that 'in colour, features and language, they bear such affinity to the people of the more western islands, that no one will doubt that they have had the same origin'.

The most recent genetic work in Polynesia, particularly using HLA (Human Leucocyte Antigen) blood grouping has shown clearly that Polynesians are mainly derived from a southeast Asian population, and that east Polynesians display considerable homogeneity and are probably derived from a small number of founders. No evidence has been found at all for gene flow between South America and Polynesia – many genes found at high frequency in the one place are not found in the other – and the few similarities between them can be attributed to their source populations in Asia. Heyerdahl's view, in other words, receives no support whatsoever from genetic analyses.

Conclusion

The earliest scholars to visit Rapa Nui, such as Katherine Routledge, had no obvious preconceptions about the origins of the islanders; after a full and fair assessment of the available evidence, she, like others before and after her, concluded that they had come from Polynesia, not from South America. Likewise, the scholars brought to the island by Thor Heyerdahl in 1955, although fully aware of his beliefs, were open-minded about the issue, while he, to his credit, wanted people who would not necessarily agree with him but who would evaluate the evidence in a fair and unbiased manner. Their investigations eventually led them to the conclusion that 'most of what is known of the prehistoric culture, as well as the surviving language, suggests Polynesian immigrants from islands to the west', though a few elements might possibly be American in origin. Nevertheless, thanks to the power of public relations, popular books and television programmes, Heyerdahl's view is still

45 OPPOSITE *Modern-day Easter Islanders fishing on the rocky shores of Rapa Nui.*

the best known among the general public, and has recently been given another airing in his ten-week television biography.

Bengt Danielsson, a member of the Kon-Tiki's crew, has described Heyerdahl's theoretical procedure as follows: 'Thor builds his pyramids upside down.' This simple metaphor is perfectly accurate and is extended by Christopher Ralling, who writes: 'The whole structure of Thor's thought sometimes rests on a single, slender premise... he has grown impatient with those who build their pyramids the right way up, and never get beyond the bottom layer.'

In this chapter, we have examined all the different kinds of evidence relevant to the problem of origins, and found that Heyerdahl's theory of a South American source for Easter Island culture is indeed a tottering edifice precariously based on preconceptions, extreme subjectivity, distortions and very little hard evidence. In putting it together so singlemindedly over the years, he has come to resemble someone who has painted himself into a corner with no means of escape, but is loath to admit it.

On the other hand, his work has certainly caused scholars to check their assumptions, and above all his first expedition was the direct cause of much of today's research. The fact that Heyerdahl's theories arouse deep scepticism or vehement rejection reflects not so much any prejudice about the source of Polynesian culture, but rather the selectivity of his data and his cavalier disregard of the problems of dating and distribution, as well as for the work of those whose findings contradict him. In the eyes of virtually all specialists, any contact that the island may have had with the New World did not precede its settlement by Polynesians, and influences from South America, if any, had a minimal impact on the island's cultural development.

Thirty years ago it was still possible to claim that the evidence linking certain elements of Easter Island with South America was the same as that used to derive others from Polynesia, so that scholars who supported either hypothesis while rejecting the other were applying double standards. Today, however, the variety and solidity of the Polynesian case contrasts strikingly with the tenuousness and subjectivity of the evidence for links between Rapa Nui and South America.

The inescapable conclusion is that, while there may perhaps have been sporadic contact between the two places – and most scholars are prepared to admit the possibility of some influence in either direction – Peruvian culture is notable by its absence. If Amerindians had the place to themselves for centuries, there should be far more physical evidence of them and their culture; but as American researcher JoAnne Van Tilburg has pointed out, 'there is absolutely no hard data known from the cumulative effort of nearly 100 years of investigation which would archaeologically link the island to the mainland'. Until such evidence turns up, it has to be accepted that Easter Island was colonized from eastern Polynesia.

CHAPTER 3

HOW DID THEY GET THERE, AND WHY?

Sailing into the unknown with women and pigs aboard
to find an island has always seemed to me a foolhardy
business no matter how intrepid and adventurous the
Polynesian might be.

Edward Dodd

Days, weeks at sea, at the mercy of the waves, without a glimpse of land. Braving the elements. Kept going through faith in their leader, Hotu Matua, a group of people – scores of them, men, women and children – were crowded into a catamaran with their animals and plants, their material possessions, and food for a journey of unknown duration. Their navigator stood by the upturned bow of the long vessel and scanned the eastern horizon for tell-tale signs of the 'promised land' which could be their new home....

Having decided that Easter Island was colonized from eastern Polynesia, we must now turn to the fascinating question of how such an amazing and hazardous journey was accomplished, and speculate as to the possible reasons that lay behind it. In the absence of written records, alas, the precise nature and cause of the journey can only be a matter of informed guesswork, based on a knowledge of Polynesian ethnography as well as on the islanders' own legends which, though not wholly reliable for details as we have already seen, nevertheless give a flavour of the likely events.

'Star-Compass' Navigators

Ethnographic study of prehistoric Polynesia does, indeed, provide us with intriguing glimpses of the way of life of the first Easter Islanders. In the colonization of the world, modern people had settled in New Guinea and Australia by at least 50,000 years ago, and had reached the northern Solomon Islands *c.* 28,000 years ago, but there is no evidence of any settlement in Polynesia until many millennia later, presumably because further exploration had to await the required navigational expertise enabling people to sail far offshore and survive.

In western Polynesia, where the islands are rich, comparatively large and close together, the early settlers (installed by *c.* 3200 years ago) were able greatly to develop these new navigational skills in conditions of comfort and relative safety. They could then spread further east (for example, to the Marquesas by 150 BC), where the islands were poorer in natural resources, smaller and further apart, requiring greater risks in exploration. It is thought likely that voyages of exploration occurred before actual colonization took place, using a strategy of 'search and find' or 'search and return home safely if unsuccessful'. In short, the spread involved a developing strategy of directed exploration that laid emphasis not on the fastest rate of advance but, understandably, on the best chance of survival.

The Polynesians were, in fact, among the most highly skilled seafarers and navigators the world has ever seen. They had an astounding knowledge of the night sky, and could steer by star paths using 'star-compass' techniques that are still practised over much of the Pacific; some had individual names for about two hundred stars, but recognized and used many other associated stars. They had an amazing ability to detect surface currents and compensate for them. And they had the almost uncanny skill of steering by wave motion, guided by the barely perceptible swells reflected from islands beyond the horizon: as David Lewis remarks, 'The skilled navigator comes to recognize the profile and characteristics of particular ocean swells as he would the faces of his friends, but he judges their direction more by feel than by sight'. The most advanced practitioners of this art would enter the water to judge the swells against the most sensitive part of the body, the scrotum – thus giving a whole new meaning to the term 'ball-bearings'.

The most sophisticated navigational concepts were restricted to selected initiates – this was closely guarded knowledge, handed down only within the navigator families. The ocean was not the daunting barrier it appears to landlubbers, but, as Thor Heyerdahl has often rightly stressed, a highway on which violent storms or the danger of death were no greater a risk than a car accident is today. The inhabitants of Pacific islands spent a great deal of time paddling or sailing in their lagoons or visiting neighbouring islands, and trading over quite large distances. Water was their element.

It is not surprising that the Polynesians' economy was based on the intensive exploitation of marine resources, together with shifting cultivation of a wide range of tubers and fruits. The commonest crops were the taro, yam, sweet potato, coconut, breadfruit and banana, while pigs, dogs, chickens and rats provided meat. The Polynesian islands comprised territorial divisions (sometimes individual islets) which usually incorporated a portion of coastline and stretched to the mountainous interior. Settlements, concentrated along the coast or in the more fertile valleys, consisted of homesteads scattered among plantations, and often clustered around chiefly dwellings. The concept of aristocracy was highly developed in Polynesian society, with the chiefs having the power of life or death, and usually tracing their lineage back through a series of first-born sons to the tribal founder-ancestor.

What could have been the Polynesians' motive for long-distance voyaging to new lands? Romantic explanations abound in the literature – the spirit of adventure, the roving seafarer, the conqueror, the supposed stimulus of astronomical events such as stellar novae and supernovae – but Polynesian ethnography provides us with plenty of more mundane and more realistic choices. All of them may hold some truth, since no single explanation can account for the numerous Polynesian voyages of colonization over the centuries.

There may have been drastic reasons for departure: volcanic activity, tidal waves, hurricanes, earthquakes, freak droughts, famine or epidemics must have created refugees from time to time, and small and isolated atolls are especially subject to depopulation through these factors. Equally drastic, and no doubt more frequent, was manmade violence: warfare, raiding, and violent family disputes leading to enforced or voluntary exile. The native histories of the Pacific are full of references to the flight of defeated parties before their enemies – the first 'boat people' seen on this ocean.

Many people were set adrift in rafts or small canoes for crimes and misdemeanours such as murder, adultery, insults, breaches of etiquette, or even juvenile mischief. It is known that a considerable number of such 'criminals' might be deported together: could the first Easter Islanders be a Polynesian equivalent of the British convicts sent to Australia? Men of abnormal physical strength or influence, of whom people were jealous or afraid, might also be sent into exile.

There were other social reasons for the 'budding off' of new communities: in many islands, the chief's first-born son inherited the land, so restless and ambitious younger sons, seeing no chance of advancement at home, often set out in canoes 'well provisioned with fruits, animals, women and male helpers', as Dodd puts it, to seek fame and fortune in a new homeland. Some may well have gone out of sheer curiosity, or to seek new materials or partners for trading purposes. Occupants of some Polynesian islands are known to have gone very considerable distances, looking for raw materials or suitable types of stone for toolmaking or tomb-building.

Oral traditions from Easter Island itself paint a vivid picture of its first settlers, who, as we have seen (p. 50), are said to have come from a large, warm, green island to the west called 'Marae Renga', probably in the Marquesas. One tale relates that they left because of a cataclysm, when most of their land was submerged beneath the ocean. However, the most common tradition is that Hotu Matua, a chief, was forced to flee that island after being defeated in war – either at the hands of his own brother, or because of his brother's misconduct with a rival chief's woman. One of Hotu Matua's entourage, a tattooer called Hau-Maka, had a prophetic dream of an island to the east with volcanic craters and pleasant beaches, on which six men could be seen. Hotu Matua therefore sent a canoe with six picked men to search for the island and await his arrival there, in order that the dream might be fulfilled. He himself followed in a double canoe, and landed on the beach of Anakena after a voyage of six weeks.

The details of this tale may be mythological, but there is a good chance that it contains a sound framework of truth; in particular, the political circumstances leading to Hotu Matua's flight are quite believable, being typical of Polynesian history.

Apart from his human entourage, perhaps dozens of people, his vessel must have been well supplied with tools, food, and plants and animals. Its two canoes would have been joined by a bridge bearing a mast and a shelter. There would have been a supply of drinking water, to be replenished from downpours during the voyage. Provisions would have included fruits, coconuts, vegetables, and also preserved fish since, apart from flying fish, it would have been difficult to obtain seafood over the farthest deeps. A lot of cooking could have been done at sea, with a sandbox carried on board and a small bed of embers constantly nursed. It has been reckoned that even a modest double canoe, c. 15 m (c. 50 ft) long, could carry about 18,000 pounds – so there would have been no problem carrying plentiful supplies in addition to the passengers.

On the shelter-floor and in the canoes would be the plants to be used for food, together with medicine, clothing, jewelry and vessels. In small cages or simply tied to the bridge were probably pigs and dogs, and certainly some chickens and rats – the latter were considered a delicacy by the elders. All Polynesian colonizers had learned over thousands of years to bring such items along, in case their new home did not have them – and Easter Island was certainly to prove bereft of many of the resources needed to support a Polynesian colony.

Found by Chance?

As with the question of the source of the colonizers, there are two principal views about their journey to Easter Island: some scholars believe that it was a skilfully navigated voyage, like other island colonizations in the Pacific, whereas others claim that Polynesian voyages were haphazard affairs, which sometimes struck lucky and found habitable islands.

In one sense, this debate is of little consequence to us, since the crucial point is that people *did* reach Easter Island, whether purposely or accidentally. But it is worth examining the two sides of the argument for the insights they provide into the culture and capabilities of these Polynesian colonizers.

The main proponent of the 'accidental' theory, Andrew Sharp, argued in a series of books and articles that deliberate navigation to and from remote ocean islands was impossible in the days before courses could be plotted with precision instruments. In other words, he shared Captain Cook's own suspicion that the more isolated islands of the Pacific were settled by accident.

Sharp rightly pointed out that to talk of a 'deliberate navigation' actually implies three voyages: a preliminary journey of reconnaissance, a navigated voyage back home to report the discovery of the new island, and finally the navigated voyage to bring the settlers to their new home. As we shall see, a triple trip of this kind is extremely unlikely in the case of Easter Island.

Polynesian Voyagers

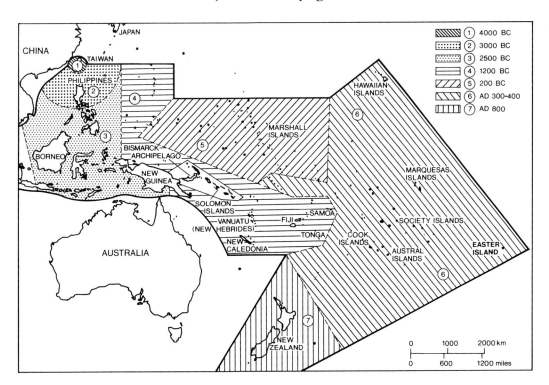

1	4000 BC
2	3000 BC
3	2500 BC
4	1200 BC
5	200 BC
6	AD 300-400
7	AD 800

CHINA
JAPAN
TAIWAN
PHILIPPINES
BORNEO
NEW GUINEA
BISMARCK ARCHIPELAGO
SOLOMON ISLANDS
VANUATU (NEW HEBRIDES)
NEW CALEDONIA
AUSTRALIA
NEW ZEALAND
FIJI
TONGA
SAMOA
COOK ISLANDS
MARSHALL ISLANDS
HAWAIIAN ISLANDS
MARQUESAS ISLANDS
SOCIETY ISLANDS
AUSTRAL ISLANDS
EASTER ISLAND

0   1000   2000 km
0   600   1200 miles

46,47 TOP *Sydney Parkinson made this drawing of a Society Island's double canoe, with sails and shelter for long-distance voyaging, on Cook's 1769 expedition.* ABOVE *Ultimately their seafaring prowess took the Polynesians right across the Pacific to distant Easter Island.*

The doubts about the possibility of deliberate navigation rest not only on the variability and unpredictability of winds and currents, but also on the frequent invisibility of stars or other heavenly bodies. Another important factor is the minute target presented by the small Pacific islands scattered through an area of 30 million sq. km ($11\frac{1}{2}$ million sq. miles) of ocean, bigger than Africa, bigger even than the Soviet Union and China combined: the distance from New Zealand to Easter Island represents one quarter of the entire circumference of the globe. The Marquesas group spans 400 km (250 miles), the Hawaiian archipelago some 600 km (370 miles), and New Zealand 1500 km (930 miles). But Easter Island's mere 23 km ($14\frac{1}{4}$ mile) span, lost in the Pacific, is a real needle in a haystack. The slightest miscalculation in course would miss it by a huge margin.

Hence, while 'local' two-way voyages of a few hundred kilometres – such as the islanders insisted they regularly undertook to Sala-y-Gómez, 415 km (258 miles) away – might be feasible since winds and currents would be familiar and relatively predictable, supposed two-way voyages over thousands of kilometres are far less likely: in golfing terms, it is like the difference between putting (where the hole provides a comparatively large target) and scoring a hole in one. The chances of Easter Island being reached even once were extremely limited; to imagine it being reached several times over vast distances is beyond belief.

Andrew Sharp was undoubtedly right that all far-flung islands must have been encountered accidentally before their first settlement, for the simple reason that nobody knew beforehand that they were there. However, the real debate centres on the degree of navigation or luck involved in these voyages of exploration. They have often been called 'drift voyages', which is an unfortunate term implying no guidance at all.

In any case, drift alone is most unlikely to have led settlers to Easter Island. Using a series of computer programmes simulating Pacific voyaging and incorporating many variations and a wealth of data on winds, currents and island locations, three scholars (Michael Levison, R. Gerard Ward and John W. Webb) have found that the likelihood of a drift or accidental voyage to Easter Island from South America was virtually nil; likewise, no simulated drifts from the nearest inhabited islands such as Mangareva or the Tuamotus reached Easter. Only two voyages from Pitcairn got anywhere near. In fact, of 2208 simulated drifts, not one reached Easter Island, and only three came within 320 km (c. 200 miles) of it. It was concluded that the island's settlers were probably following an intentionally easterly course at the time, and were lucky enough to find land; simulations modified to allow for sailing on a preferred course did reach Easter Island.

It is worth noting that this work also established that Pitcairn itself could have been reached by an accidental drift voyage from Easter – perhaps by a fishing vessel carried off in a storm. Such occurrences are by no means unknown even today: one Easter Island fishing boat was caught by a storm in 1947, and ended up in the Tuamotu archipelago thirty-seven days later after 1920 km (1193 miles) of drift.

The proponents of deliberate Polynesian long-distance voyaging argue that it is our modern technology which blinds us to the more traditional ways of doing things: our experts, astronomers, mathematics, clocks, instruments, compasses, maps and calendars have ended our reliance on the heavens for time and directions, and make it impossible for us to believe that people could go confidently across oceans without our artificial aids. We assume instead that vessels normally hugged coasts, and ventured elsewhere through accident and misfortune.

Ethnography provides plenty of evidence to the contrary, and the extent of the Polynesians' geographic knowledge suggests that deliberate two-way voyages were accomplished almost routinely over an impressive range: local histories show that Polynesian outliers were frequently visited by huge ocean-going canoes from Samoa and Tonga, and until quite recently there were two-way voyages of up to 1300 km (*c.* 800 miles) without intervening islands, and 2240 km (*c.* 1400 miles) with a single intermediate island (Raiatea to Niuataputapu). There were also multiple voyages between eastern Polynesia and New Zealand (as shown by finds there of New Zealand obsidian). Polynesians thought nothing of being at sea for two weeks or more.

One important factor is that pinpoint accuracy was not required: a radius of 80 to 120 km (50 to 75 miles) around an island brings one within the area where birds, winds, land-clouds and the altered swell patterns of the ocean can be used as guides. By 'expanding' the difficult targets in this way, it was possible simply to steer for entire archipelagos, and then use the 'radius phenomena' as one approached (ill. 52). Even the tiny Easter Island is extended tenfold by these indicators – still a small target, but easier to find than if one relied simply on visual contact with the land: Pacific islands are visible only from a distance of 100 km (*c.* 60 miles) at best, and most from far less, some a mere 24 km (15 miles).

Andrew Sharp and others have pointed out that these 'radius phenomena' are unreliable and may be deceptive: cloud effects are not always present over islands, and are frequently found over tracts of ocean without land. Sea birds do not always congregate near land, and even then are only detectable in close proximity.

Nevertheless, reliable or not, it remains true that Polynesian navigators could and did use indicators such as these to direct their vessels safely and accurately to chosen destinations. Another useful phenomenon was subsurface luminescence (thought to be a form of bioluminescence triggered by a backwash wave): these streaks of light that dart out from the directions in which land lies are best seen from 100 to 160 km (60 to 100 miles) out, and it was customary to steer by them on overcast nights when the heavens were invisible.

The active alternative to Heyerdahl's passive 'migration by drift', following prevailing winds and currents, and Sharp's passive 'migration by chance' where

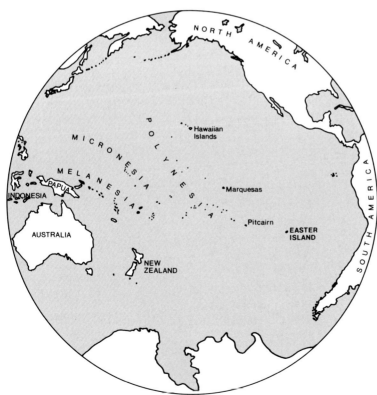

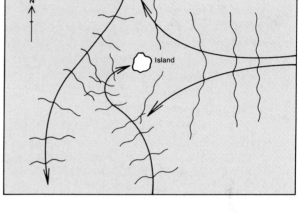

General overcast

Thickening of overcast over land

Sea

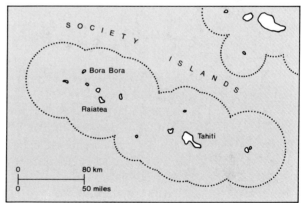

N

Island

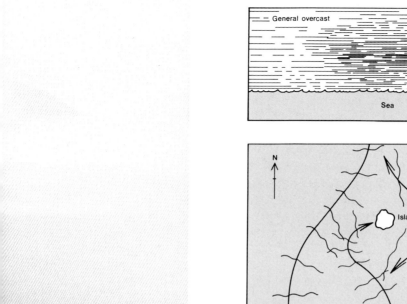

SOCIETY ISLANDS

Bora Bora

Raiatea

Tahiti

0   80 km
0   50 miles

Star-Compass Navigators

48–53 LEFT *Easter Island's isolation only
serves to increase our admiration for those
who first made the long and hazardous
journey to its shores.* ABOVE LEFT *The
'Hokule'a', a replica of a Polynesian double
canoe, was sailed from Samoa to Tahiti in
1976 using only the stars and wave formations
as navigational aids.* ABOVE RIGHT *Techniques
employed by Polynesian mariners included the
observation of (top) changing cloud formations
and (centre) variations in swells and wave
patterns around an island, which meant that
(centre right), within a radius of about 50
miles around an island group, the seafarers
could detect the presence of land even without
sighting it.* RIGHT *Boat-like forms in the rock
carvings of Easter Island.*

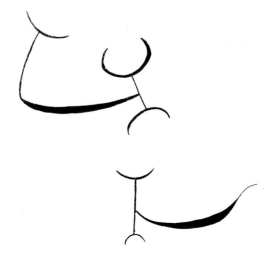

colonizations were accomplished through accidental blow-away voyages, is to see the settlement of the Pacific islands as a long, slow, skilful and largely premeditated affair, which steadily built on accumulating knowledge of geography, the elements, seamanship and provisioning. Over the centuries, it is probable that a faith was born that there were always new lands to be found: eastward, ever eastward.

Had the colonization been entirely by accidental voyages, one must suppose a staggering percentage of losses at sea, with perhaps only one boat in a hundred or even a thousand getting through. No maritime people could tolerate such losses, and their explorations would soon have ceased. The persistence of the Polynesians' expansion, together with their efficient and well-equipped vessels, argue that – despite some inevitable losses occasionally – they were eminently successful in their explorations, going boldly in their star-steered enterprises.

Since they could not rely too heavily on winds and currents, they built their vessels – the double canoe or 'catamaran' (a Malay word that originally meant 'tied logs') – for speed rather than stability. Captain Cook reported with wonder how the Tongan chiefs literally sailed rings around his ship even when she was doing her best in a fair breeze. With a sail and a favourable wind these canoes could cover 160–240 km (100–150 miles) per day, and thanks to the Polynesians' ability to preserve foods for long periods, a range of 8000 km (*c.* 5000 miles) was feasible.

The aerodynamically efficient sails and slim hulls would permit the canoes to sail to windward, though probably not for long distances if heavily laden: no sailor, even today, wants to spend days or weeks pushing hard into wind and current. This is why some scholars have argued that much of the Polynesians' spread from west to east was accomplished not by tacking against the prevailing southeast trade winds but by awaiting and using the periodic westerly wind reversals (see p. 47). During the past two centuries, such El Niño events have occurred at intervals of one to eight years, with major ones every seven to sixteen years. Similar figures may be applicable to the period of Polynesian expansion.

Thanks to the journals of European explorers and missionaries in the Pacific, we know that the 18th- and 19th-century Polynesians were well acquainted with these westerlies and did use them to sail eastward. Cook, for example, was told that when Tahitians wished to sail eastward they waited for the westerlies of November to January. They could even foretell other periodic spells of westerly wind by a day or so. There is no reason to assume that their ancestors were any less competent. In 1986, a Polynesian voyaging double-canoe was sailed successfully from Samoa to Tahiti in an experiment to show that it was possible for such a vessel to sail from west to east by using westerly wind shifts.

However, while anomalous westerlies would have been a great help in colonizing many Polynesian islands, they were not needed where Easter Island is concerned. At 27°S, the island lies in a transitional zone between the southeast trades and the westerlies of higher latitudes; as we have already seen, in winter Rapa Nui is often subjected to unsettled, rainy weather with spells of strong westerly winds. A vessel that strayed south out of the trade wind belt could have been caught by these westerlies and carried to the island. This would require an extraordinary combination of luck and seamanship, not to mention the ability to endure a cold and stormy voyage, and helps explain why Rapa Nui, far from the mainstream of Polynesian voyaging, was to remain the most isolated of colonies, largely or totally cut off from the rest of Polynesia.

The fact that animals and plants were always transported to the new settlements argues strongly against the colonization being accidental: would offshore fishermen, unexpectedly caught by a storm, happen to have not only their womenfolk but also dogs, chickens, pigs and rats on board as well as banana sprouts and a wide range of other useful plants? The transporting of complete 'landscapes' to new islands suggests organized colonizing expeditions. Only in those few cases (e.g. Pitcairn, Henderson) where small island settlements were abandoned or their inhabitants died out could one argue for colonization after accidental, unprepared voyages, though it is equally likely that these too were normal colonizations which simply failed owing to an impoverished environment or some other cause.

So were the voyages all deliberate or all accidental? As usual in prehistory – and despite the legend of Hotu Matua voyaging to a known destination – the truth probably lies in a combination of both theories: it is doubtful that many successful colonies could have been started by fishermen or coastal voyagers blown off course, but it is equally extreme to envisage nothing but systematic voyages of exploration. The Polynesian spread, whatever its degree of planning and purposefulness, must have been a hazardous and uneven affair, relying heavily on luck in unpredictable conditions and unknown seas. To realize this point only increases one's admiration for the skill and daring of these pioneers who were willing and able to face such terrible risks.

The first Easter Islanders, henceforth marooned at the 'end of the world' ('Te Pito Te Henua', literally 'land's end' or 'fragment of the earth', but sometimes translated as The Navel of the World), probably began their new life with, in the words of Patrick Kirch, a full 'transported Polynesian landscape'. However, many of their plants, as well as the pigs and dogs, became extinct – the plants, no doubt, through environmental difficulties, and the animals through accidental or purposeful extermination.

It is time, therefore, to look at the life of – and the traces left by – these first human beings ever to set foot on Easter Island: what they found there, how they adapted to the conditions and then altered them quite drastically.

CHAPTER 4

LIVING ON AN ISLAND

1400 Years of Solitude?

In attempting to retrace the islanders' prehistory, our first task is to determine when that prehistory began. As we have seen, it is extremely improbable that the island could have been reached more than once before the arrival of the Europeans. Yet genealogical studies, involving the listed names of previous chiefs back to Hotu Matua, led Sebastian Englert to conclude that the latter and his followers had arrived no earlier than the 16th century AD, while on the same basis Métraux placed their arrival in the 12th century. But archaeology has subsequently proved, through radiocarbon dating, that people were already on the island by AD 690, and possibly even by the 4th century (though isolated single dates always need to be treated with caution): this would fit with another tradition that there had been 57 generations of kings since Hotu Matua which, allowing an average of 25 years per generation, would take one back to AD 450. But where do the persistent tales of conflict between the 'Hanau Eepe' and the 'Hanau Momoko' populations fit in?

Thor Heyerdahl has sought links with South America in the famous legend of the 'long-ears' (Hanau Eepe) and the 'short-ears' (Hanau Momoko), seeing the former as the descendants of the first (Amerindian) colonizers, and the latter as the more recent Polynesian arrivals. Hence he sees the 'long-ears' as having their ear-lobes elongated and perforated for disc-ornaments, a practice still current when the Europeans first arrived (though Mrs Routledge was informed that the term 'long-ears' conveyed to the natives not the custom of distending the ears but having them long by nature). According to Heyerdahl's selected story, the 'short-ears' massacred all but one 'long-ear' (who subsequently had descendants) in the 17th century at the 'battle of the Poike ditch'.

Yet Sebastian Englert emphatically denied that these Polynesian terms referred to ears: having studied the older form of the islanders' language in more detail than anyone else, he stressed that the terms meant 'broad/ strong/corpulent people' and 'slender people' respectively. In view of the widespread notion in Polynesia associating physical size and corpulency with leadership and *mana* (spiritual power), this would suggest that the Hanau Eepe were the upper class, and the Hanau Momoko the lower. Once again, the evidence for supposed links with the New World evaporates – and in any case, as shown above (ills 41, 42), elongated ears and disc ornaments are well attested in the Marquesas Islands, and are therefore not exclusively a New World phenomenon.

Furthermore, Englert believed that the Hanau Eepe were latecomers who designed the platforms, and that the Hanau Momoko created the statues; while Thomas Barthel, after exhaustive study of the island's oral traditions, has decided that Hotu Matua arrived from Polynesia long after an initial colonization from the same direction – he was chief of the Hanau Momoko, but brought some Hanau Eepe prisoners with him as a labour force to work on the land. They were settled on Poike, away from the Momoko lands. Although the terms mean 'slender' and 'stocky' respectively, the tales concerning the two groups contain no indication of racial or cultural differences. It is far more likely that the relationship between them was one of victors and vanquished, or of lofty versus lowly status, although this clashes with the normal Polynesian association of stockiness with *mana* and the upper class.

Any attempt to fit the traditions to the archaeology is admirable, but we have already shown that they are factually unreliable: at least six different genealogies have been recorded, for example, containing different names and numbers of kings, and these were gleaned from a few surviving natives from the late 19th century onwards, by then a decimated, demoralized and culturally impoverished population which had lost most of the collective cultural-historical memory. Besides, they would mean that the island was reached not once but twice – or even three times if the tale of Hotu Matua's advance party of explorers were to be accepted. While that is theoretically possible, the most probable hypothesis is still that of a single early colonization from Polynesia, led by a chief, a culture hero who has been given the name Hotu Matua (i.e. Great Parent). The island's archaeological record is certainly one of continuous artifactual and architectural development, with no trace of a sudden influx of new cultural influences from outside.

Besides, any supposed new arrivals after the first colonization would have been few in number compared with the established population, and could have made little impact culturally other than with an idea or two – indeed, as E.P. Lanning reminds us, small groups arriving by sea would probably have been 'knocked on the head or put to work cleaning fish'. One can hardly envisage them imposing a new religion or political organization without a fleet-load of warriors. In the absence of any hard evidence for further immigration, let alone invasion, it must be assumed that the island's cultural developments and elaborations were produced by internal forces.

The earliest archaeological radiocarbon date obtained so far, as we have seen, is AD 380 ± 100 from charcoal on a buried land surface at the Poike ditch; this may indicate very early forest clearance, but the result is considered very doubtful since an obsidian sample from the same provenance gave a date of AD 1560! An even earlier 4th-century result (AD 318) came from a sample of totora reed in a grave at Ahu Tepeu I, but a bone sample from the same grave gave AD 1629. So the earliest really reliable radiocarbon date is reckoned to be that of AD 690 ± 130 from the first construction phase of Ahu Tahai, a few kilometres to the south of Tepeu; but since these platforms were already large and stylized the first settlers probably arrived long before, sometime during the first centuries AD. The earliest date for a house was obtained from a rectangular dwelling excavated on Rano Kau: AD 770 ± 239.

Overall, the evidence available points to an early centre of habitation on the island's southwest corner, more or less where the population is gathered today. Anakena, where Hotu Matua is supposed to have landed, has been revealed by recent excavations to have had its earliest habitation in the late 8th or 9th century AD with platforms present by 1100, while the south coast seems to begin a rapid build-up of population and construction only around AD 1300.

In what kind of environment would the first settlers have found themselves?

Reconstructing the Environment

Pollen analysis provides us with vital information concerning the vegetation of Easter Island at the time of the earliest human settlement.

Each year, in the Rano Raraku crater lake, microscopic freshwater algae grow and later die. Their dead bodies fall to the bottom of the lake, mixing as they do so with any clay or silt washed into the lake from the slopes surrounding it, and any particles such as pollen grains falling in from the air. Each year, a new layer of sediment is thereby added on top of what has already accumulated. This process has been going on ever since the lake first formed over 37,000 years ago. In recent millennia the process has accelerated because of the totora reed (*Scirpus riparius*) growing around the edge of the lake, and in dry periods extending its growth right over the sediment surface. The dead totora leaves and rhizomes contribute even more rapidly to the growth of sediment. Another sub-aquatic plant, a species of bistort (*Polygonum acuminatum*) is also contributory in this way.

Sediments of these types – i.e., the fine detritus muds (gyttja) formed mainly from algae, or the coarser detritus muds and peats formed from larger plants – have become well known in many parts of the world for providing a record of environmental history: a book whose pages record, in faithful detail, what was happening in and around the lake or swamp in which they are formed. Rano Raraku is not the only such site on Easter Island. Rano Kau is potentially even better, and Rano Aroi, near the summit of Terevaka, provides a third one. It is probably no accident that Rano Raraku and Rano Kau are each near major archaeological sites (the statue quarries and Orongo respectively). The likely explanation for this is that they are the major sources of fresh water on an otherwise rather dry island, and would thus have been obvious centres for human activity. These two sites, therefore, have the potential to reveal much about the palaeo-environment of the island, and of human impact on it. They

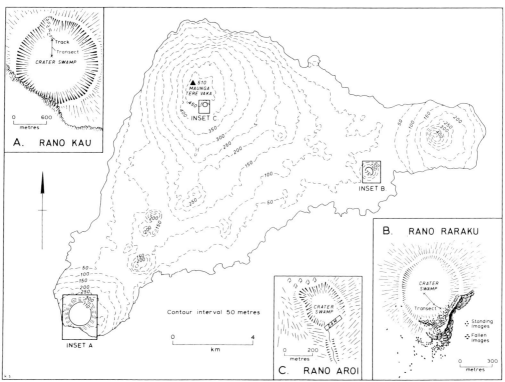

54,55 TOP *Rano Raraku crater, the quarry for the giant statues, has also proved crucial for environmental studies.* ABOVE *The three locations used by John Flenley and his colleagues to study the Easter Island environment in detail.*

are both in the lowlands: the addition of Rano Aroi, which can provide similar information from the uplands, makes Easter Island one of the finest places in the world for integrating archaeology with the history of environment; furthermore, we may come close to solving the mystery of the island's decline by charting the rise and fall of its forests.

The first attempt to discover the history of the environment on Easter Island was made by Thor Heyerdahl's expedition in 1955, which collected short sample cores from the swamps at Rano Raraku and Rano Kau and passed them to Olof Selling, a Swedish palynologist, for analysis. Selling had already made detailed studies on Hawai'i, so he was familiar with many Pacific pollen types. He concluded that the toromiro (*Sophora toromiro*) had formerly been much commoner on the island. He also found abundant pollen of a palm tree. In this family (the Palmae) many pollen types are rather similar (at least as seen under ordinary microscopes), so it was impossible to identify the pollen with a particular species, but Selling made the suggestion that it could be a species of the genus *Pritchardia*. This was a reasonable guess, for *Pritchardia* is common on Hawai'i and other Pacific islands.

Selling also found pollen of *Compositae*, which are probably derived from shrubs, and he concluded that Easter Island had once borne a rainforest. Unfortunately no radiocarbon dates were obtained, so it was impossible to say when the island had been forested. Equally unfortunately, the work was never published, although it is mentioned in the expedition monographs. Shortly afterwards Selling retired from academic life, and no further analyses of these samples were made. The problem therefore remained: what was this mysterious palm which had once been so prevalent on the island that Selling reported its pollen 'filled every cubic millimetre of the bottom strata in the (Rano Raraku) crater lake'?

Pursuing the Palm

John Flenley's first sight of Rano Raraku in 1977 convinced him that it was an ideal site for pollen analyses (palynology). In the first place, there were no inflow or outflow streams to the crater swamp; this meant that pollen would arrive mainly by aerial rather than water transport (which could have washed in older sediments), and that once in the crater it could not be washed out again. Secondly, with its diameter of *c*. 200 m (*c*. 650 ft), it was just about the right size: previous research in New Guinea had taught that larger sites collected pollen from too great an area for easy interpretation and that smaller ones might well be too young, because swamp growth is so rapid in the tropics and subtropics.

Thirdly, it *was* a swamp, and no longer the lake pictured in Routledge and Heyerdahl's publications, because the water level had recently been lowered by the pumping out of water for domestic animals. A large trench had been dug through the lowest point of the crater rim, and a pipe inserted leading to a tank outside the crater. This was a tragedy, an act of unwitting palynological vandalism, for the diggers had destroyed possible geomorphological evidence of any former overflowing of the lake, which would have been a clue to past climate. Also, the exposed sediment at the edges was rapidly drying and oxidizing. On the plus side, however, this saved a lot of work, for it proved possible to walk out c. 30 m (c. 100 ft) on to the swamp to obtain the cores, without the need to make a raft. On a subsequent visit in 1984 with Professor Jim Teller, of the University of Manitoba at Winnipeg, Canada, Flenley was relieved to find that the pumping had stopped and the water level had recovered. The result, however, was that it was necessary to make a raft in order to obtain further cores from the centre of the basin.

A further reason why the site was outstanding was its proximity to the archaeology. The statue quarries extend not only over the outside of the crater, but also down the inside on the southern side. Numerous statues, finished apart from their eye sockets and the carving on their backs, stand looking out over the lake (ills 102–6). It seemed likely that when the quarries were in use there must have been so many people active on the southern bank of the lake that the vegetation must have been modified, if not totally destroyed. The result would probably have been soil erosion, and the eroded soil should have ended up in the lake. The decision was therefore taken to carry out the sampling on the southern side of the lake, and proved a correct one (ill. 54).

A peak of pollen believed to be *Solanum* (poporo) occurred at 70 cm ($27\frac{1}{2}$ in) depth (i.e. possibly 70 years ago, and certainly within the last 200 years). If this pollen came from *Solanum forsteri*, it could represent actual cultivation of this plant within the crater. This cultivation in former times was mentioned by Métraux.

Immediately below the layer of inwashed sediment at 1.1 to 1.2 m (c. 3 ft 7 in to 3 ft 11 in) depth, there was a striking change in the pollen spectra. Grass pollen was less common, and the grass grains were larger. Pollen of the toromiro became quite common. But the big change was the *sudden appearance of palm pollen as the dominant type* – indicating, of course, that after this point living palm trees had suddenly disappeared. The grains were now well preserved and, although one could not be certain, they did not seem quite like the reference pollen of coconut. Palm grains are notoriously difficult to identify, so advantage was taken of a visit by G. Thanikaimoni, at that time the world expert on palm pollen. He could only confirm that the pollen was probably from a palm of some kind, but he refused to be more specific. It seemed pretty sure that this must be the pollen type which Selling had referred to as *Pritchardia*, so a scanning electron microscope study was now undertaken of the fossil and of various palms, including *Cocos* and two species of *Pritchardia*. The Pritchardias had a smooth surface with pits in it, whereas the fossil had a ropey (rugulate) surface: *Pritchardia* was therefore eliminated. The fossil grain had a surface like that of *Cocos* and also of *Jubaea chilensis*, the Chilean wine palm which is in the same subfamily (Cocosoideae).

Signs of the Palm

56–58 *The bare, windswept character of Easter Island today acts as a warning for humankind, for at the time of the first settlers the island was covered by forest. The once abundant palm trees – shown by archaeological research to have been very similar to the Chilean wine palm – were a vital resource for the islanders, and their over-exploitation led to ecological and social catastrophe.* ABOVE *Two examples of the Chileans' prized wine palm, 'Jubaea chilensis', in the garden of archaeologist G. Figueroa, Santiago.* LEFT *A drawing made by Frenchman R. de Noter in 1895 clearly shows the characteristic bulge in the wine palm's trunk.* BELOW *Easter Island's Rongorongo script provides several examples of palm-like 'glyphs'; indeed, these characters are called 'niu', the Polynesian term for palm tree.*

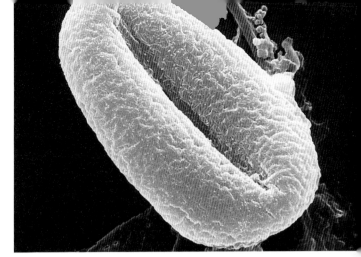

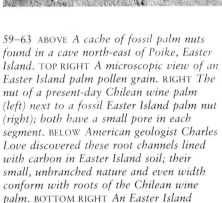

59–63 ABOVE *A cache of fossil palm nuts found in a cave north-east of Poike, Easter Island.* TOP RIGHT *A microscopic view of an Easter Island palm pollen grain.* RIGHT *The nut of a present-day Chilean wine palm (left) next to a fossil Easter Island palm nut (right); both have a small pore in each segment.* BELOW *American geologist Charles Love discovered these root channels lined with carbon in Easter Island soil; their small, unbranched nature and even width conform with roots of the Chilean wine palm.* BOTTOM RIGHT *An Easter Island palm frond petroglyph.*

Further interpretation of this pollen type might have been impossible had it not been for a fortunate accident. During Flenley's stay on the island in 1983, the Governor, Sergio Rapu, had shown him a bag containing some objects found by a party of visiting French cavers. They had been exploring one of the lava caves in the northeast side of Poike at Ana O Keke, when they had come across what appeared to be a cache of nuts. They had collected thirty-five nuts, which Señor Rapu allowed to be photographed (ill. 59). Each was almost spherical and about 2 cm ($\frac{3}{4}$ in) across, with three lines running around it like lines of longitude on a globe. Somewhere near the middle of each 'segment' was a small pore: in some cases a depression, in others a hole right through the wall of the nut. This was reminiscent of the three pores near one end of a coconut, although the positioning of the pores was different. Señor Velasco, a respected botanist who was also present, immediately suggested that these nuts were similar to those of the Chilean wine palm.

Flenley was permitted to take away several of the nuts, and sent some to Kew to be examined by Dr John Dransfield, the world expert on palm taxonomy. He telephoned in some excitement to report that the nuts must belong to a Cocosoid palm. There are eight genera of Cocosoid palms, but only two, *Jubaea* and *Jubaeopsis*, have fruits roughly resembling the fossil. After comparing the fossils with dried plant material and with fruits from the enormous specimen of *Jubaea chilensis* in the Temperate House at Kew (the largest glasshouse plant in cultivation anywhere in the world), Dransfield concluded that the French cavers had discovered what was probably an extinct species of the genus *Jubaea*, for the fossil fruits were slightly larger and more oblate than those of the living species. In any case, even if the fruits had been identical, it would have been rash to assume that all other parts of the plant would have matched those of the living species; they could have been quite different. However, Jacques Vignes, leader of the French expedition, bought fresh wine palm fruits in the street in Santiago, where they are sold as food and these turned out to be much closer to the fossils than are the fruits grown at Kew. So the possibility increases that the Easter Island palm was at least closely related to *Jubaea chilensis* and possibly of the same species: the Chilean wine palm may, therefore, turn out to be the vital evidence for which archaeologists have been searching.

Known in Chile as *glilla*, the Chilean wine palm is the largest palm in the world. It has a smooth trunk with a diameter often up to 1 m (3 ft) or more, and it is at least 20 m (65 ft) tall. The trunk is cylindrical, tapering towards the top, and sometimes with a slight bulge about one third of the way up. The leaves are large and feather-like, as in a coconut, and the fruits are borne in clusters among the leaves. Each fruit is, like a tiny coconut, provided with an outer fibrous layer, with a hard shell beneath.

The Chileans regard this, their only species of palm, as of great importance, and not surprisingly so, for it is the source of four important comestibles. The nuts contain an oily kernel which is regarded as a delicacy. In addition, by making a hole in one side of the trunk, the palm can be 'milked' of its sap. This sap can be concentrated by boiling to give palm honey (*miel de palma*), which is highly prized in Santiago. Further boiling reduces the product to a brown sugary mass (*sucre de palma*), which may be eaten straight or used in cooking. Alternatively, the sap may be allowed to ferment: this occurs naturally, through the agency of wild yeasts, and yields a highly alcoholic palm wine (*vino de palma*).

Jubaea chilensis is no longer a common tree in the wild, and it is good to know that it has conservation status. It does occur, however, near the road from Santiago down to Valparaiso at *c.* 33°S – making this the world's most southerly palm – and it grows well where planted in Tenerife in the Canary Islands (27°N). It therefore seems likely that it (or a near relative) would have experienced no difficulty in growing in the lowlands of Easter Island (27°S).

This was borne out by the subsequent discoveries on the island. Inspired by seeing the fruits from the caves, one of Flenley's 1983 party, Mike Symonds, discovered a further fruit in a crevice within the structure of Ahu Ma'itaki Te Moa on the island's north coast. Although in a poor condition, this was clearly recognizable as the same plant group, and the find was important as suggesting the survival of the species up to the time of the construction of the platforms (a Middle Period one, *c.* AD 1100–1680) or even later.

Sergio Rapu reported that many broken fragments of the same nuts had been recovered from his archaeological dig at Anakena, but of course this did not necessarily indicate where the tree had been growing. The fruits have now turned up in various other places, however. Jacques Vignes found sixteen in caves within the Rano Kau crater on a return visit to the island in 1986, while Edmundo Edwards, a resident of the island, found a large number in a cave on the island's north side. Most recently, French archaeologist Michel Orliac found two in 1988 on the south side near Ahu Vinapu, where colluvium was exposed at the coast in the mouth of a gully.

The nuts and pollen are not the only evidence of the palm. Linton Palmer reported that during his visit in 1868 he had seen the boles of large trees which he assumed to be coconuts – given the latitude, coconuts are unlikely, but *Jubaea* is not. This evidence was confused by Métraux, who reported that Palmer had seen large wooden 'bowls', but the original clearly has 'boles'. The island's rock art features a couple of probable representations of the palm: one seems to be the trunk of a large tree, while another looks like a palm frond. Moreover, some of the Rongorongo characters are called *niu* (the Polynesian term for palm tree) and do resemble palm trunks; some even feature the characteristic bulge of *Jubaea* (ill. 58).

Palm tree roots are distinctive. The trees do not produce the large, much-branched roots characteristic of broad-leaved forms. Instead they produce very large numbers of small, unbranched roots emanating straight from the base of the tree. At Ahu Akivi, William Mulloy reported finding root moulds, of undetermined nature, but which showed that the area had once been covered by quite large vegetation. More recently, American geologist Charles Love has found numbers of root channels lined with carbon in soils on Easter Island (ill. 62). These channels do not taper or vary in width as would broad-leaved tree roots: in size, density and branching they appear to conform perfectly with the morphology of present-day *Jubaea* roots and not at all with those of *Cocos*.

Love found these root casts in various lowland (under 200 m [656 ft]) sites, but especially in the deep soils of Poike. They may easily be seen by any visitor searching the area of bad soil erosion on Poike's southern side. Some are visible in the erosion platform, from which the topsoil has been removed. Others are visible in the vertical face where erosion is still proceeding: in this case, the root casts are visible only in the lower part of the section, where the original blocky soil structure is still intact. Another good place to see them is on the north side of the road from Vaitea to Anakena.

Love has also found a fragment of carbonized palm wood which provided a radiocarbon date of *c.* AD 930. The palm fruits from Ana O Keke were radiocarbon-dated by Dr Harkness at East Kilbride, giving an age of *c.* AD 1130, i.e. within the Middle Period of the island's prehistory. Those found by Michel Orliac were dated to AD 1212–1430 and AD 1300–1640. These results were sufficiently close to the present day to make one speculate that the tree might have survived into protohistoric or even historic times. A talk with Sergio Rapu confirmed these hopes: a tree called *nau-nau-opata* (literally, 'the nut tree that hangs by the cliffs') had formerly grown on the island, especially near the sea. This tree had now disappeared. Skottsberg's account of the island's botany also made reference to it. In fact, he had been sent nuts that the island children used as tops, and which were also worn around the neck as decorations, threaded through two small holes made in the shell. Skottsberg concluded the nuts were of *Thespesia populnea*, a tree still found on the island; but examination of this species revealed its nutshells to be thin and fragile, quite unsuitable as tops. It seems possible that the holes which Skottsberg observed were two of the three natural holes in every *Jubaea* shell, and that children were still wearing them in the 19th century when the necklace he examined was collected.

It is clear, therefore, that at the time of the first human settlers, Easter Island was covered by a scrubby forest. There have even been suggestions that there was once dense forestation, perhaps even rainforest: in 1983, Patrick Kirch discovered that there once existed a small snail – named *Hotumatua anakenana* after the legendary first king – of a group now confined to moist forest conditions.

What evidence is revealed by archaeology and ethnography concerning the day-to-day life of the first Easter Islanders? Until the last few decades, interest in Easter Island's archaeology understandably focused almost exclusively on its spectacular sculptures, platforms and rock art, as well as on the origin of its people. Even in recent years, these features have still been the centre of attention, though a few notable studies have been devoted to the prehistoric islanders' domestic and economic life; consequently, more is now known about these neglected areas of research.

An 'Earthly Paradise'

What was this new world in which Hotu Matua and his followers were marooned? One legend has it that the party was in some distress by the time it arrived; their vessel broke up on the shore, and they then cooked their first meal for a long time. But there is no reason to suppose that they starved, despite this rude transfer from a lush, warm island to a cooler, windy one.

Traditions claim that for the first three months the Easter Island settlers had nothing to eat but fish, turtles, ferns and fruit including 'sandalwood nuts' (which are now extinct). During the initial phase, while their plants and seedlings were being nurtured, the settlers undoubtedly relied heavily on the island's natural resources of fish, birds and shellfish. The same occurred on every other colonized Polynesian island, leading in many cases to swift extinction or impoverishment of a whole range of species, most notably the giant flightless moa birds of New Zealand. Until the recent excavations into early phases of settlement at Anakena are published, we have very little archaeological evidence for indigenous animal or bird species that may have been wiped out in the same way on Easter Island.

The breadfruit, basis of the Polynesian diet, was presumably brought but could not survive in this climate; the coconut did not fare well either. If, as might be expected, pigs were brought over, they either did not survive or were eaten before breeding. The recent discovery by Claudio Cristino of dog bones in excavations at Anakena suggests that the same was true of this animal. The chicken did manage to flourish, and eventually assumed huge importance in the island's economy. This also explains why human bones (from the thighs of deceased fishermen) were used for making fish-hooks – they were the only large mammal bones available; though the island's most common bone artifact, the small-eyed needle used to sew bark cloths together, was made of chicken, sea-bird or occasionally fish bone. Finally, the settlers' introduction of edible rats was to have dire consequences (Chapter 9).

A great deal of important information about the early islanders can be gleaned from the eye-witness accounts by the first European visitors: the Dutch reports of 1722 are obviously crucial, being our very earliest glimpses of Rapa Nui when it was, as far as we know, as yet unaffected by the outside world.

Roggeveen stated that the islanders were well proportioned, generally large in stature, very sturdy with strong muscles, and extremely good swimmers. Many had stretched and perforated ear-lobes, and both men and women were extensively tattooed (ill. 43). They were outstandingly strong in the teeth and even old men could crack large, hard, thick-shelled nuts with them (presumably the fruits of the mysterious palm; see above). Yet physical anthropologists

64,65 Sharon Long's reconstructed faces of prehistoric islanders, in the Easter Island museum.

have consistently reported that the early islanders' teeth were in poor shape: Sir Arthur Keith, for example, found decay in every adult skull he examined from the island, and remarked, 'Tooth trouble is even more prevalent in Easter Island than in the slums of our great towns.' In fact, the islanders had the highest rate of caries seen in any prehistoric people. By the age of fourteen, carious lesions were already in evidence, and increased steadily; by their twenties, the islanders all had cavities, and by their thirties the frequencies of decay, especially in women, were far higher than in other Pacific agricultural groups.

This was probably caused not only by poor oral hygiene but also by an inadequate diet, particularly in later periods, and by food high in carbohydrates that was baked in earthen ovens and eaten unpounded. Caries were even high in the front teeth, an unusual phenomenon probably produced by the habit of sucking sugar cane to relieve thirst. Sugar-cane juice was used as a liquid substitute to overcome the island's limited supply of fresh water; Captain Cook's botanist Forster reported sugar-cane stalks 'about 9 or 10 feet high'.

Although his visit came only fifty-two years after Roggeveen's, Cook noted that the islanders were not well built; according to Forster, there was 'not a single person amongst them who might be reckoned tall'. All the early visitors saw a wide range of skin tones, from white or yellow to reddish. Light skin was much prized, as in other parts of Polynesia, and it is claimed that youngsters, particularly girls, were sequestered in caves like Ana O Keke to enhance the whiteness of their skins, as an indication of high status.

The earliest 'portraits' were produced during Captain Cook's visit (ills 41, 42), but recently some prehistoric islanders have been 'brought back to life' by the technique of reconstructing the face on a cast of the skull. In this way, American sculptor Sharon Long has been able to recreate the faces of three

66,67 Two present-day islanders, their faces remarkably similar to Sharon Long's reconstructed faces.

islanders (ills 64, 65). Although inevitably approximate in some details, her reconstructions are so lifelike and accurate that excited modern islanders were able to identify the lineage of one male head from the head-shape and facial features. The family identified was descended from the royal Miru tribe of the Anakena region, and investigations later proved that this skull had indeed come from the Ahu Nau Nau area, associated with that tribe!

Physical anthropologists have found further evidence of distinct social groups on the island in their analyses of skeletal material. George Gill, of the University of Wyoming, has detected some anomalies: skeletons from the area around Anakena, but from nowhere else, had the very rare genetic condition of a defective patella (the kneecap has a corner missing), while sacro-iliac (pelvic) fusion is very common on the south coast but quite rare elsewhere. There were clearly strong social boundaries between these families which maintained their peculiarities, at least in late periods. The Anakena population in particular, thought to be of the Miru tribe or royal lineage (descendants of Hotu Matua), remained genetically isolated through inbreeding; it did not tolerate the entry of outsiders into the group by marriage.

Different parts of Rapa Nui also had different roles. The Dutch reported that the other side of the island (i.e. from La Pérouse Bay, where they landed) was the main place for cultivation and fruit trees, and all the produce brought to the Europeans seems to have come from there. The islanders divided their arable land in square fields with furrows: the lack of dividing walls thus makes them very hard to detect archaeologically, and little attempt has yet been made to study them from aerial photography.

Cornelis Bouman, Roggeveen's captain, stated that 'of yams, bananas and small coconut palms we saw little and no other trees or crops'. Roggeveen's personal judgment, however, was more favourable:

We have found it...outstandingly fruitful, producing bananas, sweet potatoes, sugar-cane of special thickness, and many other sorts of produce, although devoid of large trees and livestock, apart from fowls, so this land, because of its rich earth and good climate, could be made into an earthly Paradise if it was properly cultivated and worked, which at present is done only to the extent that the inhabitants are required to for maintenance of life.

The Dutch accepted about sixty fowls and thirty bunches of bananas from the natives, although Bouman recorded that 'they were not very well provided with these'. In 1770, the Spanish visited a banana plantation near Vinapu which they claimed 'stretched about a quarter of a league in extent and was about half that distance in breadth', but in 1774 Cook reported only a few scattered plantations of sugar cane and sweet potatoes (although the latter were the best he had ever tasted), while Forster observed bananas growing in holes a foot deep or in natural cavities to collect and preserve rainwater; their party could see that other parts of the island had once been under cultivation. By 1786, La Pérouse found that only one tenth of the island was cultivated, but the fields were tended with great care, being weeded, watered and fertilized with the ash of burned stalks. Bananas grew in regular lines. At the time of the Russian Lisjanskij's visit in 1804, he noted that every house was planted around with sugar cane and bananas.

Bouman informs us that 'they cut their bananas with a sharp little black stone. They first cut around the branch and then twist it off.' This stone was clearly obsidian, the islanders' chief raw material for tools and, later, weapons. Unlike other Polynesians they were unable to make much use of bone, as we have seen, or of shell, since they had few molluscs big enough to provide raw material.

The main obsidian outcrops occur at the southwestern part of the island, in particular the 90 ha (222 acre) scatter at Orito, but also the islet of Motu Iti which, though not easily accessible, was worth the trip since it consists almost entirely of an obsidian that is particularly good for flaking. Analysis of retouch and dulling on some of Rapu Nui's flake tools indicates that they were employed in shaving wood.

Work is currently being done on identifying the different mineral inclusions and banding of Easter Island's obsidian types, so that in the near future it will be possible to quantify and date how each source was used, and assess the distribution of its material across the island. Thanks to the constantly improving method of measuring 'hydration layers' (minute layers formed in fractured obsidian surfaces by the absorption of water from their surroundings; they increase in thickness through time), obsidian dating is proving an extremely valuable complement to radiocarbon dating for the island's later prehistory, though earlier periods are still somewhat problematical for the technique.

A series of archaeological excavations has begun to build a clearer picture of the more mundane aspects of the island's prehistory, although many results of the work carried out by Heyerdahl's team in the 1950s still await publication (notably the faunal and pollen data), and the information we have concerns the last few centuries before European contact rather than the island's early occupation phase. A further problem is that most artifacts recovered are surface finds, with no date or context, or come from the fill of structures or from cremation pits that cover long periods; and of course, the vast majority of perishable items have completely disintegrated and hence elude the archaeologist. Nevertheless, the stratigraphic excavations carried out in the past few years should eventually help us to obtain a clearer view of developments in the island's material culture through time.

The basic domestic unit of the island appears to have comprised a dwelling (a house, rock overhang or cave), plus a selection of associated features: earth ovens, stone chicken-houses, and stone garden enclosures. Most settlements consisted of two or three such dwellings dispersed in and around the agricultural plantations. Their frequency decreases away from the coast – inland they tend to be on rocky eminences or hill slopes – and they seem to have slightly higher densities around springs and the more fertile soils, as one might expect. Settlement as a whole had a strong coastal bias with exploitation of inland resources: this framework of a coast-to-inland strip closely resembles the patterns of land use and ownership throughout eastern Polynesia.

There were also 'village complexes', clustered around a religious/ceremonial site with its altar-platform, and, c. 50 to 100 m (c. 165 to 330 ft) away, five or more elliptical houses for priests, chiefs or other people of high rank. Commoners' dwellings stood a further 100 or 200 m (330 or 660 ft) inland from these élite structures.

The finest elliptical houses (hare paenga) had a foundation outlined with a kerb of cut basalt stones, an expression of social rank and wealth because of the considerable time and effort required to carve them – in fact, paenga means both 'cut stone' and 'large family'. The stones were from 0.5 to 2.5 m ($1\frac{1}{2}$ to 8 ft) long, 20 or 30 cm (8 or 12 in) wide, and at least 50 cm (20 in) high; small holes in them held the thin uprights of curved branches, which formed a series of arches attached to a ridge-pole and supporting the superstructure of plant materials (ills 68–70). Many had a crescent-shaped lateral pavement of beach stones outside, where the people worked, ate and chatted.

Hare paenga are almost always found near platforms, and often clustered in a semicircle just inland from those on the coast. Being so close to the sacred area reflected the high social status of their occupants, and in fact Aguera, one of the Spanish visitors of 1770, noted that 'others (whom I believed to be their ministers) occupy dwellings close to their statues'. These houses were first described by the Dutch visitors of 1722, who saw them as 'built of a sort of straw looking like beehives or as if a Greenland sloop has been turned upside down'. The concept of boat-shaped houses is widespread in Polynesia, and extends back across the Pacific into southeast Asia. It clearly underlines the primacy of boats in the islanders' heritage, and it is noteworthy that almost all house entrances faced the sea, and have their ovens and other structures on the seaward side.

Most had a single tunnel-entrance, up to 1 m (3 ft) high, into which one had to crawl. These offered protection from the cold and the blowing rain; small statues of wood or stone sometimes stood at either side of this entry. Some of these structures seem to have been, or become, communal, and inside there was space for dozens of people to eat and sleep. Islanders told Mrs Routledge that the evening meal was consumed inside, and that they slept parallel to the length of the house, their heads towards the door, with the old folk in the centre (which was up to 2 m [6 ft] high) and the younger people at the ends (which were less than 1 m [3 ft] in height).

Most of the elliptical houses, being for commoners, had no stone foundation-kerb; their poles were stuck directly into the ground, though they still had a stone pavement set flush against the front of the house. They averaged 12 to 14 m (40 to 46 ft) in length and 2 m (6 ft) in width, though in 1786 La Pérouse mentioned one that was 100 m (330 ft) long and could contain at least two hundred people. Since these were essentially night-time sleeping shelters, with most daytime activities taking place outside, there was little need or room for furnishings, as Roggeveen's remarks confirm: 'We found absolutely nothing... no furniture at all and of utensils only calabashes in which they keep their water. I tasted it and found it to be very brackish' (Cook's party, on the other hand, drank spring water from the west part of the island, and pronounced it sweet and delicious). Cook confirmed that the natives had very few gourds, so that a coconut shell was a very welcome gift. The houses also had reed mats on the floor, and some stone pillows, often decorated with engravings.

All of our eye-witness accounts come, of course, from the very end of the island's prehistory, but most of our domestic archaeological data also come from the later phases; this is simply because the islanders had a tendency to build their houses on top of or very near previous habitations, so that older evidence is usually masked quite effectively.

The island's most ubiquitous archaeological feature is the *umu pae* (stone-lined earth oven): hundreds have been found. The Dutch reported that the islanders prepared chicken 'in holes in the ground in which they had stones that were heated glowing hot by burning bushes' while La Pérouse observed small windbreaks enclosing the ovens.

The *umu pae* have a wide range of shapes (round, rectangular, pentagonal) and sizes since some were single-event structures, others were permanent fixtures for family or community use, while the biggest were for communal feasts. Even the largest, however, were only up to 1 m (3 ft) across: the islanders did not need huge ovens since they lacked large mammals to cook in them. Most are in front of the houses (on the seaward side) but some specialized

68–70 TOP *The foundations of an Easter Island hare paenga, or elliptical dwelling.*
CENTRE *A similar house under reconstruction, showing the framework of curved branches inserted in holes in the foundation slabs.* ABOVE *Drawing of a finished hare paenga, with its outer layer of plant material and a crescent-shaped pavement of stones in front.*

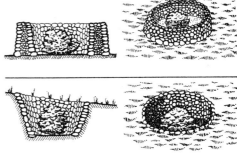

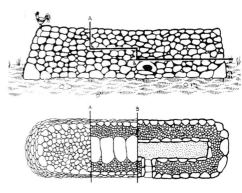

71,72 Garden enclosures called 'manavai' (place of water) provided protection from the wind. LEFT and TOP Artificial manavai above ground. ABOVE A natural manavai in a subterranean lava tube or cave.

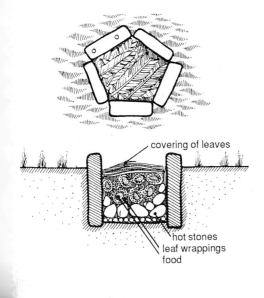

covering of leaves

hot stones
leaf wrappings
food

Providing for an Island Life

73–77 LEFT and ABOVE *Hare moa, the islanders' chicken houses, were drystone cairns with small entrances that could be secured with stones at night: a reflection of increasing competition for food supplies.* RIGHT *Engraved skulls of members of the royal Miru clan, known as puoko-moa, were believed to have the power to increase egg yields.* FAR LEFT *and* LEFT *Umu pae, stone-lined earth ovens, have been found in their hundreds. They were generally small, for no large mammals were available as a source of food.*

cooking centres are known, such as one on Rano Kau comprising thirty-three
large ovens. Domestic examples, however, were simple pits which, like the
houses, were maintained in the same spot over the centuries – a series of three
superimposed ovens spanning 250 years was found in one artificial mound,
which was probably created by the successive clearing out of food residues
and heat-fractured stones. Such trash mounds can be up to 10 m (33 ft) across
and 50 cm (20 in) high.

Manavai or garden enclosures were either walled or subterranean. It is
thought that they provided favourable micro-environments for the paper
mulberry and bananas by protecting from the wind, helping to retain moisture
and affording shade (*manavai* means 'place of water'). Certainly, they are
located primarily in the coastal zone, where there was a greater need to protect
plants from the desiccating effects of the winds from offshore. Inland settlements
may simply have used natural depressions or found them less crucial in
sheltered areas: hence they are archaeologically less visible inland, apart from
the crater of Rano Kau which can be seen as a giant natural enclosure,
providing protection from wind and a lush micro-environment – little wonder
that it contained a complex of houses and terraced gardens on its steep inner
slopes.

These garden enclosures appear in many different forms and are often in
clusters of twenty or thirty. Most of them covered *c.* 45 sq. m (*c.* 480 sq. ft),
though some were three times this size. They comprise rubble walls, about
1 m (3 ft) high, and are similar to structures in Hawai'i. Basalt hoes have been
recovered in recent excavations of one residential site. Circular garden plots
are also known, but since excavations inside them have occasionally revealed
refuse, cooking places and tools suggesting a long occupation, it is thought
that many were originally stone houses with a reed roof: González noted in
1770 that elders and leaders lived in the long houses, while 'priests' lived in
little stone houses near the statues.

The *hare moa* (chicken houses), almost impregnable to robbery, reflect the
crucial importance of this fowl to the islanders' food supply and gift exchange
system. They were solid, thick-walled, flat-topped, rectangular drystone cairns,
up to 2 m (6 ft) high, 2 or 3 m (6 or 10 ft) wide, and between 5 and 20 m (16
and 66 ft) in length, with a low, narrow chamber running down the centre;
their small entrances at ground-level could be blocked with stones at night so
that any attempt to get at the fowls would be heard in the nearby houses.
These structures have sometimes been confused with a very similar rectangular
form of platform which seems to have been used for the burial of chiefs;
however, only twenty such platforms are known, all located along the shore,
whereas we know of hundreds of chicken houses, all on commoners' land –
like the garden enclosures they are not found on chiefly sites, since the upper
classes were exempt from production.

A further source of confusion is that human skulls have sometimes been
found in the chicken houses: these *puoko-moa* (fowl heads) from the royal

Miru clan were thought to have the power to increase egg yields, and about twenty engraved 'egg heads' are known of both sexes (ill. 75). A belief in the fertilizing power of chiefs' skulls has also been documented in the Marquesas. Oddly, however, Rapa Nui's wealth of rock art includes only thirteen representations of chickens and eight of plants, which shows that this art was not a simple record of food resources but was a religious and social phenomenon tied to ritual and to things of the spirit rather than of the stomach.

Along ravines at the foot of Mount Terevaka, about four hundred square and rectangular house foundations have been identified which seem to be early in date (c. AD 800–1300 according to results from obsidian) and resemble structures in the Marquesas; they would have had a superstructure of vegetation, and are associated with crude platforms, red scoria statues and exterior pavements, all on a small scale. Excavations inside them have uncovered woodworking tools, and it is therefore probable that these were habitations – perhaps short-term or seasonal – for those who harvested the great trees that used to grow on the mountain: 'Terevaka' literally means 'to pull out canoes'. An island that was once so heavily forested would certainly have required a large labour force to be involved in the felling and working of timber for canoes as well as for the statue industry (Chapter 6). In the Marquesas it is known that four hundred men might be engaged in the construction of a single large canoe, and throughout Polynesia canoe-building involved both specialized craftsmen and communal efforts.

Over eighty rectangular house foundations are also known at Vai Atare, on the opposite side of Rano Kau's crater to the ceremonial village of Orongo. This was the area where the slabs for house foundation-kerbs were quarried, so that this cluster of houses was probably for the quarrymen.

In 1886 Thomson reported seeing a village of elliptical stone houses extending for over a mile along the west coast, north of Tahai; their entrances all faced the sea, and each had a little cave or niche at the back. Like the ceremonial houses at Orongo (Chapter 10) they were corbelled, with a keystone on the top; but whereas the Orongo houses were quite late, these seemed to Thomson to be the oldest on the island, especially as his guides knew nothing of the place, not even its name. Sadly, no trace of this village remains, but it provides evidence that stone houses and corbelled superstructures were a long-lasting tradition on Rapa Nui rather than a late intrusion.

Caves were also lived in occasionally, especially in the later phases of prehistory – for example, by fishermen exploiting the coastal zone – the always late material found in the caves excavated so far suggests strongly that for much of the island's prehistory, when it still had a heavy vegetation cover, most caves were so full of plant life, water and dampness as to be unsuitable for occupation. Even under today's relatively dry conditions, they are typically damp. A similar phenomenon is known in Hawai'i, where cave occupation seems to have begun four hundred years after the earliest settlement, while in the Marquesas the time-lag is twelve hundred years.

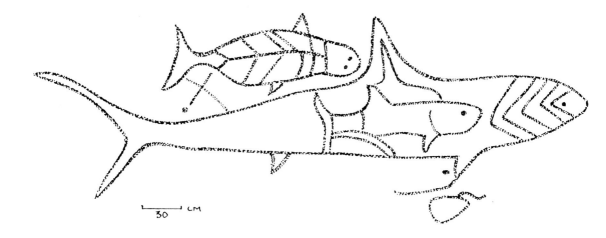

Not surprisingly, coastal caves yield more fishing tools and fish remains than inland caves, where chicken bones are far more prominent. Fire-pits and charcoal concentrations tend to be just outside cave entrances, whereas bone and shell remains form middens both inside caves and extending outside.

One large cave on the south coast has been excavated recently, and its (as yet undated) earliest occupation level yielded very high densities of food remains such as rat, chicken and fish bones, shells, and fish scales, together with obsidian tools. Thomson in 1886 reported finding little univalve shells in all the ruins and caves he explored, as well as on the beach: this resource was still highly prized as food by the islanders. Shellfish were gathered for food despite their small size (up to 4 cm [1½in]), being readily available to hand-gathering in the rocky surge zone; they were eaten raw, or cooked in water. Crustaceans such as crayfish and crabs were also probably taken, as well as bird eggs from the offshore islets – several early visitors including Cook remarked on the scarcity of land and sea birds on the island itself. As late as 1968, however, thousands of sea birds in very large flocks would still visit the island occasionally.

Turtles have never been a common occurrence, owing to the cold climate and the lack of sandy beaches – only one has come ashore in the past twenty years – but there are thirty-two represented in the island's rock art, which implies that they were considered of some importance (only two sharks and thirteen octopuses are depicted). A few turtle-shell ornaments have been found, and it is worth noting that throughout Polynesia turtles were connected with royalty and with special ritual practices. Seals were equally rare on the island, though some seal bones were discovered during recent excavations of early levels at Anakena, and twenty-three petroglyphs (rock carvings) may represent this animal.

Archaeological evidence of fish-hooks suggests that long-line fishing was of minimal importance, especially in areas such as the south coast where the

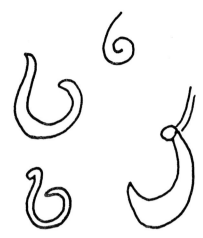

78,79 LEFT *and* RIGHT *The northern and western areas of Easter Island specialized in fishing; most petroglyphs of fish and hooks, such as those shown here, are to be found on the island's north coast.*

shallow water permitted the effective use of nets. Overall, our knowledge of fishing techniques is limited, since so much of the equipment is perishable and does not survive archaeologically: for example, the only clue to the use of nets is the presence of basalt net-sinkers and of bone netting needles. But in any case, without a lagoon, many types of large-scale communal netting operations were impossible on Easter Island. Whereas co-operative lagoon fishing with nets and sweeps up to 150 m (*c.* 500 ft) long took place on Mangareva, and over 1 km (*c.* $\frac{1}{2}$ mile) long at Tubuai in the Rapa group, communal shore fishing on Easter Island was comparatively infrequent and small in scope. Only one net appears in the island's rock art, and only one ancient draw-net over 20 m (65 ft) long, its meshes made of paper-mulberry fibres, survives in Washington from the early European visits. Geiseler reported seeing a net 60 m (200 ft) long in 1882, but most scholars think that figure is an exaggeration.

The great diversity of hooks found – of stone or human bone, and manufactured with the help of obsidian drills and coral files – was employed primarily for shore fishing of small fish rather than for open-sea exploitation. This is confirmed by the remains of marine fauna, which are dominated by small inshore species of fish and eel. The oldest hooks dated so far are bone specimens from Vinapu and Tahai, and come from the early 13th century AD; we still lack relevant data for earlier periods, though recent excavations at Anakena have uncovered an early bone harpoon of a type used in the Marquesas. Of course, many basic methods such as trapping, snaring, and hand collecting will have left no traces. A Rongorongo tablet given to Bishop Jaussen of Tahiti in the 19th century was wrapped in 6 m (19 ft) of the human hair cording that was used for fishing at that time.

Fish-hooks have been found in greater numbers on the north coast than on the south; it is thought that fish were more abundant and offshore fishing better in the north, which has yielded most of the larger and two-piece fish-hooks from the island: these were probably used for deep handline fishing by

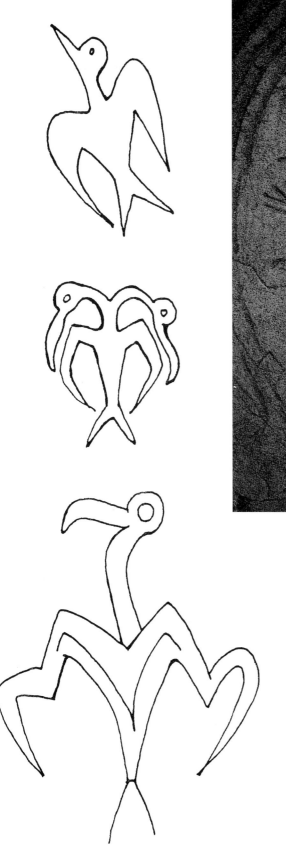

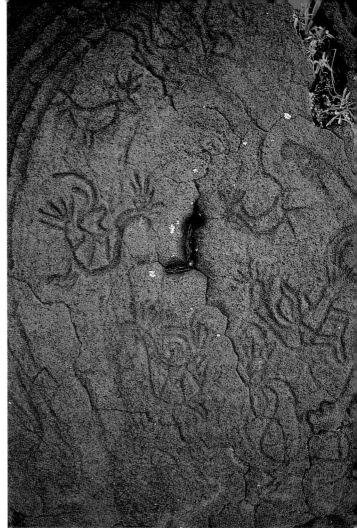

The Petroglyphic Zoo

80–82 LEFT *and* ABOVE *Birds were not only a vital source of food for the islanders, but had powerful symbolic significance, as is reflected in the island's rock carvings of both wild birds (left) and domesticated chickens (above).*
RIGHT *The high-status Miru clan controlled the distribution of prestige fish such as whales (m), dolphins (f and k), turtles (j), and seals (i). Few sharks (d) and octopuses (g) are depicted in the island's rock art, which suggests their rarity. Petroglyphs also include this octopus-like monster (l). Archaeological remains are dominated by species of small fish (a) and eel (b).*

a

b

c

d

e

f

g

h

i

j

k

l

m

experts, and it is noticeable that the forms found change from deep-sea to inshore types through the archaeological record. Moreover, of the 381 fish-hook motifs so far found in Rapa Nui's rock art, no less than 93 per cent are on the north coast, and all are the kind used for deep-water fishing, especially of tuna.

The fish-hook motif is totally absent from whole sections of the island which are, and presumably were, excellent fishing locations. A considerably greater percentage and variety of fishbone have been found in middens at sites such as Anakena in the north than on the south coast, where the small shellfish seem to have been correspondingly more important. Broadly speaking, then, the north/west part of Easter Island specialized in fishing while the south/east part had the intensive dry-field agriculture, together with the terraced cultivation inside the lush, protected crater of Rano Kau. This brought about institutionalized exchange mechanisms between these areas as well as between coastal and inland zones, especially as fishing vessels may eventually have required wood from the toromiro trees of the south coast, and caulking mosses from the crater lakes.

We know from the island's ethnography that there were restrictions (*tapu*) on marine resources, which were controlled by the high-status Miru clan of the north; this explains why most petroglyphs not only of fish-hooks but also of sea creatures are located on the north coast. The island's highest chief redistributed the prestige fish (a common phenomenon in Polynesia), while resources of great economic value, such as tuna, turtles, seals and dolphins, were reserved exclusively for the aristocracy at certain times. Only the Miru nobles could continue to enjoy larger fish like tuna during the *tapu* months from May to October, and lesser mortals would supposedly be poisoned or develop asthma if they too tried to eat them then. This reflects the political domination of the Miru, their monopoly of these resources and perhaps, at the same time, the growing difficulties experienced in exploiting the open sea (Chapter 9).

However, undoubtedly the most remarkable display of respect for the island's élite is embodied in the great statues, to which we must now turn our attention.

PART II

ANCESTORS OF STONE –
A PETRIFIED DREAM

In Easter Island . . . the shadows of the departed builders still possess the land . . . the whole air vibrates with a vast purpose and energy which has been and is no more. What was it? Why was it?

Katherine Routledge

83 *This toppled head has travelled to numerous exhibitions abroad and is now supported on a bed of stones at Tongariki; the slopes of the Rano Raraku statue quarry are visible in the background.*

CHAPTER 5

STATUES AND CEREMONIES

*...empty repetition, like a caged animal going round
and round and making always the same thing, these
frozen faces, these frozen frames in a film that's
running down...*

Jacob Bronowski

'Living Faces'

The most famous and most astonishing feat of the Easter Islanders' Stone Age culture was the production of hundreds of standardized gigantic stone statues without the use of metal tools. How and why did they do it?

The Easter Islanders' origins partly explain their motivation: even some of the 19th-century visitors to Rapa Nui compared its statues to those of other Polynesian islands. The carving of large, human figures in *stone* was not common in Polynesia, in part perhaps through lack of suitable material: all Pacific statuary is in igneous rock. In the Marquesas, where volcanic tuff was used, there are large ancient stone statues of rotund men associated with ceremonial platforms – a massive statue called 'Takaii' on the island of Hiva Oa, for example, is 2.83 m (9¼ ft) high – these figures are unlike those of Rapa Nui, but certainly hint at a shared heritage and tradition of statue-carving. Herman Melville, in *Typee*, relates how, in the Typee valley of the Marquesas, he came upon a huge wooden statue with staring eyes, standing on a stone platform. The Australs too have monolithic stone sculpture – at Ra'ivavae, there was a *tiki* figure some 2.3 m (7½ ft) tall; and it is known that Pitcairn Island also had hard red tufa statues standing on shrines: unfortunately, the Bounty mutineers threw them off a cliff! However, investigations by Mrs Routledge and others showed that the Pitcairn platforms were smaller versions of those on Easter Island, with a similarly sloped inner façade 12 m (39 ft) long; and one surviving fragment of a statue, found under the veranda of a modern house there, was a torso with large hands clasped on its abdomen. Parallels have also been drawn between Easter Island's statues and a type of pumice figure from New Zealand, with a narrow rectangular head, jutting brow and long curving nose.

The vast majority of the Easter Island statues are made of Rano Raraku tuff, including all those erected on platforms, but a few are made of red scoria,

84–86 OPPOSITE *The long, tapering fingers of this moai at Anakena make the hands look almost wing-like.* OVERLEAF LEFT *This statue at Rano Raraku carries the carving of a European sailing ship on its chest (see ill. 182).* OVERLEAF RIGHT *A statue toppled from its ceremonial platform near Rano Raraku quarry.*

or basalt, or a dense white stone from Poike – indeed, a recent survey has discovered dozens of previously unknown statues on Poike, but only a couple of them are made of Rano Raraku tuff. The finished statues on platforms range from 2 to almost 10 m (6 to 33 ft) high: the biggest, at Ahu Hanga Te Tenga, is 9.94 m (32½ ft) long, but appears to have fallen and been broken in the course of being erected, since its eye sockets were never cut. The statue known as 'Paro' (which was erected on Ahu te Pita Kura) is almost as long, 3.2 m (10½ ft) across the shoulders, and weighs 82 tons. There might be up to fifteen *moai* in a row on a statue platform; it is a common misconception that they were absolutely identical, whereas, in fact, no two are exactly alike. A certain amount of variety can be seen within the rows (ills 131, 134); some platforms seem to have had all their statues erected in one episode, while other rows were built up over time.

The largest statue ever made, nicknamed 'El Gigante', was a monstrous 20 m (65 ft) in length, weighing up to 270 tons, and it is generally reckoned to have been well beyond even the remarkable ingenuity of the Easter Islanders to move it, let alone erect it somewhere (the obelisk in Paris's Place de la Concorde is not much taller, at 22.8 m [75 ft]). Lying unfinished in the Rano Raraku quarry (ill. 109), it represents an enigma in itself: was it a commission from some power-mad individual or group? Did the workers abandon it once they recognized the futility of carving a figure they could not possibly move? Was work on it simply abandoned as part of the general cessation of statue building? Islanders told Thomson in 1886 that the platform Takiri was the last to be built and had been intended for that statue. Or was it, as some scholars believe, never intended to be a standing statue, but simply an enormous petroglyph, like the recumbent funerary statues in European cathedrals?

Dozens of statues have detailed designs in bas-relief on their backs that may represent tattooed signs of rank: for example, curved lines at each shoulder plus a vertical line for a spine appear to make the kind of abstract human face that is widespread and significant in the island's art (for example, on wooden ceremonial paddles) and elsewhere in Polynesia. On statues at Anakena there are also bas-relief spirals on the buttocks.

Between the fingertips and below the navel of a typical statue is a feature in bas-relief believed to be a *hami*, the fold of a loincloth. Lines that curve across the small of the back are likewise thought to represent the *maro*, the sacred loincloth of authority, which was important in denoting the rank of chiefs and priests throughout Polynesia. Specimens of *maro* were recorded in 19th-century Easter Island, made of *tapa* or of human hair.

It is generally assumed that most of the figures are male, though in fact the vast majority are unsexed: a gender can only be assigned safely to the few (in the quarry and at Tongariki) with a goatee beard, or to a couple of specimens with a vulva marked. Some scholars see the *hami* as indicating a male. Others have seen the occasionally very developed nipples as a sign of femininity, but this is unfounded. One or two statues have well-rounded breasts but no other

87 OPPOSITE *Carved spiral patterns on the backs of two of the moai on Ahu Nau Nau, Anakena. The white number on the right-hand figure results from Sebastian Englert's attempt to catalogue the island's statuary earlier this century.*

The Giant Statues

88–90 LEFT *One of the slim, angular moai standing on the slopes of Rano Raraku quarry.* BELOW *The range of sizes and shapes of moai.* OPPOSITE *Katherine Routledge's excavation of a statue standing in a hole on the inner slopes of the quarry.*

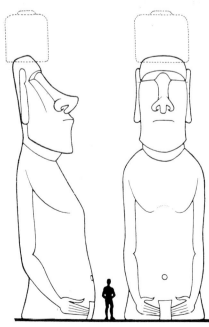

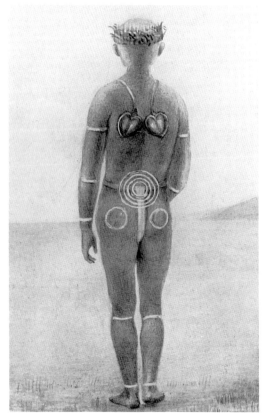

Spirals and
Sacred Loincloths

91–93 ABOVE LEFT *Bas-relief spirals on the buttocks of a moai at Anakena, together with the sacred loincloth of authority.* ABOVE RIGHT *A view of the elaborate decoration on the back of a statue excavated by Routledge (see ill. 90).* LEFT *Routledge's drawing of the ceremonial ornamentation on a 'Bird-Child' (Poki-Manu) undergoing an initiation ceremony at Orongo; the circles of white pigment recall those on the Anakena figure.*

94 OPPOSITE ABOVE *The front of a standing statue excavated by Routledge on the outer slope of Rano Raraku quarry, the 'hami' or sacred loincloth visible between its fingertips.*

sign of being female, whereas at least one of those with a vulva has nothing at the bust that gives the slightest hint of its gender. The vulva may have been a later addition, and in any case sexual ambiguity is by no means uncommon in Polynesian art.

A clear distinction can be drawn between those statues which were erected on platforms, and those – whatever their intended function – which were not. Apart from the fact that only the figures on platforms were given eye-sockets, head-gear, and perhaps colouring, the average height of the platform-statues is 4 m (13 ft), whereas that of those not on platforms is 6 m (20 ft); and many of the platform figures are stockier and less angular than those at the quarry, with less accentuated features and less concave or prominent noses and chins.

The eye sockets had generally been assumed to have remained empty, adding to the brooding appearance of the figures, although one scholar, Francis Allen, did suggest as long ago as 1884 that the statues might have had inlaid eyes of obsidian like the island's wooden figures. In 1978, excavations by Sonia Haoa, a native archaeologist, uncovered fragments of white coral and a circular red scoria pebble under a fallen statue at Anakena; when fitted together they formed an oval eye of cut and polished coral, about 35 cm (14 in) long, which fitted the empty socket of the figure (ill. 97). When restored to their original appearance, the statues with fitted eyes provide a startlingly different image from that to which the world had grown accustomed (ill. 96).

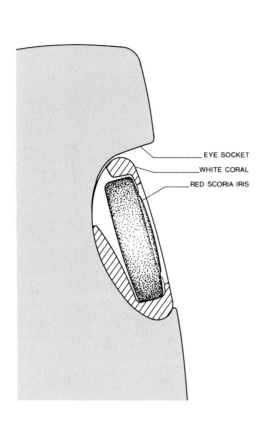

EYE SOCKET

WHITE CORAL

RED SCORIA IRIS

Restored to Sight

95–97 *It was once thought that the statues had always been 'blind', but in 1978 fragments of white coral and red scoria were discovered under a fallen statue of Anakena – when pieced together, they formed an eye that fitted the statue's empty socket perfectly.* ABOVE LEFT *A cross-section of a statue's eye.* ABOVE *A pair of reproduction eyes fitted in an erect moai showing how they gaze slightly upward.* LEFT *An eye placed in the socket of a moai head in the island's museum.*

When reproduction eyes were fitted, it was found that the statues had stared not directly at the villages before them – which would doubtless have been rather disconcerting – but slightly upward, perhaps explaining a Mangarevan name for the island, 'Mata-ki-te-Rangi', meaning literally 'eyes towards the heavens'. Less romantic observers have commented that the eyes make the statues 'look like a worried businessman at tax time'!

The reason that so few of the coral eyes had survived the toppling of the statues is that islanders had burned the coral fragments found around wrecked platforms to make whitewash for their houses: coral was scarce, since the island has no lagoon, and the only supply came from fragments washed up on the shore. William Mulloy found an almost intact eye under a fallen statue's face at Vinapu in the 1950s, but it was very eroded, and its round shape led him to think it was a fragment of a 'beautifully made coral dish' which had been elliptical with pointed ends. Since Sonia Haoa's discovery in 1978, fragments of eyes of white coral or pumice have been found all over the island, some of them with pupils of obsidian rather than of scoria. One curious fact, however, is that none of the European explorers who saw statues still standing on their platforms ever mentioned these eyes, and in fact González in 1770 stated that 'The only features of the face are simple cavities for the eyes' ... is it possible, therefore, that these eyes, embodying consciousness and intelligence, were only inserted at certain times or for particular ceremonies to 'bring the figures to life'?

The outside world's first recorded comment on the famous statues appears in the journal of Cornelis Bouman, one of Roggeveen's captains, who wrote, on 8 April 1722: 'On land we saw several high statues in the heathen fashion' – whereas the Spanish in 1770 at first mistook them from out at sea for big shrubs symmetrically set up! Roggeveen's log states that the islanders 'set fires before some particularly high erected stone images, and then, sitting down on their heels with bowed heads, they bring the palms of their hands together, moving them up and down'. It has been suggested that the fires the Dutchmen saw may simply have been preparations for earth ovens, so that food could be offered to the unexpected guests, but Bouman's account shows that the Dutchmen saw chickens being cooked in the ground, so they could presumably differentiate the two phenomena.

Many of the first European visitors expected the giant statues to be gods, although La Pérouse wrote in 1786 that 'we never came across traces of any cult and I do not think that anyone could suppose the statues to be idols, although the islanders do show them respect'. None of the statues is known to have had the name of a deity. Instead they were all known by the collective name *aringa ora* (living faces): they are clearly generalized rather than individualized portraits. Captain Cook's party heard the term *ariki* (chief) applied to some, while others had nicknames such as 'Twisted Neck', 'Tattooed One' and even 'Stinker' (even today, the islanders frequently use nicknames for each other and for visitors).

From the islanders' testimony and other Polynesian ethnography it is virtually certain that the statues represented high-ranking ancestors, often served as their funerary monument, and kept their memory alive – like the simple upright slabs in front of platforms in the Society Islands, which represented clan ancestors, or the statues dominating the terraces of sanctuaries in the Marquesas, which were famous old chiefs or priests.

This would explain the special features of the platform images: one can speculate that statues were commissioned during the lifetime of elders – rather like the pyramids or tombs of Egyptian pharaohs – but their eyes were left uncarved to indicate the person was still alive. Only after death were the sockets hollowed out, the statue moved to its platform, and its eyes and sometimes a head-dress set in place, perhaps to 'activate' its *mana* (spiritual power); if this is correct, then the eyes had far more than an occasional ceremonial significance.

But in addition to their 'identity', the statues may also have incorporated distinct symbolism of other kinds: display is a constant in Polynesian culture. These towering vertical figures on their horizontal platforms around the coast served as a sacred border between two worlds, as intermediaries between the living and the gods, between life and death – transitional areas of this kind tend to be of ritual significance in all human societies. The ancestor figures, facing inland towards the villages and with their backs to the sea, probably provided considerable reassurance and protection. One can compare the Indonesian island of Sulawesi, where wooden effigies of the deceased, wearing clothes and head-gear, and with staring inlaid eyes, are placed on high balconies in cliffs so their spirits can forever watch over their village.

It has been suggested that the Easter Island statues' location, as close to the shore as possible, implies a role in preventing encroachment by the sea, particularly if the legend about Hotu Matua and his followers fleeing a partly submerged island has any basis in fact. In that case, however, one might expect the ancestors to be placed facing the potential threat rather than with their backs to it, and the location might equally well be explained as a convenient way of keeping these structures away from the limited agricultural land available; there was little point in having fields by the shore, where heavy salt spray would damage the crops.

Max Raphael, the German art historian, pointed out that the sheer monumentality of the figures, their grandeur in relation to the viewer's relative smallness, fulfilled the need to feel protected, and must have created a sense of security and repose: monumentality always commands respect and awe. These were not works of art that carried on some dialogue with the individual, they were repositories for conserving the ancestors' spiritual power – concentrated in the head or eyes – which protected the community. The attraction exerted by each individual figure is limited, since they are so stereotyped, but in groups their effect is greatly magnified.

Raphael noted how the back of the head is flat, the cheeks and ears are 'static', but the nose and mouth jut forward aggressively – moreover, the straightness or concave curve of the nose contrasts markedly with the frequently arched noses on the island's wooden figures. He therefore believed that, consciously or unconsciously, the nose was shaped as a symbolic phallus, a vertical part above a horizontal part whose base bulges at both sides (phallic noses also occur in petroglyphs, as well as on some wood carvings), while the 'pouting' or protruding thin lips with a groove between them suggest the form of a vagina. In short, he saw these heads as sexual symbols – monuments to dead men that were somehow involved in the process of rebirth. Other scholars have seen the entire *moai* as symbolic of the phallus and procreative power – there is at least one legend on the island that the penis provided the model for the design – and we have already pointed out the statues' inherent ambiguity of gender.

The hands resting on the stomach may also have specific meaning. In the traditional Maori carving of New Zealand the hands were placed there to protect ritual knowledge and oral traditions, because it was believed these were carried in the belly. Figures with hands on the abdomen are also common in the Marquesas and elsewhere in Polynesia.

In many societies around the world, the very presence of the ancestors, whether as images or in the form of their bones (or both), frequently serves as a group's best evidence that the land has always belonged to them. The figures can therefore, in a sense, be seen as literally staking a claim, connecting a lineage to its ancestral land through a founding father (or mother). Moreover, the roles assigned to the eminent dead in this way may bear little resemblance to the roles they performed while alive: it is very common for individuals or groups in pursuit of power and authority in a changing society to call upon the dead to help them and bolster their claims. The deifying of great men who were either direct descendants of the gods, mighty warriors or people with great prestige was a deeply rooted characteristic of Polynesian culture. In Polynesia, only the nobility had ancestors and a genealogy stretching back to the gods, and Polynesian art as a whole is dominated by almost stereotyped portraits of these ancestors.

However, on Easter Island it seems that the statue carving was done not by a population under the control of some central power, but rather by a number of fairly independent kin groups from different parts of the island. It is likely that they were in competition with each other, trying to outdo their neighbours in the scale and grandeur of their religious centres and ancestor-figures. There is some evidence of an overall tendency for the statues being carved to increase in size over time.

But exactly how was the carving accomplished with a simple Stone Age technology?

Phallic Heads, Phallic Noses

98–101 *Details of moai heads at Rano Raraku and on ahu showing the vaguely phallic shape of the head, the elongated ears – sometimes with disc inserted (right) – and the possible sexual symbolism of the nose, lips and nipples.*

CHAPTER 6

THE RIDDLE OF THE QUARRY

The Statues' Maternity Ward

The volcanic crater of Rano Raraku is one of the world's most extraordinary and evocative archaeological sites, filled with unfinished statues and the empty niches from which hundreds of others have already been hacked out. If you are lucky enough to have the whole place to yourself, rather than swarming with visitors, its stillness and silence become eerily overwhelming. But imagine this unique quarry bustling with activity on the inner and outer slopes, with many different groups of tattooed and painted workers, the rhythmic noise of countless hammers striking rock, and no doubt songs or chants ringing out...

In our modern age, with its advanced technology and its emphasis on speed and impatience, it is hard to understand how prehistoric people could spend vast amounts of time and hard manual labour on carving, transporting and erecting huge stones, whether they be the megaliths of Western Europe or the Rapa Nui statues. On the other hand, it can be argued that in prehistoric times – and particularly on a small isolated island – there was little else to do, and stone-carving became a ruling passion; in 1786 La Pérouse reckoned, perhaps somewhat optimistically, that three days' work in the fields annually was all that each islander needed to do in order to obtain food for the year, while in the 1860s the missionary Eugène Eyraud reported that the islanders did no real work at all. A day's exertion assured them of a year's supply of sweet potatoes. The other 364 days of the year were spent 'walking about, sleeping and visiting'. They made their own entertainment in those days!

It is the lack of comprehension by modern people of what can be achieved with simple technology, lots of time and muscle-power, and some ingenuity, which has permitted the lunatic fringe of archaeology to flourish. The most obvious example is the theory, proposed by the Swiss writer Erich Von Däniken and others, that the prehistoric world was visited sporadically by extraterrestrial astronauts who are responsible for anything in the archaeological record that strikes us as impressive or enigmatic. In addition to being a lazy and simplistic *deus ex machina* solution to supposed ancient 'mysteries', this view provides the comforting reassurance that 'we are not alone', and that human progress is being monitored and occasionally nudged in the right direction by some benevolent power in the universe.

It is therefore somewhat ironic that the Easter Islanders' own efforts to reassure themselves – through their colossal carvings – that they were not alone have been seized on and distorted by the proponents of ancient astronauts. Such views ignore the real achievements of our ancestors and constitute the ultimate in racism: they belittle the abilities and ingenuity of the human species as a whole.

Von Däniken's view of the Easter Island statues is very simple: being made of 'steel-hard volcanic stone' they could not have been made with 'rudimentary tools . . . . Nobody could ever have freed such gigantic lumps of lava with small primitive stone tools . . . . The men who could execute such perfect work must have possessed ultra-modern tools.' He proposed that a small group of 'intelligent beings' was stranded on the island, taught the natives various things, made the statues – he emphasizes their 'robot-like appearance' – and were then rescued before all the figures were finished. The natives tried to complete the carvings with stone tools, but failed miserably.

The yellow-brown volcanic tuff of Rano Raraku (Raraku was the name of a local ancestral spirit) is made of ash and lapilli. It is, indeed, steel-hard on surfaces exposed to the weather: the Spanish visitors of 1770 struck a statue with a hoe or pickaxe, and sparks flew. Underneath, however, it is not much harder than chalk, being formed of compressed ash, and can be cut and shaped quite easily even with stone tools: Métraux found that 'the modern sculptors consider this material easier to work than wood. With nothing but an axe they cut out a large block of tuff in a day and in a few hours transform it into replicas of the great statues.' The quarry is littered with thousands of flaked and pointed stone picks (*toki*) of compact basalt: if Von Däniken's theory were correct, it seems bizarre that so many of these should have been made by the islanders before they realized the tools were useless!

During Thor Heyerdahl's expedition in the 1950s, he discussed with the islanders how the statues were carved, and they insisted that these picks had been used for the task; it is uncertain whether any of the tools were hafted on handles, though one or two hafted adzes are known in the island's rock art. In a now famous experiment, Heyerdahl hired six men who used some of these tools to outline a 5 m (16 ft) statue. It was first measured out on the rock-face in arm and hand lengths, and then the bashing began, each blow raising a bit of dust. The rock was frequently splashed with water to soften it (the spongy rock also absorbs rainwater, which makes the statues fragile and hard to preserve today), and the picks quickly became blunted and had to be sharpened or replaced. It took three days for these unpractised men to produce a statue-outline, and on the basis of this somewhat scanty evidence it was somehow calculated that six men, working every day, could have completed a figure of this size in twelve to fifteen months (Katherine Routledge, the first person to make a detailed study of the quarry, had estimated that a statue could be roughed out in fifteen days, while Métraux had thought this figure too small).

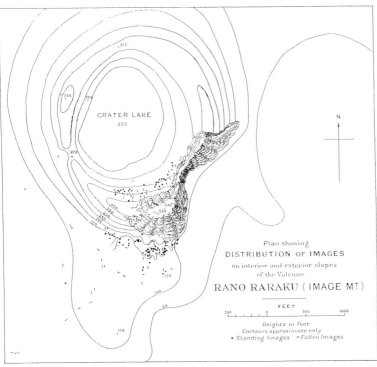

Plan showing
DISTRIBUTION OF IMAGES
on interior and exterior slopes
of the Volcano
RANO RARAKU (IMAGE M.T)

FEET

Heights in feet
Contours approximate only
• Standing Images –Fallen Images

CRATER LAKE
253

N

1/14,000

The Rano Raraku Quarry

102–6 ABOVE *Routledge's contour map of the Rano
Raraku quarry showing locations of some of the giant
statues.* ABOVE CENTRE *View towards the quarry, the giant
heads poking up on the hillside.* ABOVE, FAR RIGHT *Two of
the heads on the outer slope.* BELOW CENTRE *View looking
south towards the coast.* BELOW RIGHT *Aerial view of
Rano Raraku today.*

Rano Raraku: The Inner Quarry

It follows that twenty practised workmen, perhaps in alternating teams of ten with plenty of elbow-room, could have produced any of the island's finished statues, even 'Paro', in a year. Allowing a thousand statues on the island, and an estimated period of at least five hundred years of carving activity (from *c.* AD 1000 to 1500, based on radiocarbon dates from Norwegian excavations at the quarry), it is clear that even a small population could have achieved this number of figures. But since the Rano Raraku quarry contains so many unfinished statues, of a variety of sizes and types, it seems likely that there were numerous different groups at work, and the timespan necessary to account for a thousand statues could be far shorter. The high number of unfinished figures at the quarry also implies that carving them was much easier than moving and erecting them, and production was far outstripping demand. Excavations have revealed the abundant foundations of houses both inside the crater and, in regular terraces, between Rano Raraku and the coast, which are thought to be those of the numerous quarrymen.

107–8 ABOVE LEFT *The interior of Rano Raraku, showing erect moai facing the crater lake; in the foreground, face-up with its head towards the camera, is a statue still attached to bedrock at the rump.* ABOVE RIGHT *Routledge's view of the quarry's southeastern inner slopes, seen from across the lake.*

What is certain is that specialized master-craftsmen were at work here; the islanders reported that the sculptors had been a privileged class, their craft being hereditary in the male line, and that it was a matter of great pride to be a member of a sculptor's family. According to legend, the statue carvers were relieved of all other work, so that the fishermen and farmers had to provide them with food, especially valuable seafood; the carvers were also paid in fish, lobsters and eels.

Large areas of the quarry lie hidden under slope deposits, so it was actually bigger than we can recognize today (it should be remembered that this quarry was the 'maternity ward' for over 90 per cent of the island's statues). At present, it is *c.* 800 m (*c.* 2600 ft) long, and contains numerous now empty niches from which statues were once removed, as well as 394 figures visible on the outer and inner slopes illustrating every phase of the carving process (ills 109–14); the information they provide shows us just how systematic this process was.

Quarrying the Statues

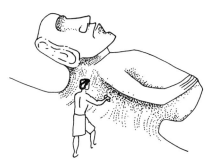

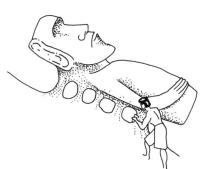

109–14 ABOVE *The monstrous 'El Gigante', the biggest moai ever carved.* LEFT *Three stages in the release of a moai from bedrock and its erection at the base of the quarry slope.* OPPOSITE ABOVE *Routledge's photograph of a statue with a complete keel, located high in the outer quarry of Rano Raraku.* OPPOSITE CENTRE *Easter Island rock carvings of hafted adzes.* OPPOSITE, BOTTOM LEFT *One of the thousands of basalt 'toki' which were used to carve the moai. They often fit the hand very comfortably.* OPPOSITE, BOTTOM RIGHT *The statue-outline carved in the quarry by a group of islanders for the Norwegian Expedition of 1955.*

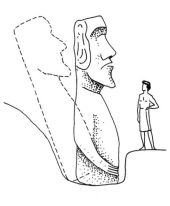

The figures were carved on their backs, with their base usually pointing down-slope (though some point the other way, others lie parallel to the mountain, and some are almost vertical). As they were cut away, a keel was left along the back, keeping them attached to bedrock. All the basic details of the head (except the eyes), the hands and so on were carved at this stage, and the surface smoothed, probably with pumice, of which fragments have been found: the tuff, while excellent for carving and smoothing, is not good for polishing.

With the statue held firm by a packing of stones and fill, holes were punched in the keel, until it was completely pecked away. Some were probably broken at this point, and it is noteworthy that the quarry displays abundant evidence of breakage or of figures abandoned due to defects in the stone. The tuff was in plentiful supply, so it was simpler to abandon a faulty statue and begin a new one than to persist with a bad one. Carving might also be abandoned if there was a slip during the work, which in Polynesia was seen as a sign of evil affecting the carver's *mana*.

The next task was to move the statue down the slope (of about 55 degrees) without damaging it. Depressed runways or channels of earth seem to have been used, with the remains of the keel serving to maintain the statue's direction. The islanders claim that cables were used, perhaps attached to the statue's neck as well as to some 'bollards' which are still visible.

On the rim of the crater, 150 m (*c.* 500 ft) above the plain, though apparently only of use to operations at one part of the inner slope, are some pairs of pecked cylindrical holes over 1 m (3 ft) in depth and width, with horizontal channels connecting them at the bottom. Scars suggest that cables *c.* 7.5 to 10 cm (3 to 4 in) thick were fastened here, and the islanders have confirmed this. Since the revelation that large trees were readily available (Chapter 4), it

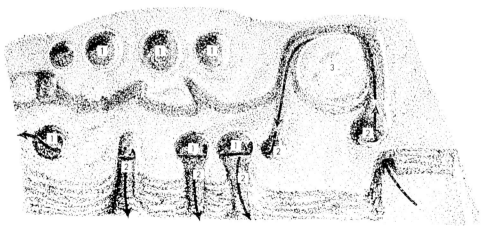

115 *Francis Mazière's plan of the statue-hoisting system high on the inner face of Rano Raraku. 1, postholes; 2, channels for ropes; 3, the movement of the hoist was checked by winding it around the 'capstan', or drum.*

is also thought probable that large trunks stood in these holes, with the ropes around them: the islanders themselves had told their German visitors of 1882 that colossal tree trunks had been set in these holes, and held cables used to lower statues down to the plain. Ropes may also have been attached to horizontal wooden beams set transversely in the channels leading down the slope: traces of these runways and of beam-seats remain in the quarry. Some accidents certainly happened: at least one head was left in place while its body continued down the slope. But, by and large, the system seems to have worked well.

Over *c*. 400 m (*c*. 1300 ft) of the bottom of the exterior slope stand about seventy essentially completed statues erected in pits in the ground: it is these figures, buried up to their shoulders or even chins by sediments, and with their backs to the mountain, which have produced the classic cartoonist's view of Easter Island heads gazing out to sea. Excavations by Katherine Routledge and, more recently, by Thor Heyerdahl's teams have revealed that these are, in fact, full statues like those on the platforms, and the tallest is over 11 m (36 ft) in height. It has been assumed that these were figures of people not yet dead, or that they had not yet been moved to *ahu* because of lack of room on the platforms or simply lack of resources for the transportation.

At the edge of the adjacent plain about thirty more statues lie on the surface, mostly on their fronts. Others are scattered along prehistoric 'roads' heading vaguely southward and westward along the south coast. We now arrive, therefore, at the question that has perplexed every visitor to the island: how were these figures brought down from the quarry and transported, sometimes miles, to their final destinations?

CHAPTER 7

ROCKING OR ROLLING: HOW WERE THE STATUES MOVED?

*[They] seemed to be triumphing over us, asking:
'Guess how this engineering work was done! Guess
how we moved these gigantic figures down the steep
walls of the volcano and carried them over the hills to
any place on the island we liked!'*

Thor Heyerdahl

Over the years some ingenious or far-fetched explanations have been put forward as to how the finished statues were moved from the quarry. In 1722 Roggeveen, clearly not a geologist, was misled by the tuff's colour and its composite nature (the numerous lapilli embedded in it) and claimed that the statues were in fact moulded *in situ* from some plastic mixture of clay and stones; some of Cook's officers in 1774 came to the same conclusion. In 1949 a psychologist, Werner Wolff, even imagined that the figures were roughed out, then blown from erupting volcanoes to the platforms, and finished where they fell! Others have suggested electromagnetic or anti-gravitational forces and, as we have already seen, visiting extraterrestrials. The islanders themselves cling to a legend that the statues walked to the platforms thanks to their spiritual power, or at the command of priests or chiefs. It was said that the statues walked a short distance each day towards their platforms, and also that they walked around in the dark and uttered oracles!

It may be true that faith can move mountains, but archaeologists have sought more mundane explanations. The first point to be made is that the problem in transportation was not necessarily the statues' weight (this could be considerable, though the average is no more than about 18 tons) but their fragility, since the Rano Raraku tuff is not very dense (its specific gravity – i.e. the ratio of its density to that of water – is light, only *c.* 1.82), and it was important not to damage the elaborate detail already carved on the figures.

Hundreds of statues were moved from the quarry, some of them as far as 10 km (6¼ miles) though it is noticeable that only the smaller ones were moved quite so far, a potent argument against spiritual forces alone being responsible! No doubt, the effort and distance involved in setting up particular statues added to the ostentation of their size, further enhancing their prestige and that of their village.

To early observers, who thought that the island had always been bereft of wood or material for cordage, the method of moving the statues remained obscure. The first real progress on this topic came, once again, during Heyerdahl's expedition of the 1950s, when an experiment was carried out with a 4 m (13 ft) statue weighing around 10 tons. Following the elders' instructions, the islanders made a wooden sledge out of a tree fork and lashed the statue on its back on to it; ropes of tree bark were attached to it. About 180 men, women and children came to feast and dance, before setting about the task of pulling the statue a short distance on its sledge, using two parallel ropes.

Since 180 people could pull a 10 ton statue, then 1500 could certainly have moved even Paro's 82 tons (plus its heavy sledge); as we shall see (p. 179), such a number is well within the estimated prehistoric population. Sledge transportation could have been rendered much smoother and more efficient – reducing the required workforce by one third – by applying lubricants to the track: taro, sweet potato, totora reeds or palm fronds could all have been used, and there is an oral tradition on the island that mashed yams and sweet potatoes were indeed used as lubricants for moving the statues.

Since we know that timber was once in plentiful supply (Chapter 4), it should be borne in mind that the work – and the workforce – could have been almost halved again by dragging the sledge over a lubricated wooden track rather than over the ground. The wood of the toromiro would have been suitable for rollers of 50 cm (20 in) diameter, and also for levers, which were probably crucial to handling the statues.

William Mulloy suggested a simple and economical method of transportation involving a curved Y-shaped sledge, made from the fork of a big tree, on which the statue would rest face-downwards. A large pair of shearlegs is attached to the figure's neck by a loop, and as they are tilted forward, the rope partially lifts the statue and takes some weight off the sledge (ill. 119). The statue therefore follows the shearlegs, in a kind of rocking movement caused by the bulging abdomen.

Mulloy estimated that, by this method, Paro could have been moved the 6 km (4 miles) to its platform by only ninety men. Specialists in ancient technology have pointed out that a flat-bottomed sledge would serve just as well, and that the estimate of ninety men for Paro is much too low. It has been calculated that, while possible (assuming the presence of trees big enough to serve as shearlegs, palms being flexible and unsuitable for the job), Mulloy's method is no more efficient than other techniques. It also puts special stress on the statues' fragile necks. Besides, most of the statues apparently abandoned in transport do not have the protruding stomachs ideal for this method, which suggests that it was not the one being employed.

The simple sledge method has become a little more plausible now that we know about the presence of the palms, since they could be used for both sledges and trackways. Palm wood is not very durable, on the whole, and the trunks of most species split on drying, and rot in a damp environment. The timber used would therefore need replacing frequently, so if the palms were used for statue transportation, this activity probably contributed heavily to the depletion of this resource; it is worth noting, however, that the present-day *Jubaea chilensis* or Chilean wine palm – the modern species closest to that which was once prolific on the island – is quite resistant to decay.

A further obvious use for palm trunks is as rollers, provided they were at least 20 cm (8 in) across: as mentioned earlier (Chapter 4), modern specimens of *Jubaea* can reach a height of over 25 m (82 ft) and a diameter of 1 to 1.8 m (3 to 6 ft), and although the trunk consists of a spongy, fibrous mass within a thin hard rind (ill. 124), it dries out to considerable hardness. To be really efficient, rollers must be fairly uniform and run on a well-constructed track. British and French experiments in moving prehistoric megaliths have found that this technique reduces the workforce required to about 6 or 7 men per ton. Hence to drag Paro on palm rollers would need 500 to 600 people. On roughly made tracks, rollers can jam; but a well-constructed track plus lubrication can make the task relatively easy.

A different technique for moving the largest statues horizontally has been suggested by the French architect and archaeologist Jean-Pierre Adam. Observing fishermen of the Ivory Coast, he saw two men move a very heavy canoe up the beach with the greatest of ease, whereas four people could not have dragged it. One man sat on one end, to raise it enough for a single roller to be placed beneath; the other man could then swivel the whole canoe through 180 degrees (ills 120–21). They then changed places and repeated the operation until the canoe had travelled the required distance.

If a series of rollers were to await each statue at the base of the runway down from the quarry, then the figures would be slightly raised above the ground. The rollers would have to be beneath the centre of gravity or almost under the axis of rotation. The head would then be weighted with rocks in bags, and a post or rock solidly planted in the ground next to it. With ropes attached to the base, it would then be simple to swivel the whole figure through 180 degrees. The ropes, counter-weight and post would have to be moved for each subsequent operation. Adam has calculated that, by this method, Paro could have been moved by 590 men, just over a third of the total needed for the sledge method. Both this technique and Mulloy's also require only short bursts of pulling, with welcome rests in between, unlike sledge-dragging.

It is worth noting that a little-known Dutch drawing (ill. 118) produced in 1728, just a few years after the island's rediscovery and probably based on information from Roggeveen's companions, shows a big sculpture (bearing no resemblance to a *moai*) being moved by only nine natives; it is difficult to assess the method used, but the block seems to rest on a stone slab, and may well have rollers beneath it – so this might add weight to Adam's suggestion.

The statues, if transported on their fronts or backs, must have required considerable wrapping and padding with vegetation because of their fragility

116 OPPOSITE *Giant statues on the outer slopes of Rano Raraku quarry. Only their heads are now visible above the ground; they have been partially buried by rubble and silt deposits running down the sides of the crater.*

118 *The earliest known depiction of Easter Island, in a Dutch drawing of 1728, seems to show, far left, a large block of stone being moved by a group of islanders.*

and to protect their decoration. But what if they were moved upright, to reduce the friction surface, perhaps swivelling on their bases like a refrigerator?

Katherine Routledge had 'seriously considered whether they could have been moved in an upright position'; Heyerdahl was told by the islanders in the 1950s that the statues had 'wriggled along' (this was displayed with the feet together and stiff knees), while a few years later French·explorer Francis Mazière was told by a native 'that the statues moved standing upright, making half turns on their round bases'.

In recent years, two independent experiments have been carried out into the feasibility of this technique. A Czech engineer, Pavel Pavel, began with a 26 cm (10 in) statue of clay, which proved to be very stable owing to the large circumference at the base and the narrower upper section, placing the centre of gravity at about one third of the total height. He then made a 4.5 m (15 ft) concrete statue weighing 12 tons, and in 1982, at Strakonice, carried out experiments in moving it upright; it was given a slightly convex base for easy swivelling (a flat base would result in longer 'steps'). Ropes were fastened around the head and the base, and seventeen people in two groups tilted the figure on to its edge and pulled it forward. With practice, good progress was made, the team working rhythmically and without strain.

117 OPPOSITE *An aerial view of statues scattered on the hillside at Rano Raraku.*

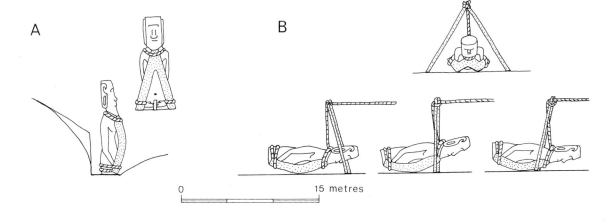

A

B

0   15 metres

Moving the Statues: Theory and Practice

119–25 *The enigma of how the prehistoric islanders could have moved the giant statues often long distances from the quarry and erected them on platforms has provoked a host of theories and experiments.* ABOVE *Stages in Mulloy's bipod method.* LEFT *and* BELOW *Adam's 'canoe-swivel' method as applied to a moai.* OPPOSITE ABOVE *Love's concrete moai being swivelled, and,* CENTRE, *the damage caused to its base as a result.* OPPOSITE, BOTTOM LEFT *A cross-section of a Chilean wine palm, showing the thin, hard rind and fibrous interior.* OPPOSITE, BOTTOM RIGHT *Love's moai being moved on a sled and rollers.*

In 1986, Pavel was able to repeat the experiment on the island using two real re-erected statues. First, a 2.8 m (9 ft) statue of 4 or 5 tons was tried (with padding to protect it from the ropes); only three men were needed to tilt it, and five to pull it forward. Next, a 4 m (13 ft) statue of 9 tons was moved. It proved so stable that it could tilt at 70 degrees to either side without falling. Only sixteen people were required to move it a distance of 6 m (20 ft): seven tilting and nine twisting forwards. Pavel therefore concluded that, with practice, this figure could have been moved 200 m (*c.* 650 ft) per day, and that even the largest statues on the island could have been transported in this way – though moving Paro's 82 tons for 6 km (4 miles) over rough terrain is a very far cry from a small figure moving 6 m (20 ft). Thor Heyerdahl has estimated that a 20 ton statue could move an average of 100 m (*c.* 330 ft) per day by this method.

American geologist Charles Love also had a replica of a giant statue made in Wyoming; the 4 m (13 ft) concrete figure weighed 10 tons, being denser than Rano Raraku tuff, and is equivalent to the smallest 20 per cent of the island's figures. With two hemp ropes, each 2.5 cm (1 in) thick, attached to its brow, he found that crews of fourteen to twenty-two men could move it a few feet by alternate pulling, which caused chips to come off the front of its base (ills 122, 123). This was a precarious method, and the figure toppled over twice, so it is likely that this simple technique was used only for moving very short distances or for the statues' final positioning. Placing logs under the lateral edges stabilized the statue and protected its base, but made it no easier to move forward.

However, a breakthrough occurred when Love's statue was placed upright on two green logs carved into sled-runners to fit its base, and was then raised on to a track of small wooden rollers. The statue could now be moved 45 m (148 ft) in two minutes using twenty-five men and two ropes – indeed, the problem was not moving the figure but stopping it! This appears to be the best method for long-distance transportation: it is convenient, stable, and fast, causes no damage, and requires little wood, not much rope, and few people (ill. 125). Pavel's tilt-and-swivel technique is more likely to have been employed for final positioning.

There are three major questions concerning upright transportation: first, as shown above, swivelling damages the base, and it has been said that the friction would have worn the soft tuff so severely that the statues would have been down to their nostrils in no time. Clearly, however, if Love's method were used, this would not be the case. Secondly, what of hilly terrain? Would the statues not topple as they tried to ascend or descend a slope? In fact, the statues have a slightly forward-slanting base – stones had to be placed under some of those on reconstructed platforms to prevent them leaning forward – and this would help to counter-balance an ascending slope of 10 or 12 degrees; on the descending side, the statue could simply be turned around and moved backwards. Horizontal figures or sledges, on the other hand, would lose contact with some rollers on hilly terrain. Thirdly, no rope marks have been found on the statues' necks and no wear on their bases; this could be explained simply by the use of effective padding beneath the ropes, and, as we have seen, Love's roller method causes no damage to the bases.

A vital ingredient in all these methods of moving the statues is a plentiful supply of strong rope. If one assumes that Paro was pulled using only 10 ropes, each having to resist the combined force of at least 50 and perhaps even 150 people, as shown earlier, it has been calculated that the ropes would have to be several centimetres in diameter, and they would need to be about 80 m (260 ft) long: in other words, hundreds of metres of very thick rope were necessary, weighing a ton or more. The more efficient the transportation method, the less cable is needed, but a section of the population must have been engaged in permanent rope-making to meet requirements, especially as rope deteriorates even faster than wood and would have to be constantly replenished.

The only good rope-making material known to have existed on the island was the inner bark of the *Triumfetta* shrub, which the islanders called *hau*, and possibly also the crowns of the now-extinct palm. *Hau* is a remarkably strong fibre, and was much used in historic times for small twisted cordage, but it no longer exists in quantities sufficient to provide the kind of ropes mentioned above, and no accounts survive of the heavy cables that must have been made. It is quite possible that a decline in availability of heavy-duty rope contributed as much as the scarcity of timber to the end of statue-building.

Much attention has been paid over the years to the statues at the foot of Rano Raraku and those between the quarry and the platforms, in the hope of obtaining clues to the particular transportation method used. Since many of those on the quarry slopes are standing in pits, while others on the plain have clearly broken after falling from an upright position, it has sometimes been assumed that all were being transported upright. Other scholars, however, believe that many of them were not being transported at all, but were set upright in these positions either temporarily (for their backs to be finished, for rituals to be performed, or to await the death of the person they represented) or permanently, lining the avenues of approach to the quarry. They may also have simply been abandoned in the course of transportation, perhaps because of strife, or a failed ritual, or the commissioning group's inability to muster the necessary manpower.

Many of the intact horizontal statues in this area lie face-down, which might support Mulloy's idea of transportation in this position (as opposed to being moved on their flat backs on rollers), while others lie face-up and broken, which suggests that they were set upright along the road and later thrown down – or perhaps that they fell and broke while being transported upright.

In fact, statues are found along the ancient roads on their backs, fronts and sides. At points where they were apparently being moved uphill they are

By Road or By Sea?

126–28 ABOVE *The basalt pedestal revealed by excavation behind a fallen moai along one of the roads discovered by Routledge.* RIGHT *An aerial view showing traces of the prehistoric roads below the outer slopes of Rano Raraku.* BELOW RIGHT *A restored canoe ramp between two platforms at Tahai.*

generally on their backs with their base towards the hill; where going downhill, they are usually on their fronts, again with their base towards the hill. Many have their heads pointing away from the quarry, but there is no fully consistent pattern. In some cases, groups of two to four statues are fairly close to each other, in varying positions, occasionally even at angles to one another.

Mrs Routledge believed that Rano Raraku was approached by at least three magnificent avenues, each lined at intervals by statues with their backs to the hill, and that none of the figures now lying around the island was in the process of being moved. Possible support for her view has come from excavations in 1986 by Thor Heyerdahl's expedition, which found that a 7.8 m (25½ ft) statue of 40 tons, lying face down near Rano Raraku along Routledge's 'southern road', had an irregular circular pavement or pedestal of basalt stones behind it, bearing clear traces of the statue's base; it was therefore probable that this *moai* had been carefully and purposely set up at this spot. The buried face of the figure was unweathered, suggesting that it had not stood upright for long. However, excavation of a statue of similar size, also face down, some 700 m (2300 ft) away, found no trace of such a pavement. At least some

of the upright statues buried at the foot of Rano Raraku still stand on stone pavements.

The island's 'roads' are still visible by the slanting light of the setting sun. These tracks, slightly raised on lower ground and depressed through higher ground, are *c.* 3 m (*c.* 10 ft) wide, and radiate out from Rano Raraku, generally following the lie of the land and avoiding sharp alterations in terrain. They must certainly have been cleared of any unevenness and of stones, but today, thanks to decades of neglect and of sheep grazing, they are again covered in small stones, though clear of boulders.

The condition of the roadbed must have been critical: the clay surface becomes very hard and stable if pressed heavily, but soft or muddy going would make statue transportation impossible. This implies that transportation took place during the drier summer, and was perhaps completely interrupted by wet wintry conditions: if so, and if statues were being moved upright, it is possible that those which had reached soft or potentially wet ground (like the first of those excavated by Heyerdahl in 1986) would have been given a stable temporary pedestal to prevent their tipping over; those on drier or solid ground (like the second) would not need a platform.

Another possibility that has received little or no attention – perhaps owing to the constant crashing of the waves (though it did occur to the Americans in 1886) – is that some figures might have been transported the short 500 m (*c.* 1600 ft) distance from the quarry to the shore and then floated on timbers or rafts around the coast to the platforms where they were required. At several points around the coast there are lava-flow causeways, and also some paved ramps, which run into the sea. These *apapa* (which literally means 'unload') are generally seen as canoe-ramps, places for large vessels to land or unload: there is one next to Paro's platform, and Mulloy restored a fine sloping ramp of beach boulders at Tahai. It is therefore quite possible that some large blocks, and perhaps some statues, were transported by water. It is also worth noting that fragments of Rano Raraku tuff at a platform-like structure dating to AD 1174 on the offshore islet of Motu Nui have led to claims that at least one statue was taken there.

One can only conclude, as so often in archaeology, that no single explanation suffices for all the statues: the giant statues found between the quarry and the platforms vary from 1.77 to 9 m (*c.* 6 to 30 ft) in length, and there is no reason to suppose that the same method of transportation was used for the smallest as for the biggest. Different techniques were probably used according to the size and style of figure, the distance to be travelled, and the manpower, timber and ropes available.

CHAPTER 8

PLATFORMS AND PUKAO: ERECTING THE STATUES

So far, then, we have a large statue that has arrived from the quarry: where is it to go? At this point, it is worth pausing to consider the phenomenon of the *ahu*, the rectangular platforms which have tended to be overshadowed – literally and metaphorically – by the statues. Even without any statues on them, Rapa Nui's platforms would be an archaeological wonder, for they are remarkable pieces of massive communal engineering, sometimes requiring the moving of 300 to 500 tons of stone: for example, the Tahai complex comprised three structures requiring about 23,000 cubic metres (*c.* 30,000 cubic yards) of rock and earth fill, estimated to weigh 2000 tons.

This tiny island has between 250 and 300 platforms, which form an almost unbroken line round its coast except for areas of high cliffs (though a few are on cliff-edges), with distinct clusters around coves or good landing places and areas that are specially favourable for habitation. They range in size from quite small to over 150 m (*c.* 500 ft) in length and up to 3 m (*c.* 10 ft) in height, and comprise a rubble core faced with masonry, for which no mortar was used. The seaward façades often seem to have been placed as close to the shore as possible, and parallel to it, forming impressive walls which seem to rise straight out of the sea. These façades vary from uncut local stones to precisely carved and fitted blocks. To the landward side was a ramp, paved with lines of beach boulders and sloping down to an artificially flattened plaza (ill. 129): one such 'court' at Tahai measured 55 by 40 m (180 by 130 ft). Around the coast, there seem to be major platform complexes on average every 0.7 km (*c.* $\frac{1}{2}$ mile), marking boundaries and serving as residential and socio-political and religious centres.

Rapa Nui's platforms are very clearly variations of the *marae* platforms of central and eastern Polynesia – this word, which clearly postdates the departure of the Easter Islanders from Polynesia since it is not part of the old Rapa Nui tongue, originates from the proto-Polynesian *malae* meaning 'meeting place', and different island groups have used such open spaces and platforms for similar purposes throughout the area: for example, the *tohua* of the Marquesas, or the *heiau* of Hawai'i. In the southern Marquesas, Tuamotu, Society and Austral Islands, the word *ahu* referred only to the raised platform at the end of a rectangular court, whereas in the northern Marquesas and on Easter

Island it meant the whole ceremonial centre. The Polynesian *marae* are likewise coastal platforms, usually parallel to the shore.

A few platforms on Easter Island seem to have been built specifically to contain burials. This does not seem to have been the original function of the image-platforms, though Thomson's investigation of the immense Tongariki structure revealed a narrow corridor at its centre, full of human remains; instead, the normal *ahu* had multiple functions such as serving as a social and ritual centre, and a lineage and boundary marker. Burial seems to have been the exception rather than the rule in early periods on Rapa Nui, since no early skeletons have yet been found: cremation was far more common, and elaborate cremation pits have been found behind the central platform at many complexes such as Akivi. These contain fragments of human bone mixed with beach pebbles, bits of obsidian and charcoal and a variety of artifacts such as fish-hooks, and occasional bones of chickens and rats. This therefore seems to be a mixture of cremation and of votive offerings and hence presents an analogy with the slab-lined pits placed next to Polynesian *marae* for the disposal of offerings and sacred paraphernalia. Cremation, however, was not practised in the rest of eastern and central Polynesia.

The study of Rapa Nui's platforms is made especially difficult because many have been plundered over the years for building blocks and foundation stones, leaving what at first sight seem to be featureless piles of rubble. However, detailed examination of the remains can shed much light on their construction. Hydration dating (obsidian) and radiocarbon dating (charcoal) have established that some platforms were built in a single episode while others have constructions spanning centuries. At Anakena, for example, several generations of platform seem to have been built on top of each other, with the structures being enlarged over the centuries. Modifications to platforms would often incorporate old statues or old house-foundation slabs in their construction.

In the opinion of those archaeologists who have excavated and studied the island's *ahu*, they reflect an overall stylistic continuity derived from the early Polynesian settlement, starting with small platforms which gradually increased in size and complexity as the statues changed from naturalistic forms to the highly stylized *moai* of ever-growing proportions.

The islanders took the basic Polynesian architectural form and gradually developed their own local elaborations, such as adding the ramps, as well as lower lateral extensions at either side. Excavations have revealed changes in form over time, with overlapping, abutting or out-of-line architectural features; these were not, however, contemporaneous or island-wide changes, which casts grave doubt on provisional sequences developed from the excavation of a very few platforms such as those at Vinapu: subsequent excavations at Akivi, for example, showed that it belonged to a far later period than expected. Some platforms were partially and deliberately destroyed before careful modifications took place – certain architectural features are not found all over the island but are very localized, emphasizing the rivalry between different clans or kin-groups, perhaps each producing their own variation of the monuments.

The very earliest platforms on the island may have been simple open-air altars without statues on them – it is very hard to tell because of all the subsequent changes they have undergone – or they may even have carried wooden figures like some in the Marquesas. Some had courtyards marked out by walls or a piece of levelled ground. The earliest such structure dated so far (AD 690) is the first phase of Ahu Tahai, which was a narrow, flat-topped platform of rubble fill surrounded by masonry; it was later extended by lateral wings, and may possibly have had a red scoria statue on it rather than a *moai* of later, classic type. Such a scoria figure was indeed found here, and its rounded, naturalistic features, circular eyes and normal 'human' ears, together with its raw material are all reminiscent of some *tiki* figures of the Marquesas. A similar statue was exposed in the fill of Ahu Tongariki after that was destroyed by the *tsunami* (tidal wave) of 1960 (caused by an earthquake off Chile), and two partial figures were incorporated in the late-phase wings of Ahu Hekii. It is probable that such small red figures were the precursors of the *moai*, and stood on top of, or in front of, the earliest platforms just like the small statues or simple upright slabs that represent chiefs at the *marae* elsewhere in Polynesia.

The few scoria statues found on the island seem to span at least as long a time as the *moai*, and regardless of whether they ever stood on early platforms themselves, they are often closely associated with the structures and the cult activities that took place there. Red scoria was also used as a landward facing for certain platforms (Akahanga, Vinapu), and Linton Palmer said in 1868 that there was at least one 'pillar statue' in this stone (like the one found at Vinapu) at every image platform. In other words, scoria statues were probably made throughout the prehistoric period, both before and alongside the giant statues as a separate but related phenomenon.

The first phase of Ahu Akivi, unusual because it is located inland and faces the sea, seems to have been a simple 35 m (115 ft) *ahu* with two 20 m (65 ft) lateral wings but no evidence of statues; instead, it is possible that a large polygonal slab (found in the fill of the later phase) had been set upright on it like on a Polynesian *marae*, and the same may be true of a small, 1 m (3 ft) high image of Rano Raraku tuff found in the same fill. Around AD 1460, this platform was rebuilt to support seven large statues on pedestals, and the wings and ramp were raised substantially, with rows of beach stones added.

The earliest known 'classical' statue of Rano Raraku tuff that originally stood on a platform is located just north of Tahai, and dates to the 12th century AD. It is over 5 m (16 ft) high, weighs 20 tons, and shows that the quarry was operating by this time, and that the classic statue form was already well developed; the latest date we have for a statue on a platform is *c*. AD 1650, a figure at Hanga Kioe, over 4 m (13 ft) high and weighing 14 tons. In other words, we know that statue quarrying was carried out at Rano Raraku for at least five hundred years and probably rather more.

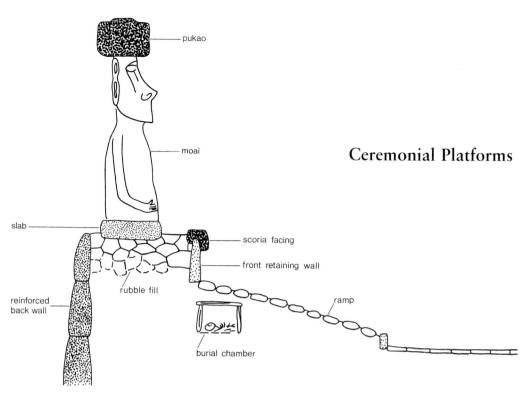

pukao

moaï

slab

scoria facing

front retaining wall

rubble fill

reinforced
back wall

ramp

burial chamber

Ceremonial Platforms

129–33 ABOVE *Cross-section of a platform (ahu), showing the major features. About 125 of the 250–300 known platforms carried statues as shown here.* BELOW *The principal features of an image ahu: (A) seaward façade of stone slabs behind the central part of the platform; (B) lateral extension or wing; (C) sloping ramp of beach boulders; (D) artificially flattened plaza; (E) moai; (F) pukao (topknot); (G) cremation pits; (H) funerary cist; (I) canoe ramp; (J) hare paenga, houses for priests and chiefs.* OPPOSITE ABOVE *The Ahu Nau Nau at Anakena, showing the pukao and reproduction eyes in place.* OPPOSITE CENTRE *The massive seaward façade of Ahu Tepeu, designed to withstand the immense lateral push exerted by the weight of the moai.* OPPOSITE BELOW *The cut-stone seaward facing of Ahu Hanga Poukura, near Vinapu.*

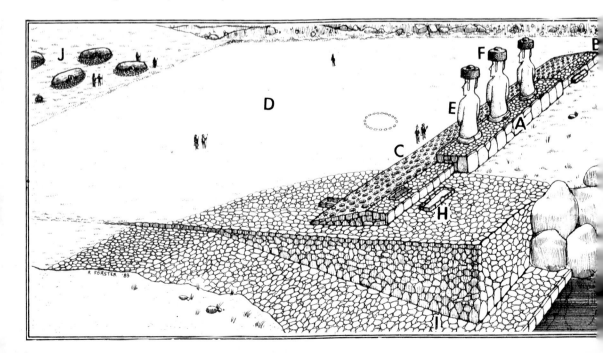

The building of platforms seems to have become an obsession by *c.* AD 1200, and this 'golden age', the peak construction time for both platforms and statues, lasted until well into the 16th century.

It is important to note that, according to astronomer William Liller, up to a dozen platforms show at least reasonable evidence of having been oriented or positioned astronomically, mostly towards important sunrise or sunset positions. More than 90 per cent of coastal platforms were built with their long axis closely parallel to the shore, as elsewhere in Polynesia where they were useful navigational aids; but six coastal platforms that are not parallel to the shore have their long axis aligned North–South and face the rising equinox. Some inland platforms seem to be directed towards the rising winter solstice, marking the time when days are shortest and the sun is lowest in the sky. It is noteworthy that the three most outstanding monuments on the island – Vinapu, Tongariki and Hekii – have all five of their central platforms oriented to the rising solstice or equinox. The summit of Poike was probably used as a calendar indicator since the winter solstice sun rises over it as seen from Orongo. Oral traditions record that priests also watched the rising and setting of particular star constellations which signalled the times for certain rituals, feasts, and agricultural or fishing activities (and it is worth mentioning that a cluster of fifty-six small cupmarks at Matariki on the northwest coast resemble a kind of star map). The islanders would have found it crucial to know the onset of the seasons for crop-planting, owing to their subtropical, somewhat temperate climate, while birds, fish and turtles all followed seasonal patterns of appearance.

The platforms were, as already mentioned, a mass of rubble encased in retaining walls of varying quality. There is now no doubt that the famous precisely fitted and smoothly pecked basalt slabs that form a façade on the seaward side of some platforms, such as Vinapu and one or two others, were the final stage in their construction, and in some cases were added as a finishing touch after the statues were already standing: their mass, together with that of the ramp at the other side, enables the platforms to resist the immense lateral push exerted by the weight of the statues. This is not, therefore, an archaic feature, and in no way points to any connection with Andean civilizations.

On Easter Island, the best façade slabs commonly weigh 2 or 3 tons: at Vinapu one slab measures 2.5 by 1.7 m (8 by 5½ ft), and probably weighs 6 or 7 tons, while one at Ahu Vaï Mata is 3 by 2 m (10 by 6 ft), weighing 9 or 10 tons. Such feats of construction are by no means unique in the region, however. In the 19th century, European visitors wondered how Tahitians could move huge masses, such as 3-ton logs, over great distances with just levers and rollers; and some of the logs transported by New Zealand's Maori to make their canoes often weighed far more than Rapa Nui's statues. Similar prodigious feats can be found all over Polynesia, and Tahiti's *marae* of Mahaiatea is over 100 m (over 325 ft) long, while platforms in the Marquesas can be 120 m

134,135 OPPOSITE: ABOVE *The late (c. AD 1460) phase of Ahu Akivi, restored by Mulloy; its statues never had head-dresses.* BELOW *A semipyramidal ahu, the last type of platform to be built, which served as an ossuary.*

(*c.* 390 ft) long and 30 m (*c.* 100 ft) wide, comprising blocks of more than 10 tons. It has been estimated that even modest platforms could require months of work by at least twenty men.

The frequent finds of obsidian flakes within the fill of excavated Rapa Nui platforms suggest that they played a role in the construction, perhaps in cutting or trimming fibres for rope (the islanders claim that stone blocks were moved around on sledges), smoothing levers, or simply in food preparation.

The last type of platform to be built on the island seems to have been semipyramidal, a dramatically different form usually superimposed on the earlier, classic statue-bearing types and often constructed of stones torn from these predecessors. Less than 75 semipyramidal platforms are known, in contrast to the more than 125 image-platforms. They never carried statues, and all of them seem to have been ossuaries, designed purely to receive burials, like some of the earlier non-image platforms.

Assuming that we have a platform that has been strengthened in preparation: how did they get the statue up there? Captain Cook reckoned that the figures were raised little by little, supported by stones. Receveur, a priest accompanying La Pérouse in 1786, agreed, suggesting that the figures had been raised quite easily by using levers and progressively slipping stones underneath. Most speculation since then has concurred, envisaging the gradual construction of a ramp of earth and stones on which the statue would be raised and then tipped over into place (ills 138–42).

This technique was first tried out on the island in 1955 when William Mulloy, during his excavations at Vinapu, needed to replace in the platform wall a fallen slab weighing over 2 tons, which lay 2 m (6 ft) in front of, and 1 m (3 ft) below, where it should be. Six islanders using two long levers set about raising each side of the slab, and sliding material beneath it to make a masonry platform, until it lay above its destination. Then it was gradually tilted, levered and pushed into place. The whole operation took one hour.

In another important experiment carried out during Heyerdahl's expedition of 1955, a fallen statue of 25 tons at Anakena was raised 3 m (10 ft) in the same simple way; by using two levers (5 m [16 ft] long) and slipping stones underneath, twelve islanders built a ramp under it, and had it standing on its platform in only eighteen days. It was first raised horizontally until it had reached the same height as the platform; then its head alone was raised, until the sloping figure could be simply slid forward and tilted to a vertical position. Since the levers were used against the statue itself, large scars were caused, suggesting that the original builders must have protected the figures with padding.

There are few archaeological traces of massive ramps on Easter Island: at Akahanga the remains of a masonry mound lie to the landward side of a platform and a statue seems to have fallen off it; other platforms, such as Te Pito Kura, do have tremendous numbers of stones nearby which may be the traces of raising operations. Ramps would also have involved colossal amounts

136 OPPOSITE *The ahu at Akivi, one of the few inland statue platforms.*

of extra labour in their construction and removal. However, the ramp idea largely arose because of the island's alleged lack of wood. Since we now know that timber was once in plentiful supply, it has also been suggested that an alternative method might have been used, namely the construction of simple, solid wooden scaffolds of criss-crossed beams; such a scaffold would have been just as effective as a ramp, but would take less time and effort to set up and dismantle. During the restoration of Ahu Akivi in 1960, Mulloy's team did use a rectangular timber armature against which the levering was done – it is worth noting that excavations in Akivi's plaza found many post holes up to 2 m (6 ft) deep. It took a month to erect the first of Ahu Akivi's seven 16-ton statues, but the seventh took less than a week, showing the benefit of experience for unpractised hands. It is safe to assume that the prehistoric islanders knew exactly how to set up the figures with a minimum of effort.

But so far, all experiments and theorizing on this topic have involved horizontal statues; what if the figures arrived upright at their platforms, as discussed above? There seems no good reason to doubt that, with care, these very stable figures could have been raised in the same gradual way, being tilted first one way and then the other, as stones or logs were inserted beneath them.

Even more extraordinary than the raising of the statues, followed by the insertion of their eyes into the sockets, was their crowning glory, the *pukao*: a soft red scoria cylinder from the quarry of Puna Pau. These seem to have been a late addition, associated only with statues on the largest and most important platforms of late phases, since most platform statues (e.g. those of Akivi) do not have them, and fewer than 100 are known to exist (Englert counted 58 fallen from statues plus 31 still in their quarry). They should be seen perhaps as a sign of the continuing rivalry between villages or kin-groups, determined to 'keep up with the Joneses' and outdo each other in the splendour of their monuments and in their homage to the ancestors with further symbolism: in the Marquesas, a great stone was placed on the image of a dead man as a sign of death and mourning, and the *pukao* may have had a similar meaning.

Debate continues about the precise nature of these cylinders; in the past, some scholars have suggested they represented grass-hats or a kind of turban made of painted paper-mulberry or *tapa* (cylindrical head-dresses are found in much of Polynesia), others that they were dressed and stained top-knots of hair, or wigs; it goes without saying that Von Däniken saw them as space helmets! Red was a significant colour associated with ritual and chiefly power throughout Polynesia, and hair was sometimes coated with red ochreous earth in Melanesia. At present, the most likely explanation is that they are a stylized version of the *hau kurakura*, a red feather head-dress worn by warriors – the early European visitors saw islanders wearing feathers on their heads, and some circular or cylindrical feather head-dresses have actually survived. Throughout Polynesia, red feathers were identified with the spiritual power of the gods.

137 OPPOSITE *Ahu Nau Nau at Anakena, with the statues' head-dresses, or pukao, restored. The platform itself incorporates the head of a former statue – a practice that was believed to imbue the new platform with the mana, or spiritual power, of the earlier moai – and a petroglyph of a horizontal ithyphallic man.*

Raise the Titan

138–43 LEFT *and* RIGHT *Stages in the experiment undertaken by twelve islanders for the Norwegian expedition of 1955. A 25 ton statue at Anakena was raised in 18 days, by using two levers and slipping stones beneath it to build a ramp.* OPPOSITE BELOW *The method envisaged by Mulloy, Adam and others for raising a statue and its head-dress simultaneously. In fact it is almost certain that the head-dresses were later additions.*

It is still uncertain how the scoria head-dresses were set in place, and no experiments have yet been carried out; those to be seen today on restored statues were all put there by cranes, not without difficulty (ill. 146). It would be a major undertaking to raise any *pukao*, but what of Paro's monstrous specimen – almost 2 m (6 ft) across, 1.7 m (5½ ft) high, and weighing about 11.5 tons? Even bigger examples lie in the quarry. Cook suggested that ramps or scaffolding were used. Some scholars, such as Mulloy and Adam (ill. 143), have even proposed that the cylinders might have been raised at the same time as the statues, and that they were solidly lashed together; most scholars, however, feel this is far too risky, and that the red cylinders were almost certainly a later addition – for example, one unfinished cylinder now lies abandoned 150 m (nearly 500 ft) from the single-statue platform (Ahu Ature Huke) for which it was intended.

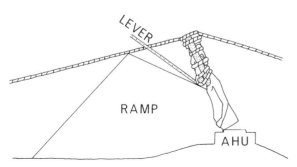

Their cylindrical shape implies that the head-dresses were often rolled from quarry to platform, using levers, and reworked there before being raised. Some were carved to a more elliptical cross-section, and a shallow mortise pecked into the base – this may have been to set it more firmly on the statue's flat head, with a slight projection over the eyes (some of the Anakena figures even have tenons on their heads to fit these mortises). Some *pukao* take the form of a truncated cone, while others were given a narrower boss or knob at the top (ill. 131). All such modifications, of course, had the advantage of reducing the cylinder's weight. One can only presume that they were lifted on a gradually rising scaffold or conical masonry-platform, though it is still uncertain how easy it would be to tilt such a squat, heavy mass. Future experimentation may help to elucidate the matter.

González in 1770 reported that the cylinders contained a slight hollow on the upper surface in which the bones of the dead were placed. Roggeveen's party in 1722 observed a 'corona' of white balls or stones on them – some scholars believe these may in fact have been whitened bones, but many white, coral-encrusted beach cobbles have been found during work at Anakena, where it is likely they were used to decorate the platforms.

The phenomenon of the giant statues and platforms is clearly far more complex than it at first appears, and some major questions remain: for example, why were some statues quarried inside the crater of Rano Raraku when this would entail much extra effort to get them out of there even before starting the journey to the platforms? Did this add to their prestige? Possibly; but on the whole the statues inside the crater are smaller and less carefully made than those outside. Is it feasible, therefore, that those inside the crater were never intended to be removed, but were set up there permanently, facing the lake? This would help explain why there were far more statues left finished or unfinished at the quarry than could ever have been allotted to existing platforms.

The Belgian archaeologist Lavachery suggested that the unfinished statues were bas-reliefs – a theory also applied to El Gigante, as mentioned earlier – but he envisaged this as the first, primitive stage in an evolution of statue carving. It is, however, possible to propose an alternative view based on hierarchy and one-upmanship: namely, that the whole spectrum of statues and platforms reflected the prestige of the commissioning groups and their wealth.

From this viewpoint, it could be argued that outlined or unfinished statues were the 'cheapest' option, involving nothing more than a little carving; those left unfinished inside the crater would be the least prestigious of all, being the least visible and not potentially movable. Presumably, work could resume later to finish the figure if funds were forthcoming. Completed and extracted statues would be more expensive, involving more carving and some effort in moving them: Routledge noticed that there were fewer completed statues inside than outside. The place where figures were set up expressed the degree of prestige they reflected: those set up inside the crater were perhaps intended

Pukao: the Crowning Glory

144–46 TOP LEFT *One of the fallen red scoria head-dresses lying around the island's coast.* ABOVE *and* LEFT *A pukao restored to its original position (above); like all the others that have been replaced, this one was lifted by a modern crane (left).*

to stay there for ever, while those moved down to the plain and set upright may have been intended to remain there, but also were potentially transportable to platforms if the commissioning group were eventually to acquire the necessary resources. This would explain the sheer numbers of statues in and around the quarry, movement of which was obviously neither imminent nor anticipated.

The most prestigious statues, of course, were those that were actually transported and erected on platforms. Here, as we have already seen, the factors of distance travelled, size and weight of statue, and size and splendour of platform all played a role in the prestige game. Some groups seem to have poured all their resources into acquiring a single enormous figure, like Paro. The really powerful centres took this to extremes, as in Vinapu's superb masonry and Tongariki's fifteen figures on a single platform, while the royal centre of Anakena featured statues with unique, elaborate designs carved on them.

The final touch, apparently a late development, and perhaps triggered, once again, by one-upmanship, was the placing of head-dresses on top of the statues, a truly awesome and prestigious feat of engineering, commanding respect and reflecting the power of the group responsible. As we have seen, only the biggest and richest platforms had such *pukao*. Other touches of splendour included the occasional use of red scoria blocks to decorate parts of the platform, and perhaps (despite lack of solid evidence) the painting of the statues.

Imagine, then, a finished platform of grey, white and sometimes red stone, on which stand a number of yellowish statues with bright white eyes and crowned by red cylinders and white stones. The statues and even the platforms may also have been painted, and smaller red figures stood in some forecourts. In other words, Easter Island was encircled by numerous impressive, vivid, highly colourful monuments testifying to the ingenuity, faith and communal spirit of its inhabitants. What happened to tear this picture apart from within?

PART III

THE AFTERMATH

Perhaps the thing that most distinguishes islands, at least oceanic islands ... is their extreme vulnerability or susceptibility to disturbance.

Raymond Fosberg

147 *A bas-relief of a birdman on a slab inside a house at Orongo (see p. 197).*

CHAPTER 9

CRASH GO THE ANCESTORS

I don't know how I am to make a fire on that island,
there is no wood!

Bailey, Katherine Routledge's ship's cook

If Captain Cook had stayed longer than the few days he spent there in 1774, there would probably never have been any mysteries of Easter Island. Cook was an astute observer and recorded what he saw with meticulous accuracy. He would probably have discovered the religious significance of the giant statues, the history of their downfall, and the meaning of the Rongorongo. He would certainly have described the island and its environmental state more fully than he did. But, as far as we know, neither Cook nor any other early visitor made these records. Easter Island was, as we have seen, visited by over a hundred ships – mostly whalers – between 1800 and 1900, but it is only a remote possibility that some unknown manuscript may survive. The history of Easter Island is therefore lost forever. Or is it? Even if written records are non-existent, and oral traditions of very limited use, there are records of another kind: those provided by archaeology and, as we have seen, by pollen analysis.

Violence Erupts

We have a rough idea of when the islanders began to topple the statues; neither Roggeveen in 1722 nor González in 1770 mentions having seen fallen statues; the Dutch saw only a small part of the island, but the Spanish saw considerably more, so it is a fair bet that all *moai*, or very nearly all, were still upright in 1770. Only four years later, however, when Captain Cook arrived, the situation was very different: he was the first to report that many statues had been overturned next to their platforms, and that the monuments were no longer maintained. Skeletal material was now strewn about the figures. One platform (probably at Vinapu) had three fallen and four upright figures, one of the latter having lost its head-dress.

Four statues were still standing in Hanga-Roa (Cook's) Bay, and seven at Vinapu, when the Russian Lisjanskij visited in 1804 (he saw at least twenty upright statues altogether), but his compatriot Kotzebue found them toppled in 1816 except for two survivors at Vinapu; all monuments on the Bay had been totally destroyed by 1825. The last eye-witness account we have of standing statues on the island is that of the French admiral Abel Dupetit-Thouars in 1838 who saw 'a platform on which were set four red statues, equidistant from one another, their summits covered with white stones'; by 1868 the visiting English surgeon Linton Palmer reported that not a single *moai* remained upright, and the missionaries of the 1860s scarcely mention the statues at all. So between 1722, when the Dutch thought the statue cult was still underway, and 1774, when Cook thought it a thing of the past, something drastic had happened.

The toppling was often no mean achievement, and must have involved ropes, levers and a number of men – this may be why Paro, the tallest and heaviest statue ever erected on a platform, was also the last to be overthrown, its huge head-dress coming to rest a few metres in front of it. But simple toppling or undermining was often not enough. In many cases, the statues were deliberately beheaded, by placing stones where the fragile neck would fall, for decapitation prevented the statue's re-erection. Most were toppled landward, perhaps to cover the eyes; in one case, a statue resting face-upward had its eye area completely pulverized, again a task of considerable effort. These attacks on head and eyes probably reflect the location of the figures' *mana* – they were not just toppled but had their power totally extinguished.

It is certain that statues had been destroyed at times throughout the centuries, to make way for new ones, with fragments (especially heads) being incorporated into new building phases in the platforms. Some figures were toppled into prepared excavations in platform ramps, and were then buried fully or partially. But the real piecemeal destruction eventually came about through feuding and wars between groups who had previously vied with each other in the size and splendour of their monuments. It was only fitting that the vanquished should therefore have humiliating damage inflicted on their proud symbols by the victors: outrages inflicted on these ancestral figures were symbolically inflicted on the whole group. Tit-for-tat acts of this kind would quickly have decimated the number of standing statues.

A further, dramatic symptom of violence and strife is the sudden appearance in the late prehistoric period of weapons made of obsidian, a material used previously only for tools. *Mataa* were large, stemmed flakes used hafted as daggers and as spearheads (ill. 154); they first appeared in the 15th or 16th century, but really proliferated in the 18th and 19th centuries when they became the commonest artifact on the island. Owing to their size, only one or two could be obtained from each slab mined, but the sheer abundance of obsidian available led to no apparent decrease in quality over time, and thousands of *mataa* were produced: Routledge reported finding hoards of fifty or sixty under stones in caves, while Mulloy's excavations uncovered 402 at Vinapu alone. The Dutch in 1722 had reported that the islanders were all unarmed, but in 1774 Cook's party saw a few clubs and spears – Forster said that 'some...had lances or spears made of thin ill-shaped sticks, and pointed with a sharp triangular piece of black glassy lava'. Most weapons must have

The Moai Toppled

148–51 TOP LEFT *A view along the platform at Vaihu showing the row of empty pedestals and, to the right, the bases of the toppled statues.* LEFT *Toppled statues face-down at Akahanga.* TOP *A moai lying on its back at Akahanga; Hotu Matua, the island's legendary first settler, is reputed to be buried in a nearby cave.* ABOVE *The severed heads of three moai at Ahu Vaihu.*

been kept hidden, however, since in 1786 La Pérouse claimed that the islanders were all unarmed. The Spanish visitors of 1770 saw conspicuous evidence of *mataa* wounds on several natives, and violence was not restricted to men, since Sir Arthur Keith's study of skeletal material from the island revealed traces of violent blows on female skulls.

Oral traditions claim that a major battle took place between the stocky Hanau Eepe and the slender Hanau Momoko at the 'Poike Ditch', a 3.5 km (*c.* 2 miles) feature which almost isolates the Poike peninsula; it comprises a series of elongated trenches, 20 or 30 of which are still visible, each *c.* 100 m (*c.* 325 ft) long, 10 to 15 m (33 to 50 ft) wide, 2 or 3 m (6 to 10 ft) deep, and 5 m (16 ft) apart, with spoil-banks alongside. This intriguing feature of the Easter Island landscape has caused a lot of ink to flow. Islanders claim that it is called the 'Cooking Place of the Hanau Eepe', and was dug by that group and filled with brush either for defence or to roast the Hanau Momoko; however, the latter turned the tables, and it was the Hanau Eepe (who had retreated to Poike after an outbreak of killing) who eventually perished in flames there after a fierce battle.

Excavations during the Norwegian expedition of the 1950s found a zone of intensive burning in the ditch that was radiocarbon-dated to AD 1676 ± 100, a figure that seemed to coincide with Englert's genealogical calculation that the battle had taken place in 1680. However, more recent excavations in the ditch have uncovered a tree hole with charcoal, at a depth of over 1 m (3 ft), which has given a radiocarbon date in the 11th century AD, which seems to cast the gravest doubt on this 'ditch' having been involved in a battle of the type and date mentioned in the traditions, particularly since no *mataa* have ever been found in it.

Early researchers believed the ditch to be entirely natural, but since the digging of test pits most geologists and archaeologists agree that it is either a natural feature that has been artificially modified, or that it is entirely man-made. A series of ancient excavations are discernible, with the soil piled up along one side, but the ditch itself has been almost filled by centuries of erosion by water and wind. But what was it for? It is a most unlikely fortification, since it is discontinuous and could be bypassed at either end. One suggestion is that it was a series of ovens for preparing the food for workers in the nearby quarry of Rano Raraku; this would account for the ditch's names (it is also called 'the long earth oven of Tavake') as well as for the burnt material. An alternative explanation is that it was a ditch, well protected from the elements, in which crops such as bananas, sugar cane and taro were grown for the quarry workers, and irrigated by water running down the slopes of Poike. In this case, the burning would result from the disposal of stalks and leaves after the harvests.

A more convincing clue to warfare is the late adoption of the custom of taking refuge in caves and on the offshore islets; none of the latter has a permanent water-source, and they are difficult to reach across the pounding

Conflict and Starvation

152–54 ABOVE *Aerial view of part of the 'Poike ditch',
a series of trenches visible between the two modern
trackways.* RIGHT *A* moai kavakava *with its
characteristic hollow cheeks and prominent ribs; legends
hold that such figures are in the likeness of two ghosts
found sleeping in the top-knot quarry.* BELOW *Some of
the thousands of obsidian* mataa – *dagger or
spearheads – which reflect the rise of violence on the
island.*

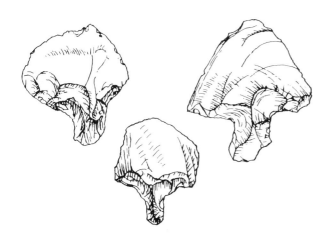

waves, so they were clearly not for permanent occupation. However, the refugees (as well as those who came here for fish or bird eggs; see p. 188) adapted the caves here, often building stone-walled entryways – some cave walls were fortified with kerbstones from the high-status elliptical houses, the *hare paenga* (ills 68–70), an obvious and convenient prestige item to steal from one's enemies. It is thought that these low, narrow crawlways were designed to retain the heat and protect from wind and driving rain, rather than as defensive measures. However, recent excavations in the cave of Ana Kionga, in the southwest part of Easter Island, found that it had been enlarged, purposely fortified and camouflaged: a small interior chamber had been walled off with stones, and an entrance tunnel built but concealed beneath debris from the enlargement. The cave, which yielded thousands of fish, rat and chicken bones from layers only 5 cm (2 in) deep, seems to have been used as a refuge for a brief period sometime after 1722 (as proved by the presence of a European glass bead).

Why did the islanders not build defensive habitations, or even hilltop fortresses, like the Maori of New Zealand? They had some hills and plenty of stone at their disposal, even if timber was by now in short supply. The answer is simply that Rapa Nui has an abundance of large, usable underground hiding places which are often impossible to detect from the surface. Since it was not possible to flee in canoes from the warfare, as their ancestors might have done, refugees went underground or to the islets.

What clues do we have that point to possible causes for such strife? The most obvious evidence to look for is scarcity of food, and there are abundant indications in the archaeological and ethnographic record of significant changes in the islanders' diet through time, and perhaps even of famine: the well-known wooden statuettes from the island, known as *moai kavakava* (ill. 153), depict men with goatee beards and hooked noses, but also hollow cheeks, a spinal ridge and prominent emaciated ribs which are often seen as indicators of famine. However, the bottom half of these figures seems normal, healthy and well built, with rounded buttocks; they embody a complex symbolism, representing secondary gods, spirits of dead people or supernatural beings, and were used in dances to ward off evil spirits (Melville reported that Typee priests in the Marquesas kept little wooden figures as oracles). Like all of the island's portable art objects, they have no date or stratigraphic provenance; nevertheless, they certainly imply that the islanders were well acquainted with some of the physical results of mineral deficiency or starvation. We have already seen (p. 92) the dramatic change in the islanders' appearance and health between 1722 and 1774, perhaps even merely in the four years between the Spanish visit and that of Cook, who was the first to find the natives in a very poor and distressful condition: 'small, lean, timid and miserable'.

The first European visitors reported that sea birds, fowls and fish were scarce by 1722 and particularly by the 1770s, and the rise of the stone chicken house – probably between 1786 and 1868, since Cook and La Pérouse did not mention them, whereas the Spanish said that chickens were bred in little runs scraped out in the ground and thatched over – reflects the increased value of this precious resource and the need to protect it from theft (the structures may have had some other function before this time). Excavations at some sites have revealed a dramatic decrease in the numbers of chicken bones (compared with other foods) after AD 1650, and also an increase in human bone fragments and teeth in late prehistoric times.

This has inevitably given rise to the spectre of cannibalism on the island as a solution to hunger. Cannibalism is certainly very prominent in Rapa Nui's oral traditions, and the name of the painted cave of Ana Kai Tangata (ill. 161) is often translated as 'eat man cave', though it could equally mean 'place where men eat'. Recent surveys of ethnography all over the world have failed to come up with any solid evidence for the existence of cannibalism (other than for survival) anywhere, in any period, so at first glance these emphatic oral traditions on Easter Island may have as little factual basis as those elsewhere. However, given the unique cultural developments in this isolated place turned in on itself, as well as the strife and undoubtedly serious shortages of food it experienced in late prehistory, the existence of cannibalism here cannot be totally discounted.

It is also worth noting that the legends explaining the end of the statue quarrying all point to quarrels over food as the cause: e.g. an old woman or witch was denied her rightful share of a giant lobster, and angrily caused all statue production to cease. The tales are reckoned to indicate that it was a breakdown of the system of distribution, the exchange networks and the feeding of the craftsmen by the farmers and fishermen that finally halted the group co-operation that was so vital to the enterprise. The abandonment of work at Rano Raraku was not necessarily the sudden dramatic downing of tools so beloved of the mystery writers, but is more likely to have been a more gradual winding down and disintegration of the system: in short, work quickly ground to a halt because of an ever-increasing imbalance between the production of essentials (food) and that of non-essentials (statues).

There appears to be a change towards the end of the island's prehistory to a greater dependence on marine resources that could be gathered rather than fished, and even these were being overexploited: the increasing collection of the shellfish *Nerita* is thought to reflect overexploitation of the more highly prized *Cypraea*. By the historic period, fishing had become relatively unimportant, though its former prominence survived in the number of legends with fishermen as heroes. Excavations in some of the island's middens have revealed a slight decrease of fish remains relative to other resources from about AD 1400 to the present. Evidence of the use of rock shelters for activities connected with fishing (e.g. hook manufacture) also shows a marked decrease after AD 1500.

The major reason for the decline in fishing – enforced, as we have seen, by seasonal *tapu*, restrictions on marine resources by the high-status Miru clan –

must be the limitations on offshore fishing caused by the decreasing number and size of canoes. The Dutch in 1722 reported that the islander who came out to their ship had a boat made of small, narrow pieces of wood glued together with some organic material, and so light that one man could carry it easily. The other canoes were poor and frail, and so leaky that the islanders spent half their time baling. Bouman added that most natives came swimming out to them on bunches of reeds. They saw very few canoes, and the largest was only 3 m (*c.* 10 ft) long. In 1770 González saw only two canoes. Four years later, Cook said the island had the worst canoes in the Pacific – small, patched and unseaworthy. He saw only three or four small canoes, 3 or 4 m (10 to 13 ft) in length, and built of sewn planks of wood only up to 1 m (3 ft) long, and stated that most natives simply swam out. Beechey in 1825 saw three canoes on the beach which did not put to sea, while the Russian Kotzebue in 1816 had likewise seen three, each carrying two men. This is all a far cry from Hotu Matua's vessel which legend claimed was 30 m (*c.* 100 ft) long and 2 m (6 ft) high, and carried hundreds of people. Canoes, including possible double-canoes and Polynesian sails, are clearly depicted in the islanders' rock art, proving that they were acquainted at some time with more impressive vessels, a fact also supported by the numerous canoe ramps found near platforms.

What, then, was the ultimate cause of all these changes? The answer must lie in deforestation, and particularly the disappearance of the palm. The first European visitors all commented on the island's bare, barren, treeless appearance: Roggeveen in 1722 described the island as 'destitute of large trees', and González in 1770 wrote, 'Not a single tree is to be found capable of furnishing a plank so much as six inches in width'; Forster in 1774 reported that 'there was not a tree upon the whole island which exceeded the height of 10 feet'. So clearly, timber was in very short supply. Dupetit-Thouars in 1838 said that five canoes came out to his ship from the island, each carrying two men; what they most wanted was wood. Even driftwood was looked on as a treasure of inestimable value, and a dying father frequently promised to send his children a tree from the kingdom of shades. It is highly significant that the Polynesian word *rakau* (tree, wood, timber) meant 'riches' or 'wealth' on Rapa Nui, a meaning recorded nowhere else.

Why, then, did the palm become extinct? Possibly the coup de grâce was administered by the sheep and goats introduced in the 19th and 20th centuries, but the species had clearly become rare before that, if Cook and La Pérouse are correct. One answer lies in tooth marks: every *Jubaea* nut so far recovered (Chapter 4), apart from the fragments from Anakena, had been gnawed by rodents. Both in Kew and in Orotava, Tenerife (where the wine palm is grown in the Botanic Gardens), it is difficult to recover many intact fruits: almost all have the same hole, surrounded by toothmarks, as one sees on the nuts from Easter Island caves. In each case, a hole large enough to eat out the kernel has been made, and the edge of the hole bears distinctive tooth marks. Some of the gnawed nuts found on Easter Island were submitted by Flenley to Dr A.J. Stuart of Cambridge University, a specialist on Britain's Quaternary mammals, in the hope that he would pronounce them the product of rats' teeth. He did not. He said the tooth marks were more the size that would be produced by the teeth of mice. This was disturbing, for mice are not abundant on Easter Island. It then transpired, however, that the archaeological dig at Anakena had turned up numerous remains of the Polynesian rat, *Rattus concolor*. The island's present rat, *Rattus rattus*, had been introduced only after European contact, when it had rapidly ousted the Polynesian rat.

The latter, as already mentioned, was regularly introduced, quite deliberately, by all Polynesian voyagers, wherever they settled. It was, in fact, a source of protein food for them. Furthermore, *Rattus concolor* is a very small species – mouse-sized, in fact. Dr Stuart's findings were now explicable. Clearly, the nuts in the caves had been gnawed by *Rattus concolor*, probably the only rodent on the island at the time. Reconstructing the likely course of events was facilitated by examining modern sagas of the introduction of rats to islands. Almost everywhere they had become a nuisance, and often they had been disastrous. The effects on ground-nesting birds were the best reported: the rats stole so many eggs that species became extinct. A case more apposite to that of the Easter Island palms was that of Lord Howe Island, home of the *Kentia* palm, that denizen of coffee-bars. Rats ate so many of the palm fruits that the export trade in seed was ruined and the regeneration of the species was totally prevented.

It therefore seems likely that it was the introduction of the Polynesian rat that may have prevented regeneration of the Easter Island palm and contributed ultimately to its extinction. But it was human activities that actually removed the trees themselves. Significant among these must have been canoe-building (e.g. at Terevaka): palms are not ideal for this role, because their timber is somewhat porous, but it is known that coconut trunks are used for canoes in the Marquesas. It seems likely that the Easter Island palm was simply the best tree available for this purpose, and we know that the islanders made large canoes: not only do such vessels appear in their rock art (ill. 53), but regular visits seem to have been made to Sala-y-Gómez, 415 km (258 miles) ENE of Easter Island, probably to collect sea birds; and, as we have already seen, the large fish-hooks imply offshore fishing for sharks and other large species, which would be very dangerous from a small canoe.

Other possible causes of decline in palms could include general felling of forest for firewood and to produce agricultural land, and also the specific felling of palms for use in the moving of the giant statues, as described in Chapters 6 and 7.

The details of forest clearance are not too well represented in the Rano Raraku pollen diagram, though there is a marked abundance of charcoal near the deposit's surface, compared with its absence at earlier times. Chemical analysis, however, demonstrated a huge increase in the amount of metallic

RANO KAU, alt. c. 110m: Easter Island

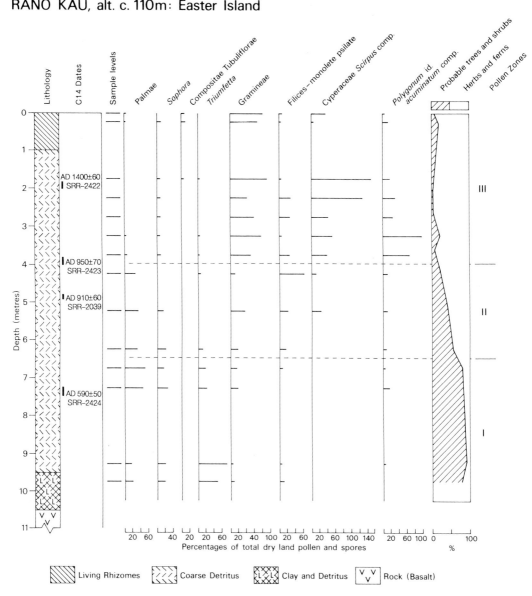

Lithology | C14 Dates | Sample levels | Palmae | Sophora | Compositae Tubuliflorae | Triumfetta | Gramineae | Filices – monolete psilate | Cyperaceae Scirpus comp. | Polygonum id. acuminatum comp. | Probable trees and shrubs | Herbs and ferns | Pollen Zones

AD 1400±60 SRR-2422
AD 950±70 SRR-2423
AD 910±60 SRR-2039
AD 590±50 SRR-2424

III
II
I

20 60   40 20   20 60   20 40 100 20 60   20 60 100 140   20 60 100 0   100
Percentages of total dry land pollen and spores   %

Depth (metres)

⧄⧄ Living Rhizomes   ⧄⧄ Coarse Detritus   ⧄⧄ Clay and Detritus   ⌄⌄ Rock (Basalt)

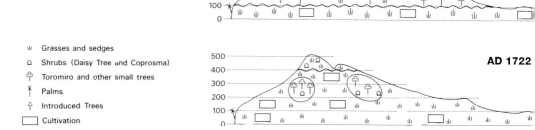

AD 950

AD 1722

ıl Grasses and sedges
Ω Shrubs (Daisy Tree and Coprosma)
⚘ Toromiro and other small trees
✗ Palms
⇡ Introduced Trees
▭ Cultivation

The Disappearance
of the Palm

155–57 FAR LEFT *The Rano Kau crater is a caldera, formed by the collapse of a volcanic cone into its own magma chamber. The swamp itself is largely a floating mat, often only a metre or so thick; if you were to fall through, it would probably be fatal, and one geologist has already disappeared there without trace. This pollen diagram reveals the results of a core sample taken from the edge of the swamp. Notice the marked decline in tree and shrub pollen in the right-hand column, reading upwards from the earliest period at the base of the diagram.* LEFT *Taking a core sample in the Rano Kau crater.* BELOW *Although Easter Island is not very high, pollen analysis at Rano Aroi, the smallest of the three main craters, has shown that the island did support an altitudinally zoned environment.*

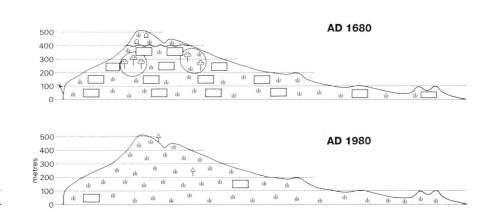

ions entering the crater lake during the last 2000 years. Clearly something fairly dramatic had happened, even before the soil erosion of which there is visual evidence in the cores. The sort of changes suggested could be those which exposed the soil to more leaching within the crater without actually causing erosion: perhaps selective felling of trees. Alternatively, and perhaps more plausibly, the deforestation by burning of areas outside the crater could have provided smoke containing wood ash rich in minerals. A third possibility which could not yet be eliminated from the investigation was climatic change: an alteration in total rainfall, or in the intensity of rainfall, could have produced these effects. Most likely would have been an increase of seasonality, leading to a less dense vegetation cover and hence to more leaching in the wet season.

The situation was soon clarified by the pollen diagram from Rano Kau, which is truly dramatic (ill. 155) and one of the most striking records of forest destruction anywhere in the world. The early samples (near the base) show a dominance of hauhau (*Triumfetta*), the tree used for rope. Perhaps it was the natural dominant inside the crater, or perhaps the sequence begins after some initial disturbance of the forest had encouraged this tree. It could even have been cultivated. From about AD 750, however, all trees start a decline, so that the pollen indicates fairly complete clearance by *c.* AD 950. The forest pollen reaches its lowest values at *c.* AD 1400. After this, there is a slight recovery, and eventually historical introductions like *Melia* ('miro Tahiti') make their appearance in the record.

The date *c.* AD 1400 is important because it is *before* the estimated date of collapse of the island's civilization in *c.* AD 1680 (see p. 213). If there is to be a causal relationship between the two events, clearly the cause must precede the effect. That the forest clearance should precede the collapse of civilization by so much (*c.* 280 years) probably relates to the progressive nature of forest clearance. It is unlikely that Rano Kau would be the last part of the island to be cleared. Probably the last part of the island to be cleared of forest would have been the summit region around Rano Aroi.

In Zone VIII of Rano Aroi's pollen diagram (AD 950 to the present) woody plants start to disappear and carbonized particles make their appearance in the record. It seems that the vegetation was being burnt, presumably by people. Grasses appear with pollen grains much smaller than earlier types, and must represent different species. Presumably these are introduced weeds or previously rare species responding to interference with the vegetation. Ferns also exhibit an increase, perhaps as a response to disturbance. The subaquatic plant *Polygonum* appears, for the first time with certainty, in the swamp. The chemical record shows striking increases in many metallic ions, suggesting their arrival in the swamp either by washing in from eroding soils or perhaps airborne in wood ash from the burning forest.

About AD 950 (the date is approximate at this site) people began to disturb the vegetation, resulting in destruction of forest and scrub and its replacement

Soil Erosion and
Water Shortage

158,159 LEFT *John Flenley at Poike,
pointing out changes in the soil
brought about by deforestation: the
soil below his hand has the original
blocky structure, before
deforestation allowed erosion; the
effects of damaging slopewash
erosion are clearly seen in the
horizontal banding above his hand.
BELOW Carved face-petroglyphs at
Vai Tapa Eru, one of the island's
scarce springs; the art here may
denote how precious such places
became.*

with grasses, sedge and weeds. Burning and soil erosion occurred and several species became extinct.

To sum up, therefore, forest clearance began at least 1200 years ago at Rano Kau, and around AD 950 at the other two sites. At Rano Kau the main forest clearance was complete by c. AD 950, and the last remnants of forest were destroyed by c. AD 1400. The forest was replaced mainly by grasses and introduced weeds. In other words, although it has often been suggested – from La Pérouse in 1786 up to some present-day scholars – that the island's trees disappeared because of drought, the situation appears more gradual and complex than this. Droughts may indeed have played a role – after all, they still occur here frequently – but the activities of the human settlers were clearly a persistent and major factor, together with the depredations of their rats.

The loss of trees had consequences not only for fishing and statue-building. The loss of fertile forest soils must have caused a shortage of food. Even water was affected: at Ava O Kiri, inland from Ovahe, there is a deep ravine that was clearly cut by running water in ancient times; these days it contains water only after a heavy rain, but the ravine's depth shows that before deforestation the island must have had intermittent streams like this one. The decline in water sources must have made those that remained extremely precious, which may explain the presence of carved face-petroglyphs at Vai Tapa Eru, a spring inland from Tepeu.

Easter Island's small size and isolation made its human population especially sensitive to the effects of any environmental alterations, such as the loss of the non-renewable forest resources. When ecological disaster struck, they had nowhere to go, but had to sit it out, with the catastrophic results outlined at the start of this chapter.

The Human Population

Could population pressure lie behind the deforestation? As in any other part of the world, it is a daunting challenge to calculate the prehistoric population of Easter Island. Estimates are inevitably vague, and the situation is little better during the first period of European contact: Roggeveen in 1722 guessed at 'thousands', but his party went ashore only on one day. González in 1770 thought it was 900 or 1000; Cook, only four years later, estimated 600 or 700, and his naturalist Forster thought 900. However, since these first visitors saw very few women and children, it is clear that much of the population was hidden from them, probably in their subterranean refuges: González actually reported that most islanders lived in underground caves with narrow entrances into which they sometimes had to crawl feet-first, while Forster stood on a hill near Hanga Roa and 'did not see above 10 or 12 huts, though the view commanded a great part of the island'.

La Pérouse, who came in 1786, saw a much more representative range of people – the islanders 'crawled out of their subterranean dwellings' – and estimated the population to be 2000. Lisjanskij, who saw 23 houses near the shoreline in 1804, guessed at a population of about 1800, while Beechey, in 1825, reckoned it was about 1500. Salmon, who spent many years on the island, told Thomson that its population between 1850 and 1860 was about 2000. It is known that the figure in 1862 was about 3000, just prior to the devastating arrival in 1862/3 of slave traders who took numerous islanders off to Peru; by 1877, there were only 111 people left on Easter Island. In 1886, this had risen slightly to 155; 68 men, 43 women, 17 boys and 27 girls under 15; by 1915, there were 250 people. Since then, the population has grown, albeit with considerable contributions from Chile to which the island has been attached since 1888; at the time of writing, the population is 2100 (including about 800 children), mostly concentrated in the main village of Hanga Roa.

In short, despite the low estimates of the first European visitors, it is likely that La Pérouse's estimate of 2000 was quite near the mark. So we have a boatload of settlers in the first centuries AD, and 2000 people some 1400 years later. What happened to population numbers during that time? The normal model applied to Polynesian islands is that the founder population grew exponentially and rapidly until stabilizing at a level just under the carrying capacity of the environment, with possible oscillations above that level. On Easter Island, however, one estimate is that numbers may have doubled every 150 years; some scholars even reckon that island populations with simple horticultural techniques may double their numbers *every generation* until they run out of land. Clearly, on Easter Island something cracked and the system collapsed.

Roggeveen reckoned that the island could have supported a larger population than was living there in 1722; and, as we have already seen, La Pérouse found that only one tenth of the island was being used to support the 2000 people. Cook's party noticed that much of the inner part of the island showed evidence of having been cultivated in the past, though as mentioned earlier (p. 93) there would have been few traces visible of abandoned unbordered fields even in the 1770s, and far fewer survive today.

To what figure could the prehistoric population have risen? Mrs Routledge was told by the natives that their ancestors had been 'thick as grass'; she was also informed that half the island – about 15,000 acres – could grow bananas and sweet potatoes, and if one allowed 2 acres per family of 5 to 7 individuals, this would give a potential population of 37,500 to 52,500, a highly theoretical figure which was probably never even approached in reality. Using population densities from Tahiti, Métraux reckoned on 13.7 people per square kilometre and hence a population of about 3000 or 4000. Most archaeologists who have worked on the island in recent years estimate that the prehistoric population may have reached 6000 to 8000, while some speculate about figures of 10,000 or even 20,000. Such estimates are made difficult by the uneven distribution of settlements, which were dense along the coast but sparser in the interior due to lack of irrigation.

Recent surveys have estimated that this small island has over 10,000 sites, and those are only the data visible on the surface. The southeast coast alone has 17 platforms within less than 3 km (less than 2 miles), and over 100 houses. This high population density probably reflects the high agricultural production of the south and east parts of the island, and the proliferation of major platforms in the 15th century on the south coast is thought to indicate an influx of people from other parts of the island together with a period of sustained population growth. One survey of the south coast's residential sites in each period has concluded that the population level remained fairly low until *c*. AD 1100, after which it doubled every century, only slowing down after 1400, with a decline setting in after a maximum *c*. 1600.

There are a number of other archaeological indications of population increase: for example, caves and rockshelters were not much used until *c*. AD 1300, when their extensive utilization implies a greater exploitation of marine resources, which may reflect a rising number of mouths to feed and/or a decrease in productivity of the land resources, caused by excessive deforestation and leaching. There is a noticeable decline in food remains, especially marine foods, in the shelters after AD 1650, which may denote a significant fall in population.

A similar clue to the rise and fall of population lies in the dating of obsidian from habitation sites, which shows that the exploitation of obsidian sources rose from *c*. AD 1300 to 1650, and then decreased for the next fifty years before rising again. The first increase has been attributed to a rising population, while the drop may reflect a decline in numbers. The subsequent rise is thought to indicate a social change, either an increased clustering of population, with larger residential units, or perhaps a collapse of the previous system of territorial control over the quarries, leaving them open to all. Such a theory would fit the oral traditions which point to big socio-political changes on the island *c*. AD 1680, with a shift in religion, burial practices, architecture and leadership. It is now time, therefore, to look more closely at some of the consequences of these changes.

160 OPPOSITE *Rock carvings of the birdman on cliffs at Orongo, with a view of the islets Motu Nui and Motu Iti.*

161 OVERLEAF *Wall paintings of birds inside the cave of Ana Kai Tangata, which is translated as either Man Eat Cave or Eat Man Cave – the latter is horribly suggestive of cannibalism, particularly in view of the food shortages that came to threaten the islanders' very existence.*

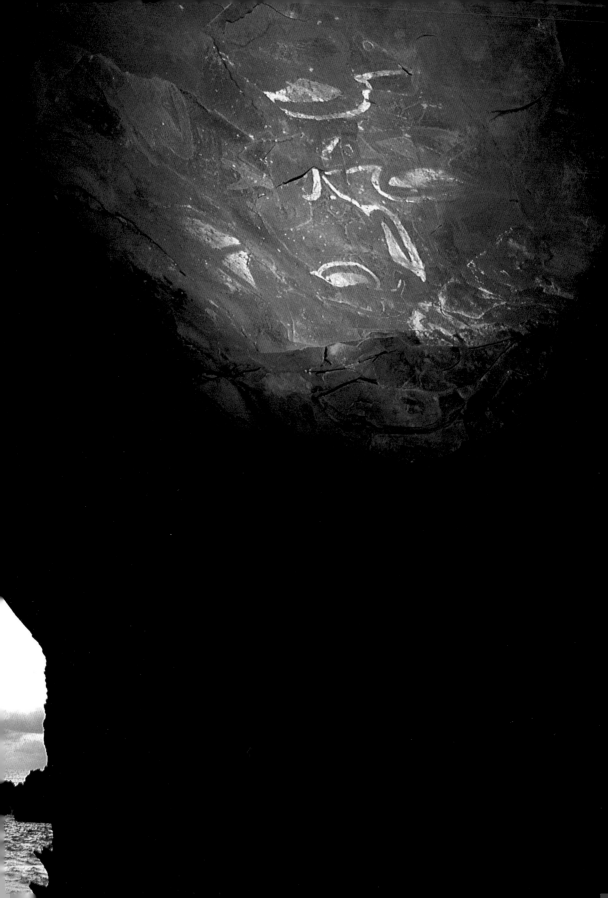

CHAPTER 10

ORONGO AND RONGORONGO

Inevitably, our information on social and political developments comes primarily from oral traditions and the reports of the first visitors. During at least the island's final prehistory, it was divided up into different clan territories (ill. 163) – with fairly blurred and overlapping edges owing to the lack of physical boundaries – though there was a centralized control of religious and economic activities through the Miru, a royal lineage descended from Hotu Matua, centred at Anakena, and headed by the hereditary chief, the *Ariki henua*. Although the most important person on the island, he was, however, not really a king or political leader, but rather a religious symbol, the main repository of *mana*, or spiritual power; he was, as it were, to the *mana* born.

There was a rigid class structure, and all surplus produce was assigned to those of high status: the chiefs, priests, possessors of ritual knowledge and arts, and the warriors (*matatoa*). The emphasis was on continually increased production, and the authority to focus manpower on particular activities was supernaturally ordained. Effective networks of exchange must have arisen since, as shown earlier, different parts of the island specialized in particular activities (fishing, cultivation) or had access to crucial resources: tuff, scoria, basalt, obsidian, timber and paper mulberry, reeds, red ochre, coral for files, and even moss for caulking boats were all highly localized.

Within this framework, the islanders had laboured long and hard at clearing agricultural land of the ubiquitous stones and cultivating it, at tree-felling and carpentry, at fishing and, of course, at producing the spectacular platforms and statues. Throughout eastern Polynesia, communal or specialist labour was employed on major subsistence projects, but Easter Island's peculiar environmental conditions seem to have largely precluded this outlet, and hence similar efforts were poured into esoteric pursuits: the monumental structures and statues. It appears that the craft specialists and ordinary workers were in no way driven under the lash to do all this, but instead were paid with cooked food and they expected to derive supernatural rewards for their efforts – rather like the medieval cathedral builders of Europe. The work was accompanied by joyful feasts, and the spiritual power of the giant statues was thought to bring benefit to the communities that owned them.

Once the system crashed, for reasons outlined in the previous chapter, there were marked changes not only in subsistence and settlement patterns, with

162 OPPOSITE *'Eye-mask' motifs – probably representations of the god Makemake – carved in the rock inside Ana Mahina cave, a human skull in the shadows.*

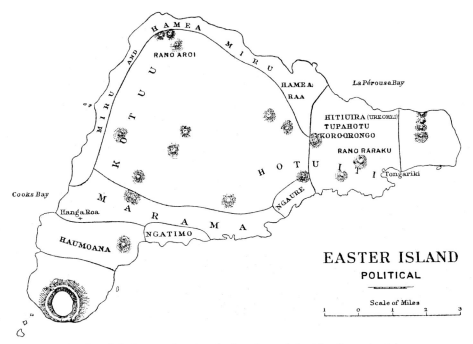

163 *Mrs Routledge's map showing the locations of the island's territorial groups;
the boundaries were approximate owing to the often uniform terrain.*

exchange networks disintegrating, but also in religion and politics: La Pérouse
noted in 1786 that the island no longer had a chief. It seems that the warrior
leaders rose to power out of the ever-increasing warfare, so that hereditary
privilege was replaced by achieved status: some have even seen it as a revolt
of the lower classes against the upper. Inter-group rivalry and competition
had always been endemic, as seen in the construction of ever more splendid
monuments, but these also required group co-operation, and until the crash
it seems – from archaeological evidence as well as from oral traditions – that
actual warfare was absent or extremely rare. Since persistent warfare (from
simple raiding to major territorial conflict) is common and ubiquitous in
Polynesia, one of the most remarkable features of Easter Island's culture is
that peace reigned for over a millennium before crisis led to violence. Once
the warriors had taken control, there was virtually persistent territorial conflict
between two loose confederations of groups, the western (Tu'u) and eastern
(Hotu Iti).

   With the change came new methods of disposing of the dead. The cremation
pits behind the platforms seem completely to have lost their significance, and
burial became dominant: bodies were often left exposed for a while, and then
the bones would be placed in family caves, in the new kinds of non-image
platforms such as a wedge-shaped form or the semipyramidal kind (ill. 135),
in crevices inside the ruined platforms, in their wings and ramps, in nooks

beneath the toppled statues, in the hollows of their fallen head-dresses, or simply scattered in the plazas. Most of the bones seen by early visitors are probably from the post-contact period, since Routledge reported that at the time of the great smallpox epidemic in the 1860s (introduced by the few surviving slaves brought back from Peru), corpses had been deposited any and everywhere; the French traveller Pierre Loti, in 1872, said the whole island was like an immense ossuary, and that merely to lift a bit of earth would reveal skulls and jaws. As recently as 1880, islanders were still stealing bodies at night from the Catholic cemetery, preferring to place the remains inside the platforms.

From a religion based on virtually deified ancestors in local kin groups (a typically Polynesian segmentary pattern), the islanders turned to the creator god Makemake (a name that is widespread in the Marquesas), and to beliefs and rituals that were strongly focused on fruits and on fertility, including human fertility. They developed a system suited to precarious times whereby leadership alternated between groups from year to year based on a ritual egg-race. The winner of this 'election by ordeal' was consecrated as the sacred birdman (*tangata manu*) for a year, during which time his group received special privileges. This was the system in place when the first Europeans arrived; the principal location of the new island-wide religion was the ceremonial village of Orongo.

Orongo: The Scramble for Eggs

The ceremonial village of Orongo is a scenic wonder, perched on the rim between the spectacular, huge crater of Rano Kau and the precipitous drop to the ocean. It originally comprised one (or possibly two) *ahu*-like terraces and a plaza. These appear to have been abandoned shortly after AD 1400, when a series of stone houses began to be used. In its final phase, after the mid-16th century, Orongo contained about fifty contiguous, oval stone houses with corbelled roofs covered in earth, and arranged in a half-ellipse facing the islets (ill. 164). They have crawlway entrances, are from 6 to 12 m (20 to 39 ft) wide inside (with walls about 2 m [6 ft] thick), and between 1 and 2 m (3 and 6 ft) high inside. Their overall shape is like an inverted canoe (like the *hare paenga*, ills 68–70). They often contained painted slabs, mostly with bird motifs. It has been suggested that they were built of thin, flat basalt slabs owing to the lack of timber by this time, but it is more probable that only stone could withstand the elements on this exposed spot from one annual ceremony to the next.

It is thought that the ceremony began as a competition for divine blessing, but by the time it finally ended in 1878 it had altered and had degenerated into a test of skills, under the influence of the missionaries in the 1860s. It is not known precisely when the ritual began: Routledge obtained a list of eighty-six sacred birdmen ending in 1866, so allowing for missing names one can estimate a start around 1760, although some scholars claim an origin several centuries earlier.

The object of the ceremony was to find a new birdman for the year, who became Makemake's representative on earth. Each candidate – ambitious warlords from dominant or victorious tribes rather than hereditary aristocrats – had a young man to represent him. Each September (i.e. in springtime), these unfortunate 'stunt-men' had to make their way down the sheer 300 m (1000 ft) cliff to the shore, and then swim 2 km ($1\frac{1}{4}$ miles) on a bunch of reeds through shark-infested swells and strong currents to the largest and outermost islet, Motu Nui (3.6 ha [*c.* 9 acres]), where they awaited – sometimes for weeks – the arrival of a migratory seabird, the sooty tern. The aim was to find its first, elusive brown-speckled egg. The winner would shout the news to his employer on the clifftop at Orongo ('Shave your head, you have got the egg'), and then swim back with the egg securely held in a headband. The master now became the new sacred birdman, shaved his head, eyebrows and eyelashes, and had his head painted, while the losers cut themselves with *mataa*.

Ceremonial Houses

164,165 LEFT *Some of the houses in the ceremonial village of Orongo, on the cliff-top between Rano Kau and the ocean; their entrances face the ocean.* ABOVE *Cross-section of one of the Orongo houses restored by Mulloy, showing the thickness of the drystone walls, the corbelled vault, and the capping of stone slabs and earth. The small island of Motu Nui is visible offshore.*

The Sacred Islet

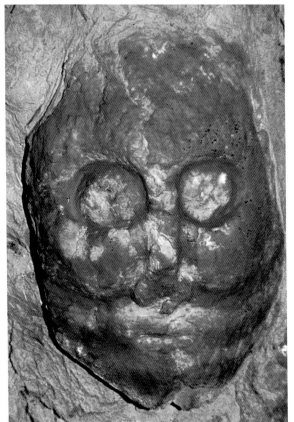

166–68 ABOVE *The site of Orongo, on the narrow cliff-top between the crater of Rano Kau and the sheer drop to the ocean; the photograph shows the distance that the egg-seekers had to travel to reach the large islet of Motu Nui.* LEFT *A large bas-relief of Makemake, painted bright red, inside one of the caves on Motu Nui.* RIGHT *The view from Motu Nui across the small islet of Motu Iti and the pointed rock of Motu Kao Kao to the imposing cliff of Orongo.*

The Stolen Friend

169,170 *The unique basalt statue removed from a house at Orongo by the British in 1868, and now housed in London's Museum of Mankind. Its name, 'Hoa Hakananai'a' means 'Friend which has been stolen'. The statue weighs 4 tons, stands 2.5 m (c. 8¼ ft) high, and bears remarkably rich decoration on its back including a raised ring and girdle, birdmen, paddles and vulvas.*

171,172 *Tracings by Georgia Lee of birdman petroglyphs, showing the development from the early type (left), comprising simple and sinuous engravings, to the more elaborate petroglyphs and bas-reliefs of the later phase (right).*

The birdman went off to live in lazy seclusion for a year in an elliptical house at the foot of Rano Raraku, where he neither washed nor bathed, and refrained from cutting his nails – this must have helped ensure his seclusion! The egg was blown and then hung up for the year, after which it might be buried in a crevice at Rano Raraku, or thrown into the sea, or eventually buried with its owner (also at Rano Raraku), who meanwhile returned to ordinary life. In the final years of the ceremony the winner's group, who took up residence in Mataveri at the foot of Rano Kau, could raid and plunder other groups with impunity.

Unlike normal dwellings, the Orongo houses were not closely associated with earth ovens, but instead a special cluster of ovens existed where food was prepared for participants in the ceremonies; they would have to take food out to the islets with them, or have it brought out by servants or relatives, because the Motu had no water, and nothing to eat but fish, seaweed and berries. Each egg-seeker's food supply had to be jealously guarded to prevent it being poached by the others.

The new religious importance of the offshore islets, previously valued primarily for their obsidian and their sea birds, led to many of Motu Nui's twenty-one caves being modified for temporary occupation by the egg-seekers, and also being used for large numbers of burials. Eight of the caves had elaborate rock art on their walls, including birdmen and a bright red mask of Makemake (ill. 167). A stockpile of red earthen pigments was found hidden in one cave, for rock art or perhaps for painting the bodies of initiates. One

cave contained a 60 cm (2 ft) stone statue which, according to Routledge, marked a boundary between the territory of the western and eastern groups.

A much larger statue, known as 'Hoa Hakananai'ā' ('stolen friend'), stood with its back to the sea inside one of the central Orongo houses, which must have been built around it: excavations revealed a great deal of charcoal in front of the entrance. The figure was buried to the chest, perhaps to lessen the necessary height of the building. Resembling a classic *moai*, it was carved in basalt – which required far more effort than carving tuff – and was richly decorated on its back with birdmen, dance-paddles, vulvas and other motifs, including traces of white and red paint. Its pointed base indicates that it was never meant to stand on a platform. This 4 ton statue, 2.5 m (8 ft) high, was removed – with ropes, levers, 300 sailors, 200 natives and considerable difficulty – in 1868 and now stands in London's Museum of Mankind (ills 169, 170).

It has been argued that it was the prototype of all classical *moai*, but in view of its veneration at Orongo it seems far more likely that this was a very late carving, forming a crucial link between the old ancestor-worship and the new birdman cult, as did the birdman's residence at the old statue quarry. Another possible sign of transition is the placing of head-dresses on some statues, which some scholars see as a sign that these figures represented warriors.

The rocks around Orongo are festooned with art, in particular at a spot called Mata Ngarau which has the heaviest concentration of rock art on the whole island, with much superimposition. It is worth noting that the basalt here is very dense, so the figures took a great deal of time and effort to produce. The most striking motif is the birdman (ills 171–79), sometimes holding an egg. No less than 481 birdmen are known so far, the vast majority

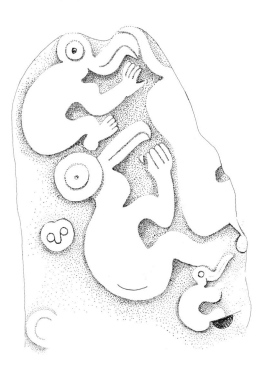

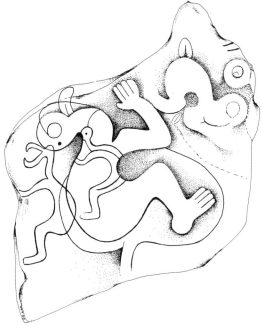

The Birdman

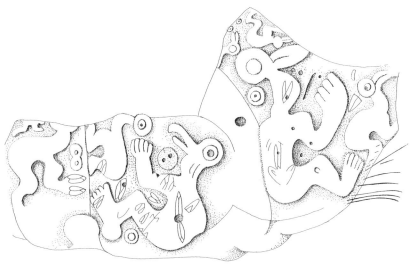

173–78 ABOVE *Tracings by Georgia Lee showing some of the many birdman carvings at Orongo. Note also the frequent eye-mask motif. At top right, this group from Mata Ngarau shows how early-phase incised, sinuous birdmen are cut through and partly obliterated by the more elaborate late-phase figures. In the lower drawing, note the komari (vulvas) engraved on top of the birdmen.* OPPOSITE ABOVE *Part of the profusion of rock art at Orongo; note the birdmen carved everywhere in various orientations; some early-phase birdmen are visible top right.* RIGHT *Birdmen carved on slabs inside a house at Orongo.* FAR RIGHT *A birdman on an exposed rock at Orongo.*

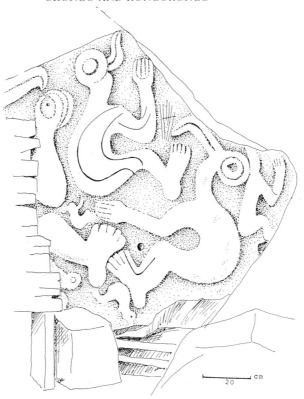

179 *Birdman petroglyphs at Orongo; since some of them are masked by a house, they clearly predate its construction. Note also the traces of early-phase birdmen.*

(86 per cent) being at or near Orongo – they rarely occur elsewhere, and then only in the earlier, more sinuous form (e.g. at Anakena); the later, fuller form, which often obliterates the earlier design, is entirely restricted to the environs of Orongo, and it has been convincingly suggested that each is a portrait of a winning contestant. Some are partly covered by houses, so they predate at least some of the buildings.

Many of these later, crouching figures, with hands and feet clearly depicted, also have the hooked bill and gular pouch of a frigate bird, although the ritual involved the sooty tern. Frigate birds were important in Pacific cults as far away as the Solomon Islands, being magnificent flyers and also notorious for being territorially and sexually rapacious – the male's red pouch under the beak is blown up like a balloon during courtship and mating. One can readily understand their significance for the islanders, for quite apart from the importance of the colour red, the birds' behaviour must have mirrored that of the islanders themselves, raiding and pillaging as a way of life, demolishing their neighbours' nests, and even stealing twigs (perhaps reflecting the islanders' desperation for timber).

It is likely that frigate birds were frequent visitors to Easter Island in the past, but today their visits are an extremely rare event, probably because they nest in trees: in 1983, forty frigate birds were seen in the skies, but none came to nest. Moreover, a frigate lays an egg only once every two years, and, if disturbed, will not nest at all. This helps to explain why the more reliable annual arrival of the sooty tern on Motu Nui was adopted as the basis of the cult: it may have been an acceptable second-best, since both birds are web-footed species with forked tails, though the tern has a straight beak and no pouch. A tern will lay up to three eggs per year if the first two are collected. Even the tern, however, is no longer reliable, perhaps owing to overexploitation in the past: in 1983, only one pair nested on the islet.

The symbolism of birds is largely self-evident; we have already mentioned their ability to fly wherever they liked and hence leave the island, unlike the natives. A combination of human and bird elements is consistent in Oceanic art from the islands of southeast Asia through Melanesia to Polynesia, and is usually associated with gods or ancestral spirits. The emphasis on bird symbols is understandable in these islands which generally lack large land mammals. Birds always occupy a prominent place in Oceanic mythology; they were often thought to have a mystical relationship with the gods, acting as messengers or as transporters of souls: sea birds were particularly symbolic since they united land, sea and sky. It is worth remembering that bird-headed humans are also known even further afield in space and time: one need only mention the ancient Egyptian gods Horus and Thoth, or the bird-headed man painted in the French cave of Lascaux, c. 15,000 BC. As shown above, the birdman concept was by no means a late arrival on the island but predated the Orongo houses and underwent some development. The concept of the birdman and Makemake may therefore have begun as a subordinate ideology: oral tradition claims that Hotu Matua brought the worship of Makemake with him; the birdman cult's eventual adoption and dominance probably reflect the need of the warrior class to justify and legitimize its rule.

The new egg cult was probably stimulated in part by the dwindling of the bird population and hence the need to protect one of the island's decreasing sources of protein. There are myths describing Makemake and other gods driving birds from Easter Island to Motu Nui so they would be safe from men. In this regard, it is significant that the few islanders who accompanied Métraux to Motu Nui devoured over a hundred eggs there in half an hour.

Goggle-eyed mask-faces are another common motif in the Orongo area's rock art, and are usually thought to represent Makemake, though they could be other gods, ancestors or particular individuals. Some have deliberately mismatched eyes. As in the rest of Polynesia, it is believed that round eyes (as on the birdmen and some masks) denote supernatural beings, whereas oval eyes (as on the statues) occurred on natural beings. Some mask-faces have long noses which make them resemble male genitalia, but it is female genitalia which really dominate here.

180,181 ABOVE *A photograph and a drawing of the same stone 'housepost' at Orongo bearing numerous bas-relief vulvas, as well as representations of Makemake. The stone's other face has two birdmen carved on it.*

The vulva (*komari*) is the commonest figurative motif in the island's rock art, and of the 564 found so far (not including those carved on stone pillows, figurines, skulls, etc.) no less than 334 are at Orongo, constituting 30 per cent of all petroglyphs at the site. Not one occurs at Anakena which, being the traditional seat of the old royal power, may have resisted the trappings of the new order like the birdman and the fertility cult. At Orongo, the vulvas are even found engraved inside the ceremonial houses. They vary from 4 to 130 cm (1½ to 51 in) in size. It is known that girls had their clitoris deliberately lengthened from an early age, with the longest and finest destined to attract the best warriors as husbands. At special ceremonies girls would stand on two rocks at Orongo to be examined by priests, and those judged best would have their genitalia immortalized in stone. This emphasis on fertility appears to be one of the last phases of Rapa Nui culture, since vulvas are superimposed at least forty-eight times on late-style birdman engravings, while one fragment of fallen statue was deeply and finely recarved into a huge bas-relief vulva,

The Cult of Fertility

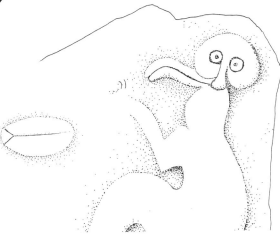

182–84 TOP *Petroglyphs abut Orongo houses, showing birdmen and Makemake faces.* ABOVE *A basalt pebble used as a pillow (ngaru'a), incised with vulvas and 26 cm (10¼ in) long, now in the Bishop Museum, Honolulu.* RIGHT *A petroglyph at Mata Ngarau showing a vulva next to a unique combination of a birdman with a Makemake face. This was the figure published so misleadingly by Thomson without its beak but with claws (see p. 57).*

46 cm (18 in) long and 25 cm (*c.* 10 in) wide, and set up in a prominent place.

The island has a remarkable wealth of rock art: about a thousand sites, and hundreds of images, clustering around coastal religious centres such as Orongo and Anakena, with very little in the interior where there are few suitable rock-surfaces. It is impressive not only for its abundance and diversity in a small island, but also for the superb quality shown in some of its designs and executions, from simple engravings to elaborate bas-reliefs, all of which may originally have had colour in their grooves. Paintings, as mentioned earlier, survive inside Orongo houses as well as in some caves: the famous cave of Ana Kai Tangata (see p. 171) contains some beautiful late paintings of terns so high up that scaffolding must have been required (ill. 161).

Much of the rock art is probably quite late – carvings, especially of canoes, and cupmarks are a frequent sight on fallen statues and their cylindrical *pukao*

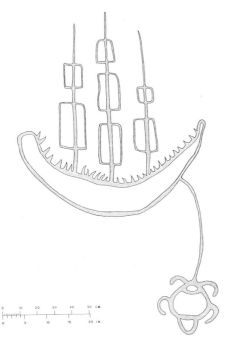

185,186 TOP *Depictions of sooty terns: painted on a slab from an Orongo house (left); engraved on a rock surface in the open air (right).*

187 LEFT *The three-masted European ship depicted on the chest of a statue at Rano Raraku (see ill. 85); it appears to have a turtle at the end of a rope.*

where they may be a sign of defeat; fifteen European ships were also depicted, including a three-master on the chest of a statue standing at the foot of Rano Raraku (ill. 187). The clustering of particular motifs in certain places or areas could also be seen as territorial marking by conquering groups during the warfaring period: the urge to mark one's clan superiority and supremacy over others clearly became a driving force on the island. Like the island's amazing richness and variety of small portable carvings, the rock art shows that the craftsmanship which produced the giant figures for centuries did not die out completely; stone and wood could still be carved with consummate skill in other ways by the 'guilds' of mastercarvers. Some of the motifs in Rapa Nui's art also provide a link with the one genuine mystery that remains from the island's past.

Rongorongo

The enduring enigma of Easter Island is the Rongorongo phenomenon: is it really a form of writing? And more crucially, did the islanders invent it for themselves?

It comprises parallel lines of engraved characters, many of them bird symbols, hooks, etc. Every alternate line is upside down, and the overall impression is of a tightly packed mass of uniform, skilfully inscribed hiero-glyphics.

According to legends, Hotu Matua himself could read and write the characters and brought sixty-seven inscribed tablets to the island with him, but since the same legends also attribute many of Rapa Nui's indigenous plants to him, we should discount them as a reliable source on this matter. The more pertinent point to bear in mind is that not one of the early European visitors ever mentioned the tablets or the characters – yet some of them spent days exploring ashore, and entered native houses. The very first indication we have of the tablets' existence is that a *rei miro* (a large, crescent-shaped, carved wooden pendant) inscribed with Rongorongo characters reached New Zealand by 1851; and the earliest written mention of the phenomenon is that of Eugène Eyraud, the missionary, who wrote to his Superior in 1864:

> In all their houses one can find tablets of wood or sticks with many kinds of hieroglyphic signs.... Each figure has its own name; but the little they make of these tablets makes me incline to think that these signs, the rest of the primitive script, are for them at present a custom which they preserve without searching the meaning. The natives do neither know how to read nor write.

Eyraud's claim that the tablets were to be found in every house is strangely at odds with the silence on this matter from previous visitors and with Mrs Routledge's belief that they used to be kept apart in special houses and were very strictly *tapu*.

The obvious conclusion is that the 'script' was a very late phenomenon, directly inspired by the visit of the Spanish under González in 1770, when a written proclamation of annexation was offered to the chiefs and priests to be 'signed in their native characters' – was this their first experience of speech embodied in parallel lines? The document survives, and the marks placed on it (ill. 189) are pretty nondescript except for a vulva, and a classic bird motif at the bottom which is identical to characters on the tablets.

The dilemma, as yet unresolved, is therefore as follows: were the islanders already producing their 'script' before the European arrivals, or did they devise a method of using written symbols as mnemonics after they had seen the annexation document?

One piece of evidence is that many of the motifs found on the tablets are well represented in the island's wealth of rock art. Some scholars therefore see this as possible proof of Rongorongo being an ancient phenomenon on the island, although there is no archaeological evidence for this and no inscriptions on stone are known; but others argue equally convincingly that, once the islanders had decided to adopt a method of 'script', they would most probably use the motifs with which they were already familiar, rather than invent a new set. In other words, the similarities of Rongorongo symbols with rock art motifs provide no solution to the puzzle. Besides, if the 'script' already existed, why did the chiefs and priests not use more of its motifs on the Spanish document?

Whatever its origin, the Rongorongo phenomenon now survives only as markings on twenty-nine pieces of wood scattered around the world's museums. Some signs also survive on paper in makeshift 'books', but these were considered by the islanders to be an 'inferior form of script'. The 29 wooden objects contain over 14,000 'glyphs', including some engraved staffs, though only the real wooden boards should be considered true Rongorongo. Their full title should be *Kohau motu mo rongorongo*, translated by Sebastian Englert as 'the lines of inscriptions for recitation'. This is often shortened to *kohou rongorongo* ('wooden board for recitation'), which Métraux believed to mean 'chanter's staff' and hence to indicate a link with Mangareva and the Marquesas where staves were used to beat the rhythm of chants.

This is certainly where the term 'Rongorongo' (chants, recitations) originates: in Mangareva the rongorongo was a class of high-ranking experts charged with the memory and recitation of sacred *marae* chants; it is therefore highly likely that the concept came to Rapa Nui with its first settlers, and the same may well be true of the 'script': according to Thomas Barthel, the foremost scholar of Rongorongo, there are oral traditions in the Austral Islands of rectangular wooden tablets with series of signs engraved on them. These symbols dealt with gods and birdmen, and were strictly *tapu*, being used by priests to sing songs relating to historical events, religion and a fertility cult.

All the surviving Rapa Nui pieces are over 125 years old: many look quite unused, and besides, some are fragments of wood foreign to the island, and

The Rongorongo Enigma

188,189 ABOVE *The wooden tablet known as 'Mamari', but called 'Kohau o te ranga' ('tablet of the prisoners') by the islanders, which was obtained by Bishop Jaussen of Tahiti in 1868; it is 30 cm long, 21 cm wide (12 by 8¼ in), and each side bears 14 lines with a total of 1000 glyphs. It is now housed in the Congregation of the Sacred Heart in Rome.* BELOW *The marks placed on the Spanish proclamation by the islanders in 1770.*

even include a European oar. It is therefore probable that they all postdate European contact. The Peruvian slave raids of 1862 removed the last islanders who could truly understand the tablets – knowledge of them was confined to the royal family, chiefs and priests, and every person in authority was carried off to Peru. Thomson's informant on the subject in 1886 had never owned or made a tablet, but had been a servant of the chief who possessed Rongorongos, and had surreptitiously memorized some texts. Mrs Routledge could find only a handful of 'man-in-the-street' informants who had merely heard readings as children but had no personal knowledge of the 'script'; there were no experts left. It has been said that the islanders were like illiterate parishioners being asked about hymnals; they honoured and revered the objects and their texts, but in the absence of their religious leaders they could provide little information.

The last tablet to come to light was a slightly charred specimen given to Englert in the 1930s. In that same period, Métraux offered 1000 pesos merely for information about new tablets, but without success. Many had been destroyed: the islanders told Thomson that the missionaries made them burn these heathen objects, though other islanders strenuously denied this. One missionary was told that the natives were using them to light their kitchen fires, and even in pre-missionary days they were often destroyed in wars or deliberately burned: one chief's funeral pyre was said to have been composed of Rongorongo tablets, while others were buried with the honoured dead. Englert believed that many tablets, once their existence had been noticed by Eyraud, had been hidden in sacred caves to protect these *tapu* symbols of paganism from the new faith.

Bishop Jaussen of Tahiti took a great interest in the boards, and had his missionaries send some to him: indeed, far from having the tablets burned, it is largely thanks to the missionaries' efforts that we have any tablets to study at all. Jaussen attempted to have one read, or rather chanted, by an islander called Metoro, but the results, while providing some valuable clues, are by no means a Rosetta Stone – it has been said that the untutored Metoro was like a schoolboy trying to explain a university textbook, and his readings were clearly full of inaccuracies. Nevertheless, they show that the boards were turned as they were read – hence the glyphs' arrangement in a 'reversed boustrophedon' (see p. 63), meaning that the characters formed a continuous sequence and the board was turned through 180 degrees at the end of every line (though one scholar has suggested an analogy with 17th-century English songbooks, where part-songs were so printed that the two parts could be read from the two sides of a table). A subsequent attempt was made in 1874 to have an islander read a text, but on three successive Sundays he provided three different versions of the same text!

According to Thomas Barthel, there are about 120 basic elements in the glyphs, mostly stylized outlines of objects or creatures, but these are combined to form between 1500 and 2000 compound signs. They were engraved with a shark's tooth, a flake of obsidian, or a sharpened bird bone. The most abundant motif is the sooty tern figure, including sitting birdmen with a sooty tern head. Barthel and other scholars have reached the conclusion that the motifs represent a rudimentary phonetic writing system, in which picture symbols were used to express ideas as well as objects. In other words, the individual glyphs do not represent an alphabet or even syllables, as in other scripts, but are 'cue cards' for whole words or ideas, plus a means of keeping count, like rosary beads. Each sign was a peg on which to hang a large amount of text committed to memory. There are no articles, no conjunctions, no sentences. The missing words had to be filled in by the reader as the tablet's content was sung – this would explain why the untutored provided different versions of a single text. They might be vaguely aware of the subject matter, but the details had to be improvised.

That being the case, there is little chance of our ever being able to produce full and accurate translations, unless the meagre collection of tablets is ever boosted by unexpected new finds from the island. Nonetheless, Barthel and others have made great progress in identifying certain symbols and assessing the subject matter of different texts: one fragment, for example, seems to be a lunar calendar. Thomson was told that each tablet relayed a specific legend, so that if the reader knew which legend was involved, it could be recited without even knowing how to read individual glyphs. Barthel and others believe that they also include king-lists, religious and cult texts, creation legends, hymns in honour of the gods, instructions to priests, lists of murdered men, etc. There appears to be a marked preoccupation with fertility, which fits with the phenomenon's late date. It is believed that some characters depict plants and animals that never existed on the island – such as the breadfruit tree which, if it ever came, must have died out quickly – and geographical names of other Polynesian islands including the Australs, and Pitcairn's ancient name.

If so, the question remains: were all these things retained within the collective memory since the time of the first settlers, or is it conceivable that Rapa Nui was visited by other Polynesians during its long isolation? Whatever the answer, and whether or not the islanders developed their 'script' alone or under outside influence, it remains a crowning glory of this unique culture, one of the most highly evolved Neolithic societies in human history.

CHAPTER 11

CONCLUSION: THE ISLAND THAT SELF-DESTRUCTED

It is common and convenient in archaeology to divide cultures or periods into three, such as Lower/Middle/Upper. Easter Island is no exception to the rule, and it was no surprise when the first attempt (by the Norwegian expedition of the 1950s) to trace the whole course of the island's history resulted in a three-phase scheme: Early (AD 400–1100), Middle (1100–1680) and Late (1680–1722). Subsequent work has questioned this scheme, only to replace it with others of a similar nature, such as Settlement (up to AD 1000), Expansion (1000–1500) and Decadence (1500–1722). An alternative chronological labelling system might be: Altars, Statues, Burials; or Architecture, Sculpture and Rock Art. The 'golden age' of platform and statue building appears to start in the mid-12th century, and the island's 'cultural peak' occurred in the 15th century. It is reckoned that no more statues (or at least very few) were erected on platforms after *c.* AD 1500, and that, economically and demographically, it was all downhill after that.

Behind the spectacular constructions and sculptures lay a religious motivation, a tribal pride in display, and an intensely competitive instinct that was characteristic of Polynesia. In most cultures, complexity seems to be closely connected to the intensity of interaction, and opportunities to exchange ideas, with one's neighbours. When such interaction and opportunities are lacking, one normally expects to find the very simplest of cultural adaptations. Easter Island is of enduring fascination because it flagrantly violates that rule.

Yet as the tremendous effort of carving, constructing and transporting the island's numerous monuments increased, it inevitably meant that the food-producers had to support ever-growing numbers of non-food producers. As the population grew, and these monumental religious activities intensified, the problem can only have grown worse. Deforestation and depletion of vegetation through burning and cutting must have led to leaching and soil erosion, more wind damage, increased soil evaporation and a reduction in crop yields. The decreased water retention by the ever-diminishing plant cover had a negative effect on water supply, with the drying up of springs and previously reliable streams. The loss of large timber eventually led to an abandonment of deep-sea fishing, and hence a further loss of badly needed protein. The islanders' counter-measures – the garden enclosures to retain precious soil moisture, and the Fort Knox-like chicken houses – reveal the kind of predicament in which

190 OPPOSITE *Juan Tepano, Routledge's informant, in 1915 by the broken base of a statue on the great platform of Tongariki, one of the fifteen that originally stood there, and the last fragment of a statue still standing. The platform was finally destroyed by the tidal wave of 1960.*

they found themselves. It is theoretically possible that a drought made things worse, but clearly the islanders brought disaster upon themselves by gradually destroying a crucial resource, the palm, and unwittingly preventing its regeneration through having imported rats. A delicate balance was put under strain and finally upset. The environmental degradation was irreversible.

The amazing peace of a thousand years – unique in Polynesia – was shattered, as old rivalries were no longer expressed in competitive construction but rather in raids, violence and destruction, aimed presumably at the acquisition of arable land or simply of food and other resources. The island-wide exchange mechanisms and the co-operation of large numbers of people required to produce the religious monuments all collapsed.

The story of Easter Island is one of amazing achievement followed by, as Patrick Kirch puts it, a 'downward spiral of cultural regression'. A remarkable and unique culture, displaying tremendous continuity combined with invention and development, crumpled under the pressures of environmental destruction and, perhaps, of overpopulation; as Kirch has said, it 'temporarily but brilliantly surpassed its limits and crashed devastatingly'. Unlike the inhabitants of other islands, the Easter Islanders could not escape in big canoes – in destroying their forests they had cut themselves off from the outside world even more than they had already been cut off by geography.

Many of the Polynesian islands took particular skills to unparalleled heights: in Hawai'i it was featherwork, in the Marquesas tattooing, while woodcarving was outstanding in New Zealand, Hawai'i and elsewhere. Easter Island achieved eminence not only in woodwork, tattoos, feathers, and tapa-work (paper-mulberry cloth), but also in rock art and the extraordinary Rongorongo phenomenon. All of these were an integral part of its culture. But the island's supreme communal efforts were poured into the giant statues and platforms – the most spectacular religious building compulsion known anywhere in Polynesia. In fact, as William Mulloy once remarked, it was a compulsion that became a little insane: 'It came to take up so much of the force of the culture that such important activities as farming and fishing were neglected, and the people didn't have enough to eat. You can carry statue-making only so far.'

The present-day Easter Islanders live amid the ruins of their ancestors' remarkable accomplishments. Mulloy saw his restoration of the monuments as a means of reaffirming the identity and dignity of the islanders. It would be a truly spectacular sight if all the statues could be re-erected on their platforms. Nevertheless, Nature, despite the abuse she has suffered on the island, will eventually reclaim everything: quite apart from the possibility of volcanic eruption, it is inevitable that not only will all the statues be worn away, dissolved back into the soil by the sun, rain and wind, but, in some millions of years, the waves and winds will batter the island itself to nothing.

THE LESSON OF EASTER ISLAND

The fact that the Easter Island civilization collapsed not long after the demise of its forests does not necessarily establish a connection between the two. Associations in time – even if established statistically – are not necessarily *causal* connections. For example, there is said to be a strong statistical correlation between the naval estimates for Great Britain (1920–38) and the changing levels of imports of bananas into the same country over the same time period. There is no obvious causal connection between these two. The association is due to chance, or may possibly be related to some third factor – in this case, the world economic situation. During the Depression, Britain spent little money on either the Navy or bananas. Before and after it, she spent more on both.

In the case of Easter Island, however, there are some grounds for believing that the connection could be causal. In the first place, the events are in the right order. If decline of the forests is to *cause* collapse of the civilization, then decline of the forests must happen *first*, as indeed the dating of the Rano Kau pollen diagram suggests that it did.

Secondly, there is a possible causal connection. That is to say, we can think of a mechanism or model for connecting the cause and effect. Such a model is shown in ill. 191. Starting at the centre of the diagram, with forest and human immigration, we can see how these could interact to produce the elements which contributed to population decline. Forest clearance for the growing of crops would have led to population increase, but also to soil erosion and decline of soil fertility. Progressively more land would have had to be cleared. Trees and shrubs would also be cut down for canoe building, firewood, house construction, and for the timbers and ropes needed in the movement and erection of statues. Palm fruits would be eaten, thus reducing regeneration of the palm. Rats, introduced for food, could have fed on the palm fruits, multiplied rapidly and completely prevented palm regeneration. The overexploitation of prolific sea bird resources would have eliminated these from all but the offshore islets. Rats could have helped in this process by eating eggs. The abundant food provided by fishing, sea birds and rats would have encouraged rapid initial human population growth. Unrestrained human population increase would later put pressure on availability of land, leading to disputes and eventually warfare. Non-availability of timber and rope would

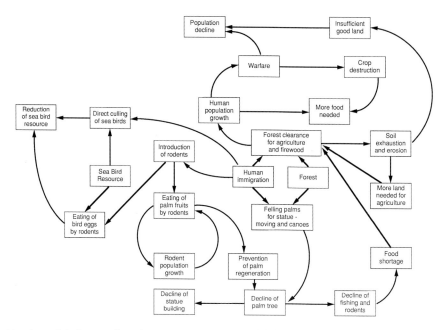

191 *A model showing how human immigration could have interacted with the indigenous
Easter Island forest to produce the elements that led to population decline.*

make it pointless to carve further statues. A disillusionment with the efficacy
of the statue religion in providing the wants of the people could lead to the
abandonment of this cult. Inadequate canoes would restrict fishing to inshore
waters, leading to further decline in protein supplies. The result could have
been general famine, warfare and the collapse of the whole economy, leading
to a marked population decline.

Of course, most of this is hypothesis. Nevertheless, there is evidence, as we
have seen, that many features of this model did in fact occur. There certainly
was deforestation, famine, warfare, collapse of civilization and population
decline. There could be explanations other than overexploitation of resources.
For example, there could have been a major drought. But it seems odd that
the forest should survive for at least 37,000 years (see p. 82), including the
major climatic fluctuations of the last ice age and the postglacial climatic peak,
only to succumb to drought after people arrived on the island. That would
be a coincidence just too great to believe. There could have been an invasion
by a new group of people, or a disease introduced. But neither would explain
all the island's history, nor is there independent evidence for either.

Even if we accept ill. 191 as a working hypothesis, so what? Are the events
of three hundred years ago on a small remote island of any significance to the
world at large? We believe that they are. We consider that Easter Island was
a microcosm which provides a model for the whole planet. Like the Earth,
Easter Island was an isolated system. The people there believed that they were

the only survivors on Earth, all other land having sunk beneath the sea. They carried out for us the experiment of permitting unrestricted population growth, profligate use of resources, destruction of the environment and boundless confidence in their religion to take care of the future. The result was an ecological disaster leading to a population crash. A crash on a similar scale (60 per cent reduction) for the planet Earth would lead to the deaths of about 1.8 billion people, roughly 100 times the death toll of the Second World War. Do we have to repeat the experiment on this grand scale? Do we have to be as cynical as Henry Ford and say 'History is bunk'? Would it not be more sensible to learn from the lesson of Easter Island history, and apply it to the Earth Island on which we live?

About twenty years ago, a group of businessmen and computer specialists known as the Club of Rome attempted to model by computer the future of the Earth into the 21st century. Various forms of the model were tried, but all those which included continuation of the present trends of economic expansion and population growth led to the same result. This is summarized in ill. 192. A rapid decline of resources was accompanied by a peak of pollution as population continued to soar. When resources became nearly exhausted at c. AD 2020, however, pollution (and economic activity) declined, followed by a sharp population crash after AD 2050. Eventually, c. AD 2100, population stabilized at a level well below its peak, but the resources available to that population were very low, giving a uniformly low standard of living.

If this kind of model has any veracity, it should also apply to the Easter Island situation. The timescale might be different – for example, the population growth on Easter might have been slower because they did not have advanced medicine, and there would be a delay because not all parts of the island were deforested at the same time – but the essential elements of resource decline, pollution peak, population growth and population crash should all be there. In ill. 193 we see that this is indeed so in the record from Rano Kau, the most detailed one we have for the relevant period. The forest pollen reduction is an index of resource decline. The decrease in organic content is indicative of soil erosion, leading to pollution of the water washing into the swamp. Charcoal fragments blowing into the swamp may be taken as a rough indicator of air pollution. The population curve is notional, but conforms to the idea of arrival c. AD 400; uninhibited growth until AD 1680 up to a population of about 10,000; a population crash leading to a population of a few thousand in the time of Cook; and subsequent historical change. The overall conclusion seems fairly clear: the Club of Rome model works.

Let us add immediately that we are not suggesting that any simplistic relationship exists between forest destruction and economic collapse. That is a message that you can take away from this book if you wish, and the analogy would certainly be timely. The present destruction of world forests must fairly soon lead to shortages of timber and all the other products which derive from forests – not just rattan cane or bark litter, but more refined products such as drugs. And then there are the knock-on effects. Soil erosion in deforested areas is already of scandalous extent. It is likely that the burning of rain forests contributes significantly to the rise of CO_2 levels in the atmosphere, probably causing climatic warming.

We should prefer, however, that the reader came away from reading our book with two more general – yet perhaps more disturbing – thoughts. The first of these is that resources are finite, and that the using up of a resource may indeed put a civilization at risk. This is true of all resources, whether potentially renewable or not. The cynic will point out that technologists will find a substitute. Often this is true, but it is most dangerous to rely on it. The Easter Islanders no doubt believed their gods would provide a solution to the problem. Nowadays we tend to rely on our gods of science and technology. But the islanders came unstuck in a big way, and we could do the same. Science is very powerful, but not infallible. Many people now consider that the discoveries of science, which have permitted humankind to make giant technological strides, have been a mixed blessing. No one, we hope, would wish to return to an age before modern medical science, yet it is medicine – and especially medical ethics combined with missionary fervour – which has led to the suicidally rapid population increase of the present day in the Third World. Few people would wish to be transported back in time to the muscle-rending tasks of pre-mechanical forestry, agriculture and construction. Yet it is the chain saw, the combine harvester and the bulldozer that have destroyed our forests and wildlife. Electricity and the motor car are true symbols of our technological success, but energy generation and car exhaust fumes are now threatening the ecology of the whole Earth, through rising CO_2 levels. We have indeed eaten of the fruit of the tree of knowledge, and we are beginning to regret it. Is the answer to be found in yet more research and more knowledge? Or is it time to ask whether true wisdom comes not from more knowledge but from better application of the knowledge we already have?

There is one final moral – the most disturbing of all – in the Easter Island allegory. Easter Island is a poor model for our world in one particular way. Like all models, it suffers from problems of scale. Easter Island is small, and its ecosystem relatively simple. It had limited topography, a rather stable climate, a limited range of rocks, soils, plants and animals. Whatever one did to alter that ecosystem, the results were reasonably predictable. One could stand on the summit and see almost every point on the island. *The person who felled the last tree could see that it was the last tree. But he (or she) still felled it.* This is what is so worrying. Humankind's covetousness is boundless. Its selfishness appears to be genetically inborn. Selfishness leads to survival. Altruism leads to death. The selfish gene wins. But in a limited ecosystem, selfishness leads to increasing population imbalance, population crash, and ultimately extinction. As Bertrand Russell pointed out, human beings are a species and like all species they will become extinct. Is it really necessary, however, to behave like the Gadarene swine, and hurry the process up?

EARTH ISLAND

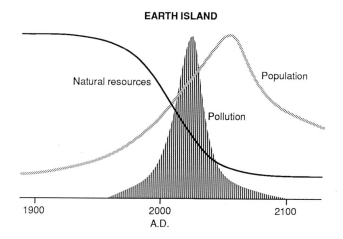

Natural resources

Population

Pollution

1900 — 2000 — 2100
A.D.

EASTER ISLAND

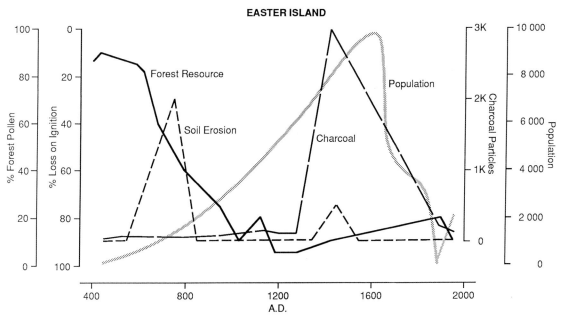

Forest Resource

Soil Erosion

Population

Charcoal

% Forest Pollen
% Loss on Ignition
Charcoal Particles
Population

400 — 800 — 1200 — 1600 — 2000
A.D.

192,193 TOP *The Club of Rome computer model of the Earth's future, which predicts that the current lethal combination of rising population and pollution, and ever-decreasing natural resources, will result in a devastating population crash.* ABOVE *The Rano Kau pollen record suggests a series of events on Easter Island similar to that of the Club of Rome model for Earth Island: a sequence of uninhibited population growth, over-exploitation of resources and sudden population decline.*

194 OVERLEAF *The central statue platform Vai Uri at Tahai, the four-masted sailing ship offshore illumined by shafts of silver light piercing the clouds.*

Could we not search for sustainability – and thus achieve stability – of population, resource use, and economic activity? It seems that human personality is against us. The feller of the last tree *knew* it would lead ultimately to disaster for subsequent generations but went ahead and swung the axe. We have already mentioned Métraux's account of how the islanders gorged themselves on eggs when visiting the Motu Nui islet; he also reported that he saw the single toromiro tree surviving inside Rano Kau, and that 'during our stay the natives were jealously watching the growth of this tree, waiting for the right moment to cut it down and turn it into statuettes and other "curios" '; even in 1984, the few terns that arrived on the island were eagerly captured and eaten. It seems the islanders' attitude to resources remains unchanged.

Our own situation is much worse, because the Earth is a large and complex ecosystem. It is all too easy to carry out an action that seems harmless – or even beneficial – and yet to endanger the ecosystem of our planet. The inventor of CFCs doubtless believed he was improving the human lot by giving people refrigerators. Now we know he was damaging the ozone layer (indirectly, of course) and causing skin cancer. The Victorian medical missionary who reduced infant mortality believed he was simply saving the lives of more children to give glory to God, and was oblivious to the fact that *their* children would destroy the rain forest in order to survive.

If there is any hope, it is surely in the idea that we must change our religion. Our present gods of economic growth, science and technology, continuously rising standards of living, and the virtues of competition – deities that we consider all-powerful – are like the giant statues on the Easter Island platforms. Each village competed with its neighbours to erect the largest statue. Platforms were constantly replaced with more grandiose ones. More and more effort went into the resource-consuming and time-consuming, but pointless, carving, moving and erecting. What we need to do is throw down our economic *moai*. To regain the sense of proportion that we have lost. To turn to a new religion centred on the environment. It could be argued that, far from being beyond salvation, the Easter Islanders did learn from their mistakes, for their response to a series of disasters was to turn to a form of nature worship: the birdman cult was tightly bound to the annual bounty of nature in providing protein in the form of sooty tern eggs. Under the discipline of this new religion, the birdman, whose young champion found the first egg, did not indulge in an orgy of eating or economic display. He humbled himself by living alone in a house for a whole year, to give thanks for the return of the islanders' protein life-line. Yes, there was war and famine, and yes, there was a population crash, but ultimately the Easter Islanders were reconciled with nature and achieved, for a time, a sustainable stability. Will we Earth Islanders have the sense to do the same thing before our skyscrapers come tumbling about our ears? Or is the human personality always the same as that of the person who felled the last tree?

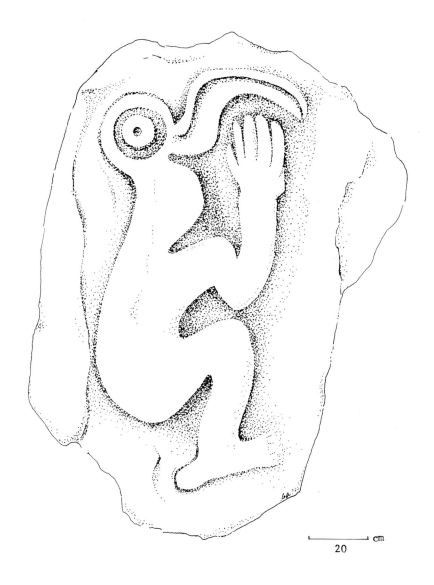

195 *A well-defined birdman petroglyph at Orongo, drawn by Georgia Lee.*

VISITING EASTER ISLAND

When to Go

Since the early 1980s tourism has become a major element of Easter Island's economy, one that is largely controlled by the islanders themselves. The best time to visit is in the summer months, that is, from the middle of January to the end of March. This is also the time of year when many Chilean students visit the island during the long vacation. However, the island never feels overcrowded, even at the height of the tourist season.

Two annual festivals take place on Easter Island: Chilean Independence Day is celebrated on 18 September, while the Semana de Rapa Nui, usually at the end of January and beginning of February, is a week of local dance and song incorporating ancient traditions.

It is well worth arranging to be on the island on a Sunday in order to attend mass at its Catholic church, to the east of Te Pito te Henua; visitors of all denominations are warmly welcomed and enjoy marvellous singing of hymns in harmony and in the islanders' own language.

How to Get There

An extension to the island's runway has recently been completed and a number of countries are now considering new routes across the Pacific via Easter Island. For the moment, however, only the Chilean airline, Lan-Chile, makes commercial flights to Easter Island. There are now two weekly flights from Santiago and from Papeete, Tahiti; flights to Santiago from Europe take about 16 hours, those from, say, Los Angeles about 11 hours. It is important to note that schedules change frequently and without warning, so departure times should be checked in advance; the airline's office on Easter Island is at Hotel Hanga Roa. All suitcases are opened by customs officials on out-going flights, and any items that form part of the island's archaeological heritage – such as the ancient fish-hooks and spear-points (*mataa*) sold by island tradesmen – will be confiscated. It is possible to visit Easter Island as part of a sea cruise, also visiting parts of the South American mainland, but cruise ships only stay on the island for a short time.

196, 197 LEFT *and* RIGHT *The Semana de Rapa Nui, or Rapa Nui Festival, takes place in the summer during late January or early February. While it is certainly of great interest to visitors, the festival is more than just a tourist attraction and is taken seriously by the islanders as a celebration of their unique inheritance of folklore and traditions.*

What to Bring

Even in summer, the island is battered by strong winds and occasional heavy showers, so a mackintosh (rather than an umbrella) and warm clothing are essential. Furthermore, the wind, dust and powerful sunlight combine to make a good-quality broad-brimmed hat, sunglasses and sunblock cream obligatory. (Any medication you may require should also be brought with you – there is no chemist's shop on the island.) Dress is informal; the one essential item is a pair of strong walking boots to cope with the rough and boulder-strewn ground. If you are planning to do any hiking, a canteen is also vital – there is very little surface water.

There is no reliable source of film on the island, so you should bring a good supply with you in a lead-lined bag; even then, it is best to ensure that it is passed around the airport's ageing x-ray machine. A polarizing filter may be useful in avoiding the problem of over exposure.

The island's currency is the Chilean peso; there are generally long queues to exchange money at the only bank, the Banco del Estado. However, US dollars are accepted everywhere and are generally preferred (except in the Chilean government-run Post Office). Only the largest hotels will accept credit cards.

Where to Stay

There is a Tourist Bureau information centre in the airport and a tourist office on Tuu Maheke street; both will provide lists of places to stay, many of which will happily provide transportation to and from the airport. Indeed, most islanders – including hotel managers – meet incoming planes at the airport, so it is easy to find accommodation on your arrival. The islanders are very friendly and it is possible to live with local families; while this may be a fascinating experience, it is important to remember that not all islanders speak English! Alternatively, there is a good choice of large hotels providing suites, room service, swimming pools and all the other facilities to which modern tourists are accustomed. Even such 'international' hotels, however, will often prepare *umu* feasts of traditional Polynesian food baked in the ground.

Camping facilities are provided on the north coast at Anakena, which has one of the island's two small beaches. It is also possible to camp at the north end of Hanga Roa village. Sleeping in the island's many caves is discouraged.

Travelling Around

Renting a car or van is the best way to travel between sites of interest; walking over the rough ground – and carrying water – is time-consuming. Vehicles often come with a driver, used to negotiating uneven dirt tracks, which may become quagmires after a rainstorm. There is only one petrol station (near the airport) and a spare tyre is essential.

198 *Dancers and musicians in traditional costume, including head-dresses of intertwined leaves and flowers.*

Renting a horse is largely problem-free and costs very little, although those for hire, while certainly well used to tourists, may be reluctant to move quickly (or at all).

What to Buy

The most popular and freely available souvenirs are wood and stone carvings, which are often copies of the ancient pieces found by early explorers. Merchandise is sold through intermediaries but can also be purchased direct from the makers: many craftsmen will accept commissions and may be able to complete them in only a few days. Small replicas of the island's giant statues are carved in pumice, most especially by residents of the leper Sanatorium (who are, it should be pointed out, no longer contagious), to the north of Hanga Roa.

On your departure from Easter Island you may well be presented with the gift of a shell necklace; important visitors find themselves draped in layer upon layer of necklaces when they take their leave from this most hospitable island.

With acknowledgments to Georgia Lee's *An Uncommon Guide to Easter Island*

FURTHER READING

The fundamental texts for Easter Island archaeology are as follows:

HEYERDAHL, T. 1976, *The Art of Easter Island*, Allen & Unwin, London.

HEYERDAHL, T. and FERDON, E. Jr (eds) 1961, *Reports of the Norwegian Archaeological Expedition to Easter Island and the East Pacific. Vol. 1: The Archaeology of Easter Island*, Allen & Unwin, London.

HEYERDAHL, T. and FERDON, E. Jr (eds) 1965, *Ibid: Vol. 2: Miscellaneous Papers*, Allen & Unwin, London.

METRAUX, A. 1940, *Ethnology of Easter Island*, Bulletin 160, Bishop Museum Press, Honolulu (reprinted 1971).

METRAUX, A. 1957, *Easter Island*, André Deutsch, London.

ROUTLEDGE, K. (Mrs S.) 1919, *The Mystery of Easter Island*, Sifton, Praed & Co., London.

Useful introductions include:

ENGLERT, S. 1948, *La Tierra de Hotu Matu'a*, Imprenta San Francisco, Santiago.

ENGLERT, S. 1970, *Island at the Center of the World*, Scribners, New York.

HOOREBEECK, A. van 1979, *La Vérité sur l'Ile de Pâques*, P. d'Antoine, Le Havre.

McCOY, P. 1979, 'Easter Island', in *The Prehistory of Polynesia* (J.D. Jennings, ed.), 135–66, Harvard University Press, Cambridge, Massachusetts.

ORLIAC, C. and M. 1988, *Des dieux regardent les étoiles*, Gallimard, Paris.

Important collections of papers are to be found in:

Circumpacifica: Band II, Ozeanien, Miszellen (Festschrift für Thomas S. Barthel. ILLIUS, B. and LAUBSCHER, M. [eds]), Peter Lang, Frankfurt.

Clava, Vol. 4, 1988, Museo Sociedad Fonck, Viña del Mar, Chile.

ESEN-BAUR, H.M. (ed.) 1990, *State and Perspectives of Scientific Research in Easter Island Culture*, Courier Forschungsinstitut Senckenberg, Frankfurt, No. 125.

Estudios sobre la Isla de Pascua, 1980. Monograph published by Los Ediciones de la Universidad de Chile, Santiago.

First International Congress, Easter Island & East Polynesia (1984), Vol. 1, Archaeology, 1988. Universidad de Chile, Santiago.

FISCHER, S.R. (ed.) 1992, *Rapanui Studies (Easter Island), Essays in Memory of William T. Mulloy*, Bishop Museum Press, Honolulu.

1500 Jahre Kultur der Osterinsel 1989: catalogue of the Frankfurt exhibition. Verlag Philipp Von Zabern, Mainz.

L'Ile de Pâques: une Enigme? 1990: catalogue of the Brussels exhibition. Musées Royaux d'Art et d'Histoire, Brussels.

Journal of New World Archaeology, VII (1), August 1986, UCLA.
Nouveau Regard sur l'Ile de Pâques, 1982, Editions Moana, Corbeil, France.
Rapa Nui Journal (formerly *Rapa Nui Notes*), since 1986.
Ulysse, Revue du Voyage Culturel (Paris), 13, 1990.

The best guidebook to the island is: LEE, G. 1990, *An Uncommon Guide to Easter Island*, International Resources, Arroyo Grande, California.

INTRODUCTION: EUROPEAN DISCOVERY

For Roggeveen's account, see SHARP, A. (ed.) 1970, *The Journal of Jacob Roggeveen*, Clarendon Press, Oxford. See also details of Cpt. Cornelis Bouman's journal, in *Rapa Nui Journal* 4 (4), 1990/1, 49–52.

CHAPTER 1: THE ISLAND AND ITS GEOGRAPHY

On climate and geography in general, see ZIZKA, G., in *L'Ile de Pâques: une Enigme?* 1990, 21–38.

For geology, see BAKER, P.E. 1967, 'Preliminary account of recent geological investigations on Easter Island', *Geol. Mag.* 104 (2), 116–22; and GONZÁLEZ-FERRAN, O. and BAKER, P.E. 1974, *Easter Island*, Guidebook, Excursion D-2, Int. Symposium on Volcanology, Santiago.

For the island's geography, PORTEOUS, J.D. 1981, *The Modernization of Easter Island*, University of Victoria, Canada; McCALL, G. 1979, *Reaction to Disaster. Continuity and Change in Rapanui Social Organization*, AMS Press, New York.

On flora, see SKOTTSBERG, C. 1956, *The Natural History of Juan Fernández and Easter Island* Vol. 1, Almquist & Wiksells, Uppsala; ETIENNE, M., MICHEA, G. and DIAZ, E. 1982, *Flora, vegetacion y potencial pastoral de Isla de Pascua* (Univ. de Chile, Fac. de Ciencias Agrarias, Veterinarias y Forestales, Boletin Tecnico No. 47); and ZIZKA, G., 1990, in Esen-Baur (ed.), 189–207.

On the toromiro, see various papers in ESEN-BAUR (ed.), 1990. On plant dispersal, see CARLQUIST, S. 1967, 'The biota of long-distance dispersal: plant dispersal to Pacific islands', *Bull. Torrey Bot. Club* 44, 129–62.

The most complete list of early European visits to the island has been compiled by McCALL, G. 'Rapanui and outsiders: the early days', *Circumpacifica* 1990, 165–225.

For the Spanish caravel, see LANGDON, R. 1975, *The Lost Caravel*, Pacific Publications, Sydney; 2nd edition 1988, *The Lost Caravel Re-explored*, Brolga Press, Canberra. For the HLA studies, see DAUSSET, J. in *Nouveau Regard*, 1982, 228.

On the American work, see THOMSON, W.S. 1891, 'Te Pito te henua, or Easter Island', in *Report of the U.S. Nat. Museum for the year ending June 30, 1889*, 447–552. Smithsonian Inst., Washington.

CHAPTER 2: WHERE DID THEY COME FROM?

HEYERDAHL's position has been set out often: see, for example, 1950 *The Kon-Tiki Expedition*, Allen & Unwin, London; 1952 *American Indians in the Pacific* (ibid); 1958 *Aku-Aku* (ibid); and, in 1989, *Easter Island: The Mystery Solved*, Souvenir Press, London.

For a different view of Kon-Tiki, see HOWELLS, W. 1973, *The Pacific Islanders*, Weidenfeld & Nicolson, London, 216–18; see also LANNING, E.P. 1970, 'South America as a source for aspects of Polynesian cultures', in *Studies in Oceanic Culture History* (R.C. Green and M. Kelly, eds), vol. 2, 175–82 (Pacific Anth. Records 11); SUGGS, R.C. 1960, *The Island Civilizations of Polynesia*, New American Library, New York; EMORY, K.P. 1972, 'Easter Island's position in the prehistory of Polynesia', *J. Poly. Soc.* 81, 57–69.

On oral traditions, see ROUTLEDGE, K. 1919; and 1917, 'Easter Island', in *The Geog. Journal* 49, 321–49.

On botanical evidence, see HEISER, C.B. June 1974, 'Totoras, taxonomy and Thor', *Plant Science Bulletin*, 22–26.

R. LANGDON's 1988 investigation of the 'chili pepper/manioc' story is: 'Manioc, a long-concealed key to the enigma of Easter Island', in *The Geog. Journal* 154, 324–36.

On the sweet potato, see YEN, D. 1974, *The Sweet Potato and Oceania*, Bishop Museum Bull. 236, Honolulu; on the Quechua term, see BRAND, D.E. 1971, 'The sweet potato: an exercise in methodology', in *Man Across the Sea. Problems of Pre-Columbian Contacts* (C.L. Riley *et al.*, eds), University of Texas Press, Austin/London, 343–65

On Easter Island material culture in general, see GOLSON, J. 1965/6, 'Thor Heyerdahl and the prehistory of Easter Island', *Oceania* 36, 38–83.

For pottery, see SMITH, C. 1988, 'A small pottery scam', *Rapa Nui Journal* 2 (3), 3–4.

On woodworking skills and the Vinapu façade, SKINNER, H.D. 1955, 'Easter Island masonry', *J. Poly. Soc.* 64, 292–4.

Tukuturi's dates can be found in SKJOLSVOLD, A. and FIGUEROA, G., 1989, 'An attempt to date a unique, kneeling statue in Rano Raraku, Easter Island', in *Occasional Papers of the Kon-Tiki Museum*, 1, 7–35.

On errors of interpretation in rock art, see LEE, G. 1986, *Easter Island Rock Art: Ideological Symbols as Evidence of Socio-Political Change*. Ph.D. dissertation, UCLA. (In press as *Rock Art of Easter Island: Symbols of Power and Prayers to the Gods*. Monumenta Archaeologica, 17, Inst. of Arch., UCLA.)

The Solomon Islands analogies were drawn by BALFOUR, H. 1917, 'Some ethnological suggestions in regard to Easter Island, or Rapanui', in *Folklore* 28, 356–81; see also BARROW, T. 1967, 'Material evidence of the bird-man concept in Polynesia', in *Polynesian Culture History* (G.A. Highland *et al.* eds), 191–213, Bishop Museum Special Publication 56, Honolulu.

On the alleged solar observatory, see LEE, G. and LILLER, W. 1987, 'Easter Island's "sun stones": a critique', in *J. Poly. Soc.* 96, 81–93; and in *Archaeoastronomy* 11, 11pp.

On linguistics, see GREEN, R.C. 1988, in *First Int. Congress*, 37–57.

R. LANGDON and D. TRYON's views are in *The Language of Easter Island: its Development and Eastern Polynesian Relationships*, 1983, Institute for Polynesian Studies, Laie, Hawai'i.

BUTINOV, N.A. and KNOROZOV, Y.V. 1957, 'Preliminary report on the study of the written language of Easter Island', in *J. Poly. Soc.* 66, 5–17.

For Thomas BARTHEL's work, see *The Eighth Land*, 1978, University Press of Hawai'i, Honolulu.

Murrill and Simmons' anthropological studies are reported in HEYERDAHL and FERDON (eds), 1965, 255, 333.

For G. Gill's work, see 1990, 'Easter Island rocker jaws', *Rapa Nui Journal* 4(2), 21.

The latest work on Polynesian genetics can be found in Hill, A.V.S. and Serjeantson S.W. (eds) 1989, *The Colonization of the Pacific: A Genetic Trail*, Clarendon Press, Oxford.

For B. Danielsson's view of Heyerdahl's work, see Ralling, C. 1990, *The Kon-Tiki Man*, BBC Books, London, and an article in *The Listener*, 19 April 1990, 6.

For J. van Tilburg's view, see 'Symbolic archaeology on Easter Island', in *Archaeology* 40 (2), 1987, 26–33 (quotation p. 28).

CHAPTER 3: HOW DID THEY GET THERE, AND WHY?

For the island's ethnology, see Métraux 1940. For anthropology, see McCall, G. 1981, *Rapa Nui, Tradition and Survival on Easter Island*, University Press of Hawai'i, Honolulu.

For Polynesian prehistory in general, see Bellwood, P. 1978, *Man's Conquest of the Pacific*, Collins, Auckland and 1987 *The Polynesians* (revised ed.), Thames and Hudson, London; Jennings, J.D. (ed.) 1979, *The Prehistory of Polynesia*, Harvard University Press, Cambridge, Massachusetts; and Kirch, P.V. 1984, *The Evolution of the Polynesian Chiefdoms*, Cambridge University Press.

For the 'accidental' view, see Sharp, A. 1957, *Ancient Voyagers in the Pacific*, Penguin, Harmondsworth; and 1961, 'Polynesian navigation to distant islands', *J. Poly. Soc.* 70, 221–26.

For the 'deliberate' view, see Lewis, D. 1972, *We, the Navigators. The Ancient Art of Landfinding in the Pacific*, ANU Press, Canberra; Dodd, E. 1972, *Polynesian Seafaring*, Dodd, Meade & Co., New York.

The two views are debated in Golson, J. (ed.) 1962, *Polynesian Navigation*, Memoir 34, The Polynesian Soc., Wellington, Supplement to the *J. Poly. Soc.* The computer simulations are reported in: Levison, M., Ward, R.G. and Webb, J.W. 1973, *The Settlement of Polynesia, A Computer Simulation*, ANU Press, Canberra.

For the 'El Niño'/westerlies theory, see Finney, B. 1985, 'Anomalous westerlies, El Niño and the colonization of Polynesia', in *American Anthropologist 87*, 9–26; 1991, 'Myth, experiment, and the reinvention of Polynesian voyaging', *Idem 93*, 383–404; and Finney, B. *et al.* 1989, 'Wait for the west wind', in *J. Poly. Soc. 98*, 261–302. Also Irwin, G. 1989, 'Against, across and down the wind', in *J. Poly. Soc.* 98, 167–206; 1990, 'Human colonisation and change in the remote Pacific', *Current Anth.* 31, 90–94; and Irwin, G., Bickler, S. and Quirke, P. 1990, 'Voyaging by canoe and computer: experiments in the settlement of the Pacific Ocean', *Antiquity* 64, 34–50.

For Polynesians' navigation skills, see Lewis, D. 1974, 'Wind, Wave, Star and Bird', in *National Geographic*, vol. 146, no. 6, 746–54.

CHAPTER 4: LIVING ON AN ISLAND

For Selling's work, see Heyerdahl and Ferdon (eds), 1961, 519, footnote.

For a study of sediments, see Flenley, J.R. 1979, 'Stratigraphic evidence of environmental change on Easter Island', *Asian Perspectives* 22, 33–40.

On the discovery of the palm, see Flenley, J.R. and King, S.M. 1984, 'Late Quaternary pollen records from Easter Island', *Nature* 307, 47–50; and Dransfield, J., Flenley, J.R., King, S.M., Harkness, D.D. and Rapu, S. 1984, 'A recently extinct palm from Easter Island', *Nature* 312, 750–52.

For studies of the palm and its nuts, see ORLIAC, M. October 1989, 'Le palmier des Pascuans', in *Saga Information* (Société Amicale des Géologues Amateurs), Paris, 94, 60–64; ZIZKA, G. 1989, 'Jubaea chilensis (Molina) Baillon, die chilenische Honig- oder Coquitopalme', in *Der Palmengarten* (Frankfurt), 1, 35–40; and ARNOLD, M., ORLIAC, M. and VALLADAS, H. in Esen-Baur (ed.), 1990, 217–19.

On root moulds, see MULLOY, W. and FIGUEROA, G. 1978, *The A Kivi-Vai Teka Complex and its relationship to Easter Island architectural prehistory*, Asian and Pacific Arch. Series No. 8, Social Science Research Inst., University of Hawai'i at Manoa, 22.

The full study of the island's pollen diagrams is in FLENLEY, J.R., KING, S.M., TELLER, J.T., PRENTICE, M.E., JACKSON, J. and CHEW, C., 1991 'The Late Quaternary vegetational and climatic history of Easter Island,' *J. Quat. Sci.* 6, 85–115.

On the new snail, KIRCH, P.V. and CHRISTENSEN, C.C., 'Extinct achatinellid snails from Easter Island: biogeographic, ecological and archaeological implications', in *Burke Museum Contributions in Anth. and Nat. History* (in press).

For dating by radiocarbon, see AYRES, W.S. 1971, 'Radiocarbon dates from Easter Island', *J. Poly. Soc.* 80, 497–504; for dating by obsidian, see STEVENSON, C.M. 1988, 'The hydration dating of Easter Island obsidians', *Clava* 4, 83–93.

The best studies of domestic aspects of Easter Island prehistory are McCoy, P.C. 1976, *Easter Island Settlement Patterns in the Late Prehistoric and Protohistoric Periods* (Bull. 5, Easter Island Committee, Int. Fund for Monuments Inc., New York), and STEVENSON, C.M. 1986, 'The socio-political structure of the southern coastal area of Easter Island: AD 1300–1864', in *Island Societies* (P.V. Kirch, ed.), 69–77 (Cambridge University Press); STEVENSON, C.M. and CRISTINO, C. 1986, 'Residential settlement history of the Rapa Nui coastal plain', in *J. New World Arch.* 7, 29–38; and regular articles by STEVENSON in the *Rapa Nui Journal*.

On dog bones, *Rapa Nui Journal*, 5 (3), Autumn 1991, 45.

On dental problems, see OWSLEY, D.W., MIRES, A-M. and GILL, G.W. 1985, 'Carious lesions in permanent dentitions of protohistoric Easter Islanders', *J. Poly. Soc.*, 94, 415–22; and 1983, 'Caries frequency in deciduous dentitions of protohistoric Easter Islanders', *Bull. Indo-Pacific Prehistory Assoc.* 4, 143–47.

On skeletal anomalies, see GILL, G.W. 1988, 'William Mulloy and the beginnings of Wyoming osteological research on Easter Island', *Rapa Nui Notes* 7, 9/13.

On obsidian, see STEVENSON, C.M., SHAW, L.C. and CRISTINO, C. 1983/4, 'Obsidian procurement and consumption on Easter Island', *Arch. in Oceania* 18/19, 120–24; also in *First Int. Congress* 1988, 83–94. See also McCoy, P.C. 1976, 'A note on Easter Island obsidian cores and blades', *J. Poly. Soc.* 85, 327–38.

For house excavation, see McCoy, P.C. 1973, 'Excavation of a rectangular house on the east rim of Rano Kau volcano, Easter Island', *Arch. & Phys. Anth. in Oceania* 8, 51–67.

For subsistence in general, AYRES, W.S. 1985, 'Easter Island subsistence', in *J. Soc. des Océanistes* 80, 103–24; and for marine resources, AYRES, W.S. 1979, 'Easter Island fishing', in *Asian Perspectives* 22, 61–92.

CHAPTER 5: STATUES AND CEREMONIES

The fullest study of the island's statues is to be found in VAN TILBURG, J. 1986, *Power and Symbol: the stylistic analysis of Easter Island monolithic sculpture*, Ph.D. dissertation, UCLA.

On possible female figures, BARTHEL, T.S. 1958, 'Female stone figures on Easter Island', *J. Poly. Soc.* 67, 252–55.

For the 'eye' discovery, see *Nouveau Regard* 1982 (J. Vignes, 'Les Yeux des statues', 183–7); Mulloy's 'bowl' can be found in HEYERDAHL and FERDON (eds) 1961, 177.

Raphael's study can be found in: RAPHAEL, M. 1988, 'Die Monumentalität in der Bildhauerkunst am Beispiel eines Kopfes von der Osterinsel', 462–526 in *Tempel, Kirchen und Figuren* (by M. Raphael), Suhrkamp, Frankfurt.

CHAPTER 6: THE RIDDLE OF THE QUARRY

For the extraterrestrial view, see VON DÄNIKEN, E. 1969, *Chariots of the Gods?*, Souvenir Press, London – and several other titles of the same kind.

The Norwegian Expedition's experiment is to be found in HEYERDAHL and FERDON (eds), 1961, 368–9.

CHAPTER 7: ROCKING OR ROLLING

For Wolff's view, see WOLFF, W. 1948, *Island of Death* (reprinted 1973), Hacker Art Books, New York, 149–61.

The Norwegian Expedition's experiments are to be found in HEYERDAHL and FERDON (eds), 1961, 370–1.

For Mulloy's theory, MULLOY, W. 1970, 'A speculative reconstruction of techniques of carving, transporting and erecting Easter Island statues', *Arch. & Phys. Anth. in Oceania* 5, 1–23.

A critical view of Mulloy's theory can be found in COTTERELL, B. and KAMMINGA, J. 1990, *Mechanics of Pre-Industrial Technology*, Cambridge University Press, 226–32.

For Adam's theory, ADAM, J-P. 1988, *Le Passé Recomposé*, Seuil, Paris, 143–54.

Pavel's experiments: PAVEL, P., 'Reconstruction of the transport of moai', in Esen-Baur (ed.), 1990, 141–44; see also HEYERDAHL, T., SKJOLSVOLD, A. and PAVEL, P. 1989, 'The "walking" moai of Easter Island', in *Occasional Papers of the Kon-Tiki Museum* 1, 36–64.

Love's experiments: LOVE, C., 'How to make and move an Easter Island statue', in Esen-Baur (ed.), 1990, 139–40.

For recently excavated statue pedestals, see HEYERDAHL, SKJOLSVOLD and PAVEL, *op. cit.*

CHAPTER 8: PLATFORMS AND PUKAO

On *ahu*, see HEYERDAHL and FERDON (eds), 1961; MULLOY, W. 1968, *Preliminary report of archaeological field work, Feb–July 1968, Easter Island*, Bull. 1, Easter Island Committee, Int. Fund for Monuments Inc., New York; and 1970, *Preliminary report of the restoration of Ahu Vai Uri, Easter Island*, Bull. 2, Easter Island Committee, Int. Fund for Monuments Inc., New York; LOVE, C. 1983, 'Easter Island research', *Chilean University Life* 16, Spring, 3–8; SEELENFREUND, A. 1988, 'Ahu Tautira', in *Clava* 4, 69–81; AYRES, W.S. 1988, 'The Tahai settlement complex', in *First Int. Congress* 95–119.

For astronomical orientations, see MULLOY, W. 1975, 'A solstice oriented *ahu* on Easter Island', *Arch. & Phys. Anth. in Oceania* 10, 1–39; and LILLER, W., 'The lost observatories of Rapa Nui', in Esen-Baur (ed.), 1990, 145–59.

On head-dresses, SKINNER, H.D. 1967, 'Cylindrical headdress in the Pacific region', in *Polynesian Culture History* (G.A. Highland *et al.*, eds), 167–89 (Bishop Museum Special Publ. 56, Honolulu).

On red scoria in general, VAN TILBURG, J. 1986, 'Red scoria on Easter Island', in *J. New World Arch.* 7, 1–27.

CHAPTER 9: CRASH GO THE ANCESTORS

On the Poike ditch, SMITH, C.S. 1990, 'The Poike ditch in retrospect', *Rapa Nui Journal* 4 (3), 33–37; see also HEYERDAHL and FERDON (eds), 1961, 385. For the new date from the ditch, see *Rapa Nui Journal* 4(4), 1990/1, 56.

For use of islets, McCOY, P.C. 1978. The place of near-shore islets in Easter Island prehistory, *J. Poly. Soc.* 87, 193–214.

For population estimates, see STEVENSON 1986 and STEVENSON and CRISTINO 1986, *op. cit.*

CHAPTER 10: ORONGO AND RONGORONGO

For social aspects, see McCALL, G. 1979, 'Kinship and environment on Easter Island: some observations and speculations', *Mankind* 12, 119–37.

For Orongo, see ROUTLEDGE, K. 1920, 'Survey of the village and carved rocks of Orongo, Easter Island, by the Mana Expedition', *J. Roy. Anth. Inst. Gt Britain* 50, 425–51; and MULLOY, W. 1975, *Investigation and restoration of the ceremonial center of Orongo, Easter Island*, Bull. 4, Easter Island Committee, Int. Fund for Monuments Inc., New York.

On the birdman cult, ROUTLEDGE, K. 1917, 'The bird cult of Easter Island', *Folklore* 28, 337–55.

On the birdman in rock art, LEE, G. 1986, *Easter Island Rock Art: Ideological Symbols as Evidence of Socio-Political Change*, Ph.D. dissertation, UCLA; and 1986, 'The birdman motif of Easter Island', in *J. New World Arch.* 7, 39–49.

On the vulva in rock art, LEE, G. 1987, 'The cosmic Komari', in *Rock Art Research* 4, 51–55.

An excellent introduction to Rongorongo can be found in DAVIS DRAKE, A. 1988–90, 'A layman's guide to Rongorongo', in *Rapa Nui Journal* 2(3) to 4(1).

For the island's first missionaries, see DEDEREN, F. 1990, 'L'évangélisation de l'Ile de Pâques', in *Circumpacifica*, 103–23.

CHAPTER 11: CONCLUSION: THE ISLAND THAT SELF-DESTRUCTED

On Polynesian display, see SAHLINS, M. 1955, 'Esoteric efflorescence in Easter Island', *American Anthropologist* 57, 1045–52.

EPILOGUE: THE LESSON OF EASTER ISLAND

For the Club of Rome, see MEADOWS, D., RANDERS, J. and BEHRENS, W. 1972, *The Limits to Growth*, Universe Books, New York.

ACKNOWLEDGMENTS

The initial interest of Paul Bahn in the story of Easter Island was kindled at an early age by television documentaries about Thor Heyerdahl's pioneering expedition and his experiments in carving and erecting statues. Later, this interest was developed in archaeological studies at Cambridge and, during the same years, by further television programmes such as a BBC *Chronicle* which took Colin Renfrew to the island, and *The Ascent of Man* which did the same for Jacob Bronowski. The fact that Bronowski had, alas, nothing very flattering or informative to say about the prehistoric islanders did not detract from the visual impact of their achievements or from the ever-growing desire to go and see for oneself.

That chance finally arrived in 1985 when, thanks to a J. Paul Getty postdoctoral fellowship in the history of art and the humanities, it was possible to start planning a first visit to the island. At that point, in the course of researching the subject, it was realized that by an amazing and lucky coincidence John Flenley – the very person who had recently made a most important breakthrough in Easter Island studies through pollen analysis – taught at the University of Hull, Bahn's home town.

In 1977, on finishing a research fellowship at the Australian National University, Flenley took a circuitous route back to England. As he was writing a book about tropical rain forests at the time, he resolved to go via South America, which he had never previously visited. The obvious way to do this was to fly to Tahiti and then transfer to the Lan Chile flight to Easter Island and Santiago in Chile. At last his own childhood ambition to visit Easter Island was to be achieved, and he decided to stop over there for two weeks, having obtained permission from the Governor to do research on the island. The important results obtained during that short stay are set out in Chapters 4 and 9.

On Bahn's return from the island in 1986, he took the advice of Graham Massey at the BBC and submitted to the then editor of *Horizon*, Robin Brightwell, a synopsis for a new television documentary on recent Easter Island research. This eventually became a successful double programme for *Horizon* in 1988 (and for *Nova* in the USA in 1989), with Bahn as archaeological consultant, and with Flenley's work featured.

We would like to express our deep appreciation for the help and documentation provided by many friends in Europe, in particular Michel and Catherine Orliac; the indefatigable André Valenta and his Paris group; Georg Zizka in Frankfurt; Annette Parkes; Pat Winker. Our thanks for documentation are also owed to Horst Cain and Annette Bierbach, Shirley Chesney, Steven Fischer, Roger Green, Johan Kamminga and Pam Russell.

Currently, the great majority of Easter Island scholars are to be found in the United States, and here above all we would like to thank Georgia Lee, founder-editor of the invaluable and indispensable *Rapa Nui Journal*; and also William Ayres, Alan Davis Drake, George Gill, Bill Hyder, Patrick Kirch, Sharon Long, Charlie Love, Chris Stevenson, and JoAnne Van Tilburg. For photographs, we are grateful to Georgia Lee, Scott Baker, George Gill, Bill Hyder, Sharon Long, Charlie Love, Emily Mulloy, Mark Oliver, Isabella Tree and Jacques Vignes.

Technical help was given to Flenley by Sarah M. King (pollen counting), Maureen Martin (pollen preparation), Joan Jackson and Christopher Chew (chemical preparation), Keith Scurr and Karen Puklowski (diagrams), and Glynis Walsh (typing).

On the island itself, Flenley would like to thank Gerardo Velasco (Director of CORFO, the Chilean Government's Agricultural Development Organization on Rapa Nui) and his wife Margherita (an islander of high birth) for accommodation and much other help; Yolanda Ika and her mother for accommodation; Sergio Rapu for help and discussions; Claudio Cristino for useful discussions, and also Earthwatch volunteers Ernest Igou, Sally Goodhue, Kathy Marine and Mike Symond.

Flenley would also like to acknowledge research grants from the British Natural Environment Research Council; the NERC Radiocarbon Laboratory (Dr D.D. Harkness); and Professor Jim Teller for his research collaboration.

SOURCES OF ILLUSTRATIONS

72–3 Drawings of *manavai* and *hare moa* by R. Förster, from *Guia de Campo Arqueologica*, Easter Island 1986.

74 Photo of *hare moa* by Georgia Lee.

75 Photo of *puoko-moa* by Mark Oliver.

76 Drawings of *umu pae* by R. Förster, from *Guia de Campo Arqueologica*, Easter Island 1986.

77 Photo of *umu pae* by Georgia Lee.

78–80 Drawings Georgia Lee.

81 Photo Mark Oliver.

82 Drawings Georgia Lee.

83, 84 Photos Georgia Lee.

85, 86 Photos Isabella Tree.

87, 88 Photos Georgia Lee.

89 Drawing R. Förster, from *Guia de Campo Arqueologica*, Easter Island 1986.

90 Photo K. Routledge, courtesy Museum of Mankind.

91 Photo Elizabeth Pendleton.

92 Photo K. Routledge, courtesy Museum of Mankind.

93 From K. Routledge, *The Mystery of Easter Island*, London 1919.

94 Photo from K. Routledge, *The Mystery of Easter Island*, London 1919.

95 Drawing Annick Petersen, after Jacques Vignes, from *Nouveau Regard sur l'Île de Pâques*, Corbeil 1982.

96 Photo Elizabeth Pendleton.

97 Photo Georgia Lee.

98 Photo Elizabeth Pendleton.

99 Photo Georgia Lee.

100 Photo Elizabeth Pendleton.

101 Photo Georgia Lee.

102 From K. Routledge, *The Mystery of Easter Island*, London 1919.

103–5 Photos Elizabeth Pendleton.

106 Photo William D. Hyder.

107 Photo Paul Bahn.

108 From K. Routledge, *The Mystery of Easter Island*, London 1919.

109 Photo Georgia Lee.

110 Drawing Annick Petersen, after Chica, from A. Valenta, *A la découverte de l'île de Pâques*, Nathan, Paris 1985.

111 Photo by K. Routledge, courtesy of Museum of Mankind.

112 Drawing Georgia Lee.

113 Photo Georgia Lee.

114 Photo Paul Bahn.

115 Drawing from F. Mazière, *Mysteries of Easter Island*, London 1968.

116 Photo Georgia Lee.

117 Photo Mark Oliver.

118 Engraving from *Two Year Journey Around the World*, Dordrecht 1728.

119 Drawings after Mulloy taken from P. Bellwood, *The Polynesians* (rev. ed.), London and New York 1987.

120, 121 From J.-P. Adam, *Le Passé Recomposé*, Edition du Seuil, Paris 1988.

122 Photo Charles Love.

123, 124 Photos Paul Bahn.

125 Photo Charles Love.

126 Photo Georgia Lee.

127 Photo William D. Hyder.

128 Photo Georgia Lee.

129 Drawing Annick Petersen after Claude Royer.

130 Drawing R. Förster, from *Guia de Campo Arqueologica*, Easter Island 1986.

131, 132 Photos Georgia Lee.

133, 134 Photos Peter Bellwood.

135–7 Photos Georgia Lee.

138–41 Photos Thor Heyerdahl.

142 Photo Georgia Lee.

143 Drawings after Mulloy from P. Bellwood, *The Polynesians* (rev. ed.), London and New York 1987.

144 Photo Elizabeth Pendleton.

145 Photo Georgia Lee.

146 Photo Nick Saunders.

147 Photo Mark Oliver.

148 Photo Georgia Lee.

149 Photo Peter Bellwood.

150 Photo Elizabeth Pendleton.

151 Photo Nick Saunders.

152 Photo William D. Hyder.

153 Photo courtesy British Museum.

154 Drawings by William Mulloy, from T. Heyerdahl and E. Ferdon (eds), *Archaeology of Easter Island* Vol. 1, London 1961.

155 Drawing John Flenley.

156 Photo John Flenley.

157 Drawing John Flenley.

158 Photo Charles Love.

159 Photo Georgia Lee.

160 Photo Paul Bahn.

161, 162 Photos Mark Oliver.

163 Map from K. Routledge, *The Mystery of Easter Island*, London 1919.

164, 165 Photos Paul Bahn.

166 Photo Mark Oliver.

167 Photo Marcía Opal.

168 Photo E. Edwards.

169, 170 Photos courtesy Museum of Mankind.

INDEX

Text page references are given in roman type; illustration numbers are given in *italic*